THE AMERICAN HORROR FILM

THE AMERICAN HORROR FILM
AN INTRODUCTION

Reynold Humphries

EDINBURGH
University Press

Every effort has been made to make proper acknowledgement of the photographs used in this book. However, if any oversight has been made, the publisher will be pleased to make the necessary arrangements at the first opportunity.

Edinburgh University Press Ltd
22 George Square, Edinburgh

Reprinted 2003, 2005

Typeset in Palatino by
Aarontype Limited, Easton, Bristol and
printed and bound in Great Britain by
MPG Books, Bodmin, Cornwall

A CIP Record for this book is available from the British Library

ISBN 0 7486 1416 8 (paperback)

CONTENTS

⟶⚬⟵

LIST OF ILLUSTRATIONS

———⚬⚭———

This one is for Archie

INTRODUCTION

———∽∽———

I would like to open with two quotes:

> One might say that the true subject of the horror genre is the struggle for recognition of all that our civilization represses or oppresses, its re-emergence dramatized, as in our nightmares, as an object of horror, a matter for terror, and the happy ending (when it exists) typically signifying the restoration of repression. (Wood 1986: 75)

> When individuals perceive that they do not have control over their lives and that they are dominated by powerful forces outside themselves, they are attracted to occultism. Consequently, during eras of socioeconomic crisis, when people have difficulty coping with social reality, the occult becomes an efficacious ideological mode that helps explain incomprehensible events with the aid of religious or supernatural mythologies. (Kellner 1996: 218)

These alert and essential observations nicely articulate politics and psychoanalysis, our main concern in this book. 'Repression', then, must not only denote its proper sense but also connote how this is reinforced and reorientated by social values under patriarchal capitalism. For Freud, we are all born into repression which takes three forms. The first is primal repression, where we 'forget' something that was never conscious to begin with: the child's incestuous desire for the mother or father, the instance of castration that is the realisation of the Oedipus complex but without the unconscious traces ever being erased. Next is secondary

1

repression, where a concrete notion or image is expelled from the conscious mind, to which it can return, uninvited and unwanted ('the return of the repressed'). Finally, repression in the sense of the acceptance of social constraints in the place of the immediate satisfaction of infantile drives (a central theme which we shall encounter frequently).

This last sense is what Marcuse calls 'surplus repression', a formula to which a political dimension is given. It is not simply, as in Freud, a question of the superego preventing drives from creating social chaos, but 'the result of specific societal conditions sustained in the specific interest of domination'. (Marcuse 1955: 44, 81) Here we find appearing the notion, central to horror in general and increasingly explicit in modern horror, of the role of the father: from bread-winner and family head he becomes the signifier of the imposition of family values, 'the representative of the family's position in the social division of labour'. (Marcuse 1955: 82) When Marcuse refers to 'irrational authority' (181), he is thinking precisely of the unthinking submission of subjects to a patriarch whose symbolic function is to shore up as 'natural' and 'rational' an economic system – capitalism – based on the survival of the fittest and the concomitant ideology of competition, success and incessant rivalry. This latter notion, be it said at once, stems from infantile narcissism where the child wishes to eliminate any person (sibling, parent) threatening its egocentric attachment to the mother.

For patriarchal capitalism, only individualism counts: a person's subjectivity is interesting inasmuch as it can be exploited for profit once it has been transformed into a compulsive drive to consume. One theorist has cogently assessed the situation:

> One of the central projects of psychoanalytic theory is to explain how social and cultural relationships produce subjectivity in individuals. Psychoanalysis argues that our conscious and unconscious minds are not 'pre-given' in a form of subjectivity that is intrinsic, essentialist, and ahistorical, but are instead produced by our entrance into social formations and symbolic systems that pre-exist our consciousness. Consciousness (and 'reality') are thus socially, culturally, and historically specific. (Sconce 1993: 108)

My concern in the pages that follow is to illustrate how these concepts take form in horror from the 30s to the present day, be they represented by Dracula or Frankenstein, latter-day vampires or serial killers, 'possessed' children or rampaging zombies, to name but a few.

A further aspect of horror, or at least of modern horror, that merits a mention is the vexed and controversial question of violence. Here we need only evoke the cinema of Arthur Penn and Sam Peckinpah – from *The Chase* in 1966 to *Bring Me the Head of Alfredo Garcia* in 1974 – to obtain some notion of the matter. The outcry provoked by Penn's *The Chase* and Peckinpah's *Straw Dogs* (1971) are already indicative of ideological forces at work in society. Critics and politicians alike were always ready to show complacency towards the often nauseating combination of sex, sadism and violence in the James Bond films: after all, the victims were foreigners, women, homosexuals and the colonised. Similarly, the sordid exploitation of voyeurism and sadism in certain 'slashers' worried nobody (except for feminists and film theorists) until a real-life criminal claimed to have been influenced by one film or another. Penn, however, committed the sacrilege of foregrounding the orchestration of lynching as a normal activity by the ruling class and making an explicit parallel between this and the murder of Lee Harvey Oswald, thus raising the question of violence inherent to right-thinking American society and its political representatives. Peckinpah touched a raw nerve by portraying the descent into the most terrible violence of an apparently mild, liberal American academic fleeing the worst aspects of his country, then re-creating them to defend himself against deranged locals in England. If David Sumner has no alternative but to defend his home – and that is what is at stake – what I want to stress here is the fact that he makes his stance at a point where it is too late. As a result he is no better than those who attack him and Peckinpah's use of montage during the scene where his wife is raped makes it patent that Sumner's lack of convictions and an unconvincing appeal to ethics are responsible. With the benefit of our ally hindsight, we can now see a most productive link between this maligned movie and early Wes Craven. Both *Last House on the Left* and *The Hills Have Eyes* turn on self-satisfied middle-class males who commit acts of atrocity beyond what even the dubious notion of 'self-defence' can justify. The complacently nihilistic aestheticisation of violence indulged in by John Carpenter (of which *Ghosts of Mars* is perhaps the most disreputable example) renders even more urgent attempts to keep committed horror alive.

This is an appropriate place to draw attention to *Targets*, a key film in the elaboration of certain themes dealt with in *Psycho* (see Part II,

Chapter 5). Bogdanovich succeeds in rendering a homage both to classic Hollywood in general and classic horror in particular (his brilliant use of Boris Karloff, aged eighty), and to modern horror. He does this by having Karloff, who plays an elderly horror film star, confront the killer in a drive-in cinema in Los Angeles showing *The Terror* (starring Karloff). As the killer is the product of a traditional family — whose members he murders prior to going on a killing spree that recalls certain real events of the period — Bogdanovich is able to introduce one of the key themes of modern horror — 'family values' — while reflecting on the interaction of those values and the social and psychic power of the image. *Targets* suggests that people in general and filmgoers in particular are conditioned to consume images unthinkingly, in which case their vocal activity during a screening cannot affect the ideological passivity they betray in so behaving. We shall see throughout Part II the various meanings the word 'consume' can take.

Too many books and articles to be mentioned here have influenced my thinking on the subject, but I feel it is pertinent to draw attention to the theoretical work of Fredric Jameson and Slavoj Zizek in the related fields of cultural studies, Marxism and psychoanalysis. I owe an intellectual debt beyond what words can express to Robin Wood who for forty years has been asking critics and students alike to take film — and themselves — seriously: *Hollywood from Vietnam to Reagan* is a model to be studied and pondered over. The bibliography attempts to do justice to my reading and the filmography lists all films viewed. Lack of space has forced me to leave aside the discussion of certain areas, such as the 40s remakes of the 30s classics and the various series based on the characters of Michael of *Halloween* (but *Halloween III: Season of the Witch* has nothing to do with the series), and Jason of *Friday the 13th*. Certain films are missing, not simply because I have not managed to track down prints, but because of my disagreement with critical opinion: I appear to be in a minority of one in not admiring George Romero's vampire movie *Martin* and in finding Brian De Palma's *Sisters* grotesque and unconvincing. Nor has it been possible to consider 'eco-horror', except in passing when analysing *Piranha* (II, 6). And the only 'exploitation' horror movie discussed is the TROMA production *Mother's Day*, admittedly better known than such interesting TROMA films as *Chopper Chicks in Zombietown* and *Combat Shock*.

A topic requiring an extended theoretical study is that of humour, black, sick or tongue in cheek; I have not been able to do more than mention the question when appropriate. Similarly, we need to extend the kind of analysis undertaken by Carol Clover on *Deliverance* (Clover 1992) to gauge the interpenetration of themes, images and conventions common to horror and non-horror films. If the example of David Lynch is well known (*Blue Velvet, Lost Highway*), of particular interest is the Clint Eastwood thriller *Tightrope* which is a serial killer movie, a 'slasher/ stalker' movie and even a werewolf movie rolled into one. Those who share my love for obscure horror movies of the 50s (there are limits: films like *She Demons* are best forgotten) can find much information (but little analysis) in Worth. The volumes by Vale and Juno and Weaver may well have readers calling for more. The extraordinary erudition and enthusiasm manifest everywhere in the encyclopedias of Hardy and Newman make these volumes indispensable companions when seeking intelligent commentary on films famous or forgotten.

Thanks go to my editor at Edinburgh, Nicola Carr, who suggested the project and accompanied it along the way; to the outside readers for their comments and suggestions; to Holly Roberts for prompt replies to my questions. Thanks also to Nina Harding and Rina Sagoo of the British Film Institute, ever courteous and helpful. And to Steven Schneider who gave me the opportunity to elaborate elsewhere a detailed theory of serial killers that has proved useful here. Special thanks go to Nicole Gabet, Frank Lafond and Archie Tait who opened their collections of horror films to me; and to my wife, Martine Lannaud, called upon yet again to help with technical computing details. Special thanks go to the unknown person responsible, in the early 60s, for programming at my local flea-pit such double bills as *The Monolith Monsters* and *Brain from the Planet Arous*. Such fare has left its mark on me, as did viewing at that distant moment in time Corman's Poe films (and reading Poe into the bargain) and the early work of Mario Bava, whose *Blood and Black Lace* (1964) is a 'stalker/slasher'. The very special climate of what the great opening song in *The Rocky Horror Picture Show* calls 'the late-night double-feature picture show' has more or less disappeared (much to my chagrin, the cinema referred to above became a bowling-alley in 1962). If such films occupy only a small place in this volume, it is heartening to notice the interest shown in them by a Joe Dante. It has been in re-viewing these movies that I have found much of the sustenance for the pages that follow.

Paris, December 2001

Part I

CLASSIC HORROR

FIGURES IN A GOTHIC LANDSCAPE

～∞～

I am giving the term 'Gothic' a wide application, the parameters of which are the following: a concern with characters of an aristocratic nature; scientific aspirations going hand in hand with a mistrust of machines; sinister, remote castles with endless corridors, hidden rooms and family secrets, hauntings and spectres, mysteries which may or may not be supernatural; repressed sexuality finding pathological outlets in a combination of terror, pleasure and the death drive. In such fictions the emphasis is more often than not on atemporal, timeless forces and a curious sense of the anachronistic that will concern us particularly in the political analysis I shall give in the next chapter. I would simply suggest at this juncture that the aristocrat – a virtually dead species in Europe and a non-existent one in the States, a factor of considerable importance for the ideological projects of 30s horror – at once fascinates and repels, especially when he is a mad doctor/scientist claiming the right of the individual to success, always at the expense of other individuals or the peasants (taken collectively as a 'class'). In this opening chapter I present, in successive sections, Dracula; Frankenstein and his monster; Jekyll and his Hyde; werewolves. Because of the overarching theme of love, I have chosen to include here the character of King Kong.

i) DRACULA

What can possibly attract us to an undead Count anxious only to suck our blood? For it would seem that we are attracted, especially women. That is a little matter to which we shall return presently, but it is patent that characters in *Dracula*, with whom we can readily identify, are scarcely indifferent to his charms. Are we seduced by his good looks, his aristocratic bearing, his power, his immortality? Clearly none of these characteristics exists without the others, so we keep coming back to what motivates him, which we can sum up as a combination of rampant sexuality and implacable aggressivity, although the censorship of the period limited sexual contact and the shedding of blood. David Punter has succinctly summed up the situation:

> Dracula's is the passion which never dies, the endless desire of the unconscious for gratification, which has to be repressed — particularly on the eve of marriage, of course — in order to maintain stable ideology. He is 'undead' because desire never dies; gratification merely moves desire on to further objects. There is, for Dracula as for the unconscious, no final satisfaction, for his very nature is desire. (Punter 1996: 19)

He goes on to insist on the 'attraction and repulsion' linking yet separating the bourgeois Van Helsing and the aristocratic, feudal Count, stressing the former's 'order, neatness, reserve' that make of him the perfect incarnation of patriarchal sexual repression and the maintenance of a conservative status quo where each thing has its place and each person knows his or hers — particularly hers. Yet class, too, is crucial and will continue to be for Frankenstein, Jekyll and Larry Talbot the Wolfman.

It is impossible to understand the seduction of Dracula without psychoanalysis. Impossible, too, to limit our findings to a structure outside society and history. Taking up Punter's comments, we need to reverse the situation and make of the vampire's victim and the spectator the subject of desire and gratification rather than simply the object of the Count's desire. I asked what made him seductive, which is another way of asking what he represents for us. Dracula is Lacan's object *a*, the object-cause of desire, that non-existent and eternally lost object that we spend our lives trying to (re)find: the maternal phallus. Dracula will enable us to find an imaginary plenitude, that which existed for the infant in its formative years where only it and its mother mattered. If Dracula symbolises the unconscious pleasure that such a relationship conjures up retroactively, he also represents the terror of separation and the horror of the realisation of the social meaning of that separation: subjectivity, castration and

Figure 1 The predatory aristocrat as vampire. *Dracula.* Copyright © 2002 by Universal Studios. Courtesy of Universal Studios Publishing Rights, a Division of Universal Studios Licensing, Inc. All rights reserved.

mortality. It is here that we must insist on the social and cultural repercussions of Lacan's theory of the mirror stage. The child both jubilates at its bodily integrity and recognises itself through its resemblance to the (m)other. Simultaneously it reacts against the presence of the other, its dependence on whom wounds definitively its narcissism, provoking in its relation to others a possibly murderous aggressivity. The shock of not seeing a vampire in a mirror – parodied in *Dance of the Vampires* where the characters are reflected in a mirror, thus betraying them to the vampires – stems from this: *not* seeing what we expect and desire is to recognise that which has been long repressed, the non-existence of the maternal phallus. Dracula is the locus of castration, which explains why he both attracts and repels: repels because he is the signifier of lack; attracts because, as object *a*, he fills that lack and fulfils our expectations:

The danger that anxiety signals is the overproximity of this object *a*, this object so *inalienable* that like Dracula and all the other vampires of Gothic and Romantic fiction it cannot even be cast as a shadow or reflected as a mirror image, and yet so *unsubstantial* that like Murnau's Nosferatu it can disappear in a puff of smoke. (Copjec 1994: 119)

What might this imply?

I have said that Dracula is particularly attractive to women; he is also attracted to them. Yet Dracula also vampirises men. That Van Helsing feels fascination for him is not just a question of knowledge, although the film wants to convince us it is. For the vampire hunter is curiously unwilling to put into practice what he preaches. He warns everyone that Dracula's strength stems from the fact we refuse to believe in him, yet takes no heed of the remarks made by a guard in Dr Seward's sanitorium to the effect that Renfield keeps exiting from his cell without having a key or without signs of violence. What is Van Helsing doing if not disavowing the testimony of the senses, continuing to believe one thing while knowing the situation is different? Here we have the structure of disavowal: the fetishist maintains a belief in the maternal phallus (= denying castration), while knowing that no such object exists. Thus *Dracula* unwittingly attributes to Van Helsing − and, hence, to the spectator too − a pathological psychic state that is a form of psychosis. We can better understand what is occurring by giving some thought to the question of bisexuality, which we must be careful not to reduce to homosexuality.

Dracula must be taken as a signifier: he is not just a symbol of castration, of loss, but he also represents the infantile. He is an unstoppable drive, demanding immediate satisfaction, a feudal Freddy Krueger. To evoke bisexuality means to remember that a child can desire union with the parent of the same sex: the pre-Oedipal drives are not limited to that caricature of Freud which claims a boy wants to eliminate father to have access to mother, however dominant that paradigm is. Dracula is seductive because he allows us to experience again that infantile omnipotence where every desire was satisfied and where others were at one's beck and call. Such is the aristocratic standing of Dracula and the dream of the patriarchal capitalist who has replaced him. He is also society's inevitable punishment for such forbidden pleasures. Just as the bourgeois thinks he alone has the right to property and luxury, obtained through the labour of those who have neither, and steps in to restrain by any means the lower orders who dare demand their share, so Dracula stands in for the punishment of our guilty desires through the terror he brings, a terror that is the fear of transgressing society's 'natural order'. A good conservative, Dracula is as much on the side of law and order as Van Helsing. His concept of law and order, however, is feudal and therefore proscribed.

Like the child who spurns his mother because he wants to identify with big, strong, phallic father, Dracula vampirises men: their blood, like the labour of the proletariat for Van Helsing and his like, keeps him going. Moreover, he enjoys it. Hence the role of men in combatting him. This sets up within a supernatural framework a supposedly natural order: men join forces to protect women and keep at bay those forces that threaten patriarchy by refusing to submit to order, restraint, marriage. They also keep women in a state of ignorance, conditioning them to believe in something women may not accept: the male right to take decisions, wield power and hold the purse strings. That strange film *Mark of the Vampire* has something to tell us here. Everything invites us to assume the characters are fighting a vampire, then suddenly the plot turns out to be a ruse to confound a character suspected of murdering the heroine's father. The hostility the film aroused is due in part to its representing spectatorial desire as based on disavowal. What we wanted to believe is a decoy: the plot is an object *a*. Unconsciously, however, the film represents an element inherent to pre-Oedipal drives: incest. By being forced to relive the circumstances of her father's death, the heroine is faced with the return of the repressed of desire, and one that is mutual between father and daughter. This is overdetermined by the fact she has to submit to the law of the film's stern but benign vampire hunter and father figure, a stand-in for the father she loved in a proscribed fashion. The fact that only her fiancé is kept in the dark is explained by the fact he would have refused to go along. This is correct, but the conscious reason hides an unconscious one: it is necessary for the vampire hunter to teach the heroine to submit to paternal law so that she will be 'free' to marry the hero at the end. The whole plot is an unconscious working through of the role of incest in desire and of the way society places young men and women in their 'proper' roles once the drama and the horror of the situation is resolved, either by social and sexual repression or, here, by a piece of sleight of hand summing up that which the film cannot say and which we are not meant to contemplate: the homosocial dimension of patriarchy.

Hence the fascination of *Dracula's Daughter*. While agreeing with the 'queer' reading proposed by Berenstein and Benshoff, I suggest things are far more complicated. (Humphries 2000) That the Countess is attracted to the young prostitute Lily is clear, but if we give this too much weight we shall miss the way the film unwittingly pillories psychiatrist Dr Garth for being responsible for the girl's death: she survives the attack of the Countess, but by forcing her to remember, Garth provokes heart failure. How? Because the girl has experienced the return of the repressed, the privileged relation of girl to mother, a relation proscribed as unhealthy simply because it jeopardises patriarchy. The experience was at once tender and aggressive, the protecting mother and the monstrous, devouring mother condensed in the Countess. Lily also experiences what the vampire symbolises: death. Moreover, the visual parallels between Garth and Sandor, the Countess's retainer, suggest effeteness, hence effeminacy: it is sufficient to notice the attention the film pays to their immaculately combed hair, a 'feminine' trait *par excellence*. If Garth wins the day and saves his young secretary, it is because a jealous Sandor has killed the Countess. Thus two men collaborate unconsciously to get rid of a woman who refuses to recognise her role as Dracula's daughter, or who refuses to be a dutiful child obeying a paternal law that is as much social and economic as psychic. The film's sympathy for her must be displaced, especially as she is psychically stronger than the weak Garth whom his secretary is forever putting in his place, or castrating. Obedience is the order of the day, as Dracula's three wives well know.

ii) FRANKENSTEIN

As an opening gambit I propose a parallel between *Dracula* and *Frankenstein*. Just as Dracula, with his unbridled drives and feudal power, is the return of the sexually and economically repressed of patriarchal capitalism represented by Van Helsing, so the monster is the return of the repressed of what Frankenstein represents in the second of the three Gothic classics to be filmed (we shall return to this when considering *Dr Jekyll and Mr Hyde*). Chris Baldick has called attention to the way Marx compared capitalists to vampires, ghouls, werewolves and grave-robbers, sucking the labour from the proletariat and thus transforming them into its victims. They are forced to sell their labour, their life's blood so to speak, and thus depend financially, without deriving any benefit, on those exploiting them. (Baldick 1987: 121–40) Certainly Frankenstein is an expert grave-robber, digging up fresh corpses to fabricate his creature. The monster is thus the signifier of alienation as he has no identity outside that given him by his creator (and Frankenstein behaves like God). He is also its signifier inasmuch as he is made up of bits and pieces; fragments of other people. Thus does the capitalist Frankenstein live off literally dead workers, getting them to work twice: the first time they get some payment for their trouble, but once dead they can be used at will. No restraint is needed, no money need change hands. The logic of capitalism is already present in *Frankenstein*. Success is all that counts, but it is unstable: 'Frankenstein has literally sown/sewn his own destruction by fusing pieces of rebellious property that fight being forced to serve an illegitimate patriarchy'. (Crane 1994: 94)

There are enough indications to show society going radically wrong. Frankenstein is presented in a positive light, which must be taken as ambiguous and indicative of competing and conflicting ideologies. The film dehistoricises the story by setting it in a never-never world of feudalism, with happy peasants who turn readily on the monster, thus transforming him into a scapegoat for their own exploitation. They mis-recognise their true social situation and cheer Frankenstein's father when he offers them festivities and alcohol. *Frankenstein*'s conscious discourse is contemptuous of the lower orders, but things keep failing to live up to that discourse. As I have indicated, Frankenstein has our sympathy, but why sympathise with a grave-robber? I would argue there are two main reasons which sit uneasily together. On the one hand, we are dealing with the ideology of success, where a brilliant individual strives to increase knowledge and better a humanity which just does not want to know. Here we have the basis of capitalist individualism: the indi-vidual, acting alone and significantly with no financial worries – how many individuals have private means? – rejected by the ignorant who must be left to their own devices. At the same time, Frankenstein's hubris and megalomania must be denounced: he is not Christian enough, always a good way to damn the overreacher. On the other hand, his work is con-demned by men – his teacher Dr Waldman, his friend Victor – whose devotion to social standing, marriage and the status quo are second to none. Then there is Henry's father, the Baron.

A doddering old fool whose only ambition for his son is that he should organise mindless activities to keep the peasants happy, the Baron is strangely horrified when the Mayor, evoking Henry's imminent marriage, hopes it will produce a son who will resemble Henry, as he does his father: 'God forbid!' he gasps. This has been interpreted as suggesting the Baron knows his son is homosexual. And the homosexuality of director James Whale and the bisexuality of actor Colin Clive (Henry) is cited as evidence of this. Using such extratextual elements to prove a theory smacks of an unconscious desire to create an imaginary gay identity. I would suggest that the father unconsciously knows his son rejects the sort of conservative, anti-feminist patriarchy he, Victor and Waldman represent, that there is at the core of Henry's being a desire which he cannot express consciously because of the repressive nature of the society which has produced him. It rejects the social and sexual values of his father in favour of knowledge and research, but cannot find expression except in a way which estranges his future wife and leads to an unconscious repetition of that exploitation of which Henry is also a victim.

It is for this reason that *Frankenstein* is of more consequence than *Bride of Frankenstein*, usually seen as an openly gay movie. That Pretorius is a misogynistic old 'queen' who confronts Frankenstein's wife in an attempt to take the passive Henry from her and that the scene where he and Frankenstein bring the Bride to life is shot so as to represent two men as mirror images of each other lends itself to a 'queer' reading I would not deny. Yet this marginalises too much: the negative representation of Pretorius can only reinforce sexist prejudices about homosexuals being effeminate and 'bitchy', hardly a progressive move. And the representation of the peasant woman played by Una O'Connor as a stupid coward who can do nothing but scream suggests a contempt for women on Whale's part that must also be taken into account. However, it is the lack of that Utopian dimension to Frankenstein's work analysed above that makes *Bride of Frankenstein* a less interesting work.

iii) JEKYLL AND HYDE

I shall concentrate on the 1931 version, incomparably superior to that of 1941. We are fortunate that Hollywood should have produced the film so early in the decade, as certain aspects – Hyde's sadism, blatant sexuality and frightening violence, the extraordinary sensuality of Ivy when she seduces Jekyll — would have caused problems several years later. As it stands the film is remarkable, one of the major works not only of the genre but also of the decade, notably in its representation of the unconscious, women and class.

After his encounter with Ivy, to which I shall return, Jekyll says to his colleague Lanyon: 'I want to be clean, not only in my conduct but in my innermost thoughts and desires. There is only one way to do it: separate the two natures in us'. From the outset the film has striven to present the notion of a split personality in terms of good and evil, cleanliness and dirtiness, restraint and its rejection. Restraint is fundamental to Freudian psychoanalysis: the notion that the human subject must give up the immediate satisfaction of many desires in the name of a civilised and responsible intersubjectivity. The film's conscious 'either ... or' tactic reflects Lacan's Imaginary Order, binary oppositions that repress the social and the cultural in favour of an eternal and an ahistorical re-working of pre-Oedipal harmony. Consciously Jekyll echoes this conservative appeal to the established order, while at other times challenging it radically and just as consciously. The film is thus riven by contradictions which prove productive. Both Jekyll and his fiancée Muriel protest at her father's refusal to allow them to marry earlier: he had to wait, so must they. Their discussions are not only couched in sexual terms, but smack of sadism on the father's part: he evokes 'training' in a way that condenses both his military training and toilet training, manifesting the unconscious social traits of retention and hence repression, both psychic and social. The couple insist they cannot wait, which fore-grounds the dimension of sexual desire and refuses to reduce marriage to having children.

One has to remember the repressive context of the censorship imposed by dour Protestant Will Hays to appreciate the scene where Jekyll treats Ivy, who has been beaten up by a client: naked in bed, she dangles a gartered leg and swings it to and fro. The subsequent dissolve to Jekyll and Lanyon talking after leaving her translates perfectly what is going on, not only in Jekyll's mind, but in Lanyon's too: the seductive leg and the two men are co-present in the image. One can understand the importance of Jekyll's remark, to the effect that 'it's the things one *can't* do that tempt me', especially in the light of Lanyon's disgust, due to his unconscious awareness of his own attraction to Ivy. However, this remark needs contextualising, to be seen as part of the film's discourse on the relation between Jekyll and his fiancée and, especially, on Hyde as a signifier of class conflict. Early in the film Jekyll and Muriel are talking alone in the garden when he comments 'you've opened a gate into another world'. Then, somewhat incongruously, he admits this frightens him and evokes the unknown which 'now looks at me with your eyes'. This juxtaposition of science and woman indicates that if the scientist must press on with his quest for knowledge then no attempt must be made to fathom the feminine, which indicates another dimension of that 'overproximity' discussed above in the context of the vampire. We are here in the realm of the Sublime and Lacan's Thing, an excessive proximity to which will transform it into something monstrous. Think of the bathroom scene in *The Shining* where the beautiful and naked young woman who approaches the hero turns into a putrescent old hag. This is male castration anxiety and all it implies: the implacable Real of mortality.

This fear is not a private affair concerning Jekyll: it is psychically and socially determined. Jekyll needs marriage because it will justify that proximity to the female body which, unbeckoned, can trigger off anxiety. His progressive arguments are thus a screen protecting him from the Real of difference and death. The situation is, however, more complex than this, as we can see in a discussion between Hyde and Ivy in a working-class pub. The 'feudal baron' aspect of Hyde – who is dressed in clothes which suggest that he belongs to the upper class, like Jekyll, Lanyon and General Carew, the father – makes an interesting link with Dracula and Frankenstein's father, particularly the former; he harks back to the Middle Ages and 'bleeds people dry', a case of class exploitation. Despite his sadism and violence, Hyde is overcome by Ivy and says she deserves better, to which she replies: 'Buckingham Palace, I suppose'. Hyde roars with laughter: 'That's the spirit!' What is happening here? Is Hyde just wanting to thumb his nose at bourgeois decorum? Not so. Let us return to the sequence where Jekyll and Lanyon leave Ivy, her leg literally on their minds. A further dissolve shows them walking through a sedate residential part of London. The juxtaposition of poverty and wealth, which are linked through a dissolve, can also be interpreted as spatial, at least discursively, in which case the film is hinting subversively at a form of dependence: wealth is attained by maintaining the vast majority of the population in a state of poverty. The master cannot do without his slave but passes off this dependence as natural, just like marriage and sexual restraint. Hyde thus represents, in his triumphant cry, Jekyll's political unconscious, a throwing-off of class barriers in the name of class solidarity, a desire for genuine change. He is also the manifestation of Carew's desire freed of the restraints of the superego: put the clock back to the 'good old days' when one could rape, torture and pillage with impunity, which is how Hyde behaves on other occasions towards Ivy.

Two elements in the politically correct 1941 version are of interest. Jekyll writes to his fiancée Beatrice of his determination to carry on with his experiments, despite her father's opposition, even if it means death. As he pens this word, cut to Beatrice waking up from a nightmare. She then rushes over to see Jekyll, sensing he has gone away. As he comforts her, who should walk in but Sir Charles, another excessively stern father. All this strains credulity on a conscious level but has its own unconscious logic. Beatrice does not fear that Jekyll is going away but, rather, wants her father to, which means that she unconsciously wants him to die. Only then can she have access to her lover. Similarly, the arrival of Sir Charles is the unconscious of patriarchy functioning: he will give up his daughter only if he dictates the conditions, the patriarch determined to impose the logic of money and social standing on Jekyll. The remake thus fleetingly asks to be read as an early proto-feminist work and is also of interest as anticipating the frequent use of nightmares in contemporary horror.

The other element concerns class. The film opens with a sermon about moral values and the need to follow the example of Queen Victoria. Suddenly a man of working-class origins starts to heckle the parson, evoking the Devil. Jekyll takes over as the man is escorted out so that he will not be imprisoned but put in his, Jekyll's, care, for Jekyll has seen in the episode the proof of his belief in the struggle between good and evil. The scene exists to show that a good man – a 'solid citizen' as Jekyll significantly calls him – can be prey to evil forces: the worker disrupting a sermon whose purpose is to defend the most smug and repressive status quo. We soon learn that the man had been living a normal life up until an explosion at work. Here we find a contradiction inherent in capitalism. 'Normal' indicates the man accepted his class exploitation as natural, but the film is forced to find a reason to explain his 'evil' outburst and, unwittingly, evokes one based on class: it is not people like the parson, Jekyll and Sir Charles who will have to risk their lives so that those who do not work can live in luxury. Both Carew and Sir Charles consider that Jekyll's aim in life is to build up a private practice and make

money, but only the 1931 version shows up systematically the ideological tensions at work.

iv) WEREWOLF OR WOLFMAN?

This is not a question of semantics but paramount in distinguishing
between *Werewolf of London* and *The Wolfman*. Dr Glendon in the former
is a mad scientist, but a sympathetic one like Frankenstein and Jekyll.
Larry Talbot the Wolfman is a victim. *Werewolf* is the first of its kind, but
feature films of the 40s – *The Undying Monster*, *Cry of the Werewolf* –
have been overshadowed by films which bring together two or more
characters from the 30s, such as *Frankenstein Meets the Wolfman*. In *House
of Frankenstein* and *House of Dracula* Dracula, Frankenstein and his
monster, the Wolfman and sundry mad scientists coexist uneasily.

Figure 2 The mad scientist transformed: classic horror. *Werewolf of London*. Copyright © 2002 by Universal Studios. Courtesy of Universal Studios Publishing Rights,
a Division of Universal Studios Licensing, Inc. All rights reserved.

Glendon is bitten by a werewolf when on an expedition to Tibet and spends the rest of the film trying to cultivate a flower that is the only antidote to his condition. However, he has a rival: Dr Yogami, none other than the Tibetan werewolf who also needs the flower to keep were-wolfery at bay. Another rival appears, this time the childhood sweetheart of Glendon's young wife, whom Glendon has neglected in the name of science. It is in this context that the journey to Tibet takes on a precise colouring. Glendon meets there a British priest who warns him not to venture further as there are 'some things it is better not to bother with'. Thus is raised the question of knowledge, but it takes on another form; Glendon calls the priest 'Father'. Now the difference of age between him and his wife places him in a paternal position, notably when he gives her orders, tells her to leave him alone and looks upon the young man Paul as a danger. There is much going on here, but I shall highlight just one element. Glendon's neglect of his wife betrays the same fear of woman as Jekyll's comparison of his fiancée with the unknown, and the fact that Glendon and his 'sibling' Yogami battle for the flower turns it into an object *a* destined to protect them from castration anxiety and difference. Paul is the providential answer to this: he is the same age as the wife, so steps in to eliminate the neurotic males and position himself as the 'natural' partner. He does this by marrying her after Glendon's death and flying off to America with her, an ending which is its own ideological project: America as fetish, answer to all problems.

It is therefore significant that Larry Talbot should return to Britain after many years in America, consciously a ploy to explain the accent of Lon Chaney, Jr., but in reality part of Hollywood's ideological unconscious. Attacked by werewolf Bela, he turns into a beast at the full moon and goes on the rampage. He is killed by his own father, the local squire. However, the father kills the son not to put him out of his misery or to protect the community, but because of what Larry has come to represent. His years in America have estranged him from the notion that his sole function is to carry on the family line and run the family home and the village in feudal fashion. For this is the function his father wishes to impose upon him: with Larry's brother dead, it is up to the younger brother to assume his phallic and patriarchal rights. Larry does not feel up to this role and hence is led, unconsciously, to question his masculine subjectivity and to entertain doubts about himself. In a society that distributes roles according to gender and class, Larry is doubly guilty, of not wanting to lord it over the locals and of failing to be a 'real' man. Psychoanalysis can help us in this explicit social context. The transformation of man to beast takes place once a month, an immediate parallel being set up with menstruation. I would argue that this transformation is a perfect case of hysteria, where the subject's repressed desire or fear of that desire inscribes itself onto the body. Psychosomatic blindness is a hysterical reaction to what one refuses to see, such as sexual difference. By refusing to shape up like a true son, Larry behaves in a non-virile manner all too quickly assimilated in our societies to weakness, a feminine trait. The father kills the son for not being man enough, according to the dominant values he represents.

v) KONG

The most famous horror film of the decade is a fascinating case of representing what one does not want to acknowledge, as can be seen by the way Carl Denham, film maker, big-game hunter and entrepreneur, blames the ape's death on its love for Ann Darrow, the woman Denham saved in the opening sequence from being yet another (female) victim of the Depression. This inversion is typical of the way both ideology and the unconscious function and should encourage us not to take Denham at his word. Let us consider the now celebrated sequence where Denham encourages Ann to experience fear, and where she, looking horrified off-screen, utters that piercing scream. Two theorists will help us here. The first is Linda Williams, discussing the difference between the male and the female look:

> The male look expresses conventional fear at that which differs from itself. The female look — a look given preeminent position in the horror film — shares the male fear of the monster's freakishness, but also recognises the sense in which this freakishness is similar to her own difference ... The strange sympathy and affinity that often develops between the monster and the girl may thus be less an expression of sexual desire (as in *King Kong*, *Beauty and the Beast*) and more a flash of sympathetic identification. (Williams 1996: 20–1).

Williams is stressing here the male fear of castration symbolised by anatomical difference and the way horror films displace the issue by equating the monster and the woman as twin sources of that anxiety. Fear, however, is the reverse of fascination, central to *King Kong*. The ape is turned into a fetish, at once representing the male phallus in order to reinforce masculine superiority and the maternal phallus that soothes the troubled male and protects him from anxiety.

Roger Dadoun has insisted on the Marxist meaning of fetish, where an object becomes fascinating by its ability to erase all traces of labour and be admired for itself, outside class, economics and history. Thus the apple Ann steals at the outset is divested of its social and economic significance – she is starving and forced to prostitute herself – and transformed into a fetish that brings man and woman together as objects of mutual fascination:

> Human relationships and their outcome gravitate around a tiny stolen apple, a radiating fetishistic centre. That's the end result of a socio-economic system in which Marxism sees the fetishism of goods, money and capital taken to an extreme, to the point of caricature. (Dadoun 1989: 44)

Dadoun rightly sees this represented in the closing sequence where Kong is exhibited to bourgeois New York, a fetish hiding all traces of colonial exploitation, working-class misery and toil in the name of the pleasure of the happy few. Ann's scream faced with an absence (the off-screen) that later becomes a presence (Kong looking down at her) is a perfect representation of fetishism in the Freudian sense; the absent maternal phallus is seen as present. Similarly, Kong's fascinating presence in the theatre is the representation of the Marxist theory of fetishism, where a presence (proletarian labour) is passed off as an absence the better to enjoy the product as natural and shoring up the ego's narcissistic identity. If we take up these observations in the light of Williams' reference to 'sympathetic identification' between Kong and Ann, then we can perhaps draw a provocative conclusion: there is no textual proof that Kong is male.

To claim that the title of the film proves Kong is male is to mistake authorial intention for textual coherence which has its own unconscious logic, here political. It is surely the height of anthropomorphism to assume Kong finds Ann sexually attractive. What evidence is there that a primate can tell the difference between a male and a female human, let alone symbolise that difference in terms of sexual desire? The ape does not have access to language, Lacan's Symbolic Order. Let us, however, for the sake of argument, go along with that line of reasoning, but turn it upside down. If this is to be the case, Kong pursuing Ann is Kong seeing in Ann a kindred spirit; someone exploited by capital and patriarchy. Kong's 'love' for Ann is an early form of female bonding, neglected in favour of its male counterpart. *King Kong* thus looks ahead to films like *Thelma and Louise*. At the same time, if we bring the strands of class, gender and colour together — remembering the film's racist representation of otherness in the island sequences — then the shot where Kong breaks the chains can be summed up in a paraphrase of Marx: 'Workers, women and blacks of the world, unite! You have nothing to lose but your chains'.

To terminate this chapter, I want to consider another manifestation of 'sympathetic identification' which is turned into its opposite: horror. It occurs in *Freaks* — still one of the most misunderstood and underrated horror movies — when Cleopatra the trapeze artist is accepted into the community of the freaks who think she sincerely wants to join them by marrying Hans. As they chant 'one of us, one of us', the camera cuts to her and her mounting horror: she sees the sympathetic identification creating a link between the freaks and her as the return of the repressed. For the freaks represent difference in a radical form and the possibility that any of us could have been born deformed. This is too monstrous to contemplate and she insults them. It is this terrifying moment that returns like the repressed for the spectator at the end of the film where the freaks crawl and slither through the mud and rain to finish off Cleopatra's lover Hercules, before turning to Cleopatra. Browning has been accused of giving in to precisely the fear of difference and 'monstrousness' that *Freaks* so implacably pillories, but nothing could be further from the truth. The freaks are simply identifying totally with the *image* of them purveyed by a benighted society. We are monsters, you tell us. Very well, we shall behave like monsters. And they turn Olga into a literal travesty of monstrousness, of the inhuman, a 'chicken woman'.

2

VARIATIONS ON A THEME

⎯⎯∞⎯⎯

Reference has already been made to the mad doctor or scientist. This chapter is devoted to him in his various guises, not necessarily as a doctor or scientist. What links the various characters is a thirst for power and recognition, a drive gone berserk. Their madness has all the traits of the death drive duly projected onto others who must suffer in their place. This madness has a precise sadistic component. I propose to broach the subject via a consideration of the theme of death.

i) BACK FROM THE DEAD

The zombie and the Mummy are other emblematic figures introduced in the early 30s in *White Zombie* and *The Mummy*. Both films also approach the occult which figures prominently in *Supernatural*, *The Walking Dead* and *The Devil Commands*. Death, then, is a central preoccupation but is handled in different ways.

White Zombie is a most complex work, bringing together as it does hypnosis, male bonding and colonialism. What is fascinating about the film is its implicit equation between women and black slave labour. Murder Legendre, the virtual owner of Haiti, turns local workers into zombies so that they will work for nothing (I refer readers to my comments on *Frankenstein*). Wealthy plantation owner Beaumont gets Legendre to transform Madeline, the inaccessible object of his infatuation, into a zombie by the use of poison so that he can possess her. The problem for Beaumont is that, unlike Legendre, he can draw no profit of an economic or a sexual nature from the situation: Madeline is as oblivious to him as Jessica is to her husband in *I Walked with a Zombie*

25

(Chapter 3). Thus Legendre has everyone in his power: workers, businessmen and politicians he has zombified in order to control the island
without hindrance, but also Beaumont and Madeline. Intriguing too is
the nature of the relation between Legendre and Beaumont. At one
point the former says, 'I have taken a fancy to you, Monsieur'. Rather
than endow this with the inevitable gay reading, we should see it rather
as placing Legendre in the same category as Dracula, symbol of drives
that brook no restraint or repression, a narcissist who has regressed to
the pre-Oedipal in striving to 'enjoy' both men and women alike. Once
we place this in an economic context, Legendre becomes a typical
capitalist, transforming every person into an object, a means to obtain
money and pleasure effortlessly.

One of Legendre's weapons in his drive for power is hypnotism, a
theme central to *The Mummy*. If we remove the theme from the context
of the love of high-priest Imhotep for his Princess and his belief that
Helen Grosvenor is her modern reincarnation, the film turns into a
reflection on the control of woman by man, albeit a control cut off from
the precise economic parameters of *White Zombie*. Contradictions,
however, abound. Imhotep is intellectually and psychically stronger than
any of the British archaeologists in Egypt and is just as capable of
producing a fatal heart attack in a man as of hypnotising a woman. Also
striking is the insipid nature of Helen's fiancé, incapable of saving her.
I refuse to put this down to the poor acting of David Manners – already
witnessed in *Dracula* and later to be exhibited in *The Black Cat* – and
see rather the fascination exerted by someone exceptional, whatever
his moral qualities, on characters and spectators alike. Imhotep is hence
a variant on the mad doctor as well as a case of 'mad love', another
theme to which we shall return. *The Mummy* thus both dehistoricises the
implications of a colonial presence through the fetishisation of a love
affair and hints at unconscious social dissatisfaction, our sympathy for
Imhotep stemming less from his status as lover than from our feeling
that here is someone who can escape the constraints of time – death as
the only 'reward' for a life of toil – in the name of desire.

Both *Supernatural* and *The Devil Commands* turn on this longing for
something other than a boring and repetitive existence, the lot of most
people forced to sell their labour without any class advantages, and boast
ghosts, mediums and mad scientists. In the former Ruth Rogen is con-
demned to the electric chair for murdering three lovers and psychologist

Dr Houston requests her body be handed over to him after execution to 'prove' his theory that personality can escape after death: he wants to prevent her 'evil' from living on. Consciously, the film presents murder as evil; unconsciously, female sexual independence as a resistance to patriarchy and capitalist expropriation. Rogen refuses: 'my body's my own', a remarkable piece of proletarian self-defence. Moreover, she is unrepentant about her crimes: 'I'd do it again and again and again'. We are entitled, given the fact that the film implies the three lovers were killed simultaneously after an 'orgy', to see this remark as a reference to the sex act, which means Rogen has committed the unpardonable sin of acceding to pleasure outside patriarchal control. A parallel, but in an inverse form, is set up between her and the heroine Roma Courtney, who tries to contact her dead twin John via medium Paul Bavian. Rogen possesses Roma's body and John's spirit must fight to save her and ensure that she marries the man of *his* choice. Just as Rogen wants to 'possess' her own body as her property, so John claims the right to 'possess' his sister's in the name of family values and Roma's huge inheritance which she must share with a suitable husband. Roma's body belongs to her dead twin and her future husband, the only way of protecting bourgeois society from Rogen's 'evil'.

This is thematically pure Gothic; an inheritance which is both psychic and economic. It is central to *The Devil Commands* where a phoney medium tries to control a mad scientist for reasons of power and money. Dr Blair (Karloff in one of his best and most interesting roles) is convinced he can record the impulses of the brain, even after death, and maintain contact with the deceased, a notion that becomes obsessive after the tragic demise of his wife. The film's theme seems to be the supernatural which it represents most effectively via the wind that rises whenever Blair tries to communicate with the dead, a sort of 'wind from nowhere' that represents Lacan's Real: the absolute of death itself (films as different as *Videodrome* and *Firestarter* use the same tactic). The textual unconscious is conveyed via a name: Karl, Blair's assistant and a victim of his experiments. We are surely entitled to express surprise that an American should be called Karl, until we remember that this was the name of Frankenstein's assistant in *Bride of Frankenstein* (in *Frankenstein* he was called Fritz). Is Karl Marx being evoked here in a distorted form? Blair's assistant is an inverse form of Karl; just as Whale's character tormented the creature in order to misrecognise his own status as exploited proletarian, so Karl defends Blair from the irate townspeople because he is already alientated. Just as the townspeople blame everything on science because they fail to see how they are exploited economically, so Karl's touching faith in Blair enables him to repress the reasons for his mental and physical deformity via a fetishisation of that very science which has abused him.

The Devil Commands is both effective and unsettling, not because it is better realised than *Supernatural*, but because it represents, in all its contradictions, the analyses of Adorno in 'Theses against Occultism':

As a rationally exploited reaction to rationalized society ... reborn animism denies the alienation of which it is itself proof and product, and concocts surrogates for non-existent experience. The occultist draws the ultimate conclusion from the fetish-character of commodities: menacingly objectified labour assails him on all sides from demonically grimacing objects. What has been forgotten in a world congealed into products, the fact that it has been produced by men, is split off and misremembered as a being-in-itself added to that of the objects and equivalent to them. (Adorno 1974: 239)

These timely remarks clearly apply to horror in general, notably to the theme of the power the mad scientist strives to obtain in an attempt to ward off the effects of alienation, which he is prompt to impose on others who become his victims. This is one of the concepts we shall return to in the following sections, but first I want to consider a rather special case: *The Walking Dead*.

What is special about the film is its mixing of genres; it is as much a gangster movie as a horror one. That this is due to its production history — made by Warners, specialists in crime movies — is clear: Curtiz's two other horror movies of the period (*Dr X*, *Mystery of the Wax Museum*) have wise-cracking reporters in key roles. This fusion of horror and gangsterism returns in later films: *Black Friday* and *The Monster and the Girl*, which boasts the finest bunch of 'heavies' outside *film noir*, and *The Face Behind the Mask*, closer to the gangster movie and devoid of the supernatural, but with a clear debt to *Mystery of the Wax Museum*. What is striking about the production is the way it was sold, with posters representing hero John Elman (Karloff) as a threatening, bald-headed Nosferatu, whereas he has a full head of hair and is an innocent victim of gangsters who frame him for a murder. Executed on the electric chair, he survives and is treated by a scientist who wants to discover the meaning of life after death. Elman can no longer reason and speak coherently and spends the rest of the film hunting down the gangsters, who die one by one. However, this is represented less as revenge than as something that drives him without his knowledge, an unconscious memory of what he was. I suspect that this unusual story, handled with intelligence and sensitivity by Curtiz, failed to correspond to what was expected from a horror movie, but also that its insistence on class and how upper-class gangsters can cheat the law (a theme more explicit here than in *The Monster and the Girl*, but less well worked out than in *The Face behind the Mask*) needed defusing. Unsettling too is the sight of Elman, a version of the zombie, tracking down his victims without knowing what he is doing, a sight that comes uncomfortably close to representing the Real of mortality for spectators, a force that is unthinking and irresistible. The film gets out of the quandary by evoking God: only He can have knowledge of life after death, which is meant to put the mad doctor in his place. However, he pays no heed.

ii) JUST WHAT THE MAD DOCTOR ORDERED

Frankenstein, Jekyll, Glendon and Blair are made sympathetic to the audience, but this is a minority situation in 30s horror, as a checklist shows: Mirakle (*Murders in the Rue Morgue*), Moreau (*Island of Lost Souls*), von Niemann (*The Vampire Bat*), Vollin (*The Raven*), Crespi (*The Crime of Dr Crespi*), Rukh (*The Invisible Ray*), Thorkel (*Dr Cyclops*) and Rigas (*Man Made Monster*) are unlikely to have spectators rooting for them. Nor are businessman Eric Gorman (*Murders in the Zoo*) and architect Hjalmar Poelzig (*The Black Cat*). Xavier (*Dr X*) is more sympathetic than not, although his colleagues are all antipathetic. Sculptor Igor (*Mystery of the Wax Museum*), the Invisible Man, Vitus Werdegast (*The Black Cat*) and Gogol (*Mad Love*) arouse conflicting responses within each of us, as men driven over the edge by hostile circumstances not of their choosing. At this juncture a question must be asked: is there such a difference between Frankenstein and Moreau — both of them seek to create a human being, the former from the dead, the latter from animals — that the former should arouse our sympathy, whereas the latter is represented in a totally negative fashion?

I shall defer a reply and tease out factors common to a number of films. Revenge for some slight that has bruised their monstrous ego can be sufficient, as *Murders in the Zoo*, *The Crime of Dr Crespi* and *The Raven* show. *Murders* opens with one of the nastiest scenes consigned to film in the decade: in the jungle Gorman sews up the mouth of a man who has shown interest in his wife, ties his arms behind his back and abandons him to be eaten by tigers. Gorman is a perfect representation of the paranoiac who is unconsciously homosexual, his suppression of the man's mouth symbolising his fear of the 'gaping wound' of the female genitals. Significantly, he murders his wife by throwing her into the gaping mouth of a crocodile. He is also the perfect capitalist, letting nothing stand in the way of economic success, his quest for power. Crespi punishes a man whom the woman he loved preferred to him by deliberately botching an operation after an accident and making it appear that the victim has died. In fact Crespi has injected him with a drug that creates a state of catalepsy so that he can have him buried alive; he will regain consciousness the next day. One scene has Crespi, speaking softly as if to the woman he loves, sitting by the paralysed victim and recounting to him, in sadistic detail that had the censors denounce the film as 'revolting', what it will feel like to hear the earth falling on the coffin. This suggests that Crespi is projecting onto the wretch his own fear of premature burial, a fear that returns implacably like the repressed for the spectator in a chilling scene later. Medical colleagues of Crespi suspect the man was murdered and dig him up within hours. They leave his body in a room and go in search of Crespi. Auer places his camera at one end of a corridor, in front of a desk where a nurse is on duty. Then a door opens in the background and the 'corpse' emerges, making its way slowly towards the nurse/us until she becomes aware of what is happening. The anxiety induced by this extraordinary shot comes from our understanding of what the man has been through, but especially of the effect on the nurse for whom it is a case of the dead returning.

In *The Raven* Dr Vollin becomes infatuated with Jean, the daughter of Judge Thatcher, after watching her perform a dance based on Poe's poem 'Leonore'. Vollin's own obsession with Poe is thus exacerbated by desire, but he is dismissed as mad when he requests her hand from Thatcher. Such a thwarting of the drive for satisfaction transforms pleasure into mental pain, a torture which Vollin, taking a leaf out of Poe's book, projects onto Thatcher. He imprisons the judge in the dungeon under his house in order to inflict on him the fate reserved for the victim of the Inquisition in 'The Pit and the Pendulum'. This most complex and under-rated movie represents remarkably the death drive and what happens when others are designated by the psychotic to submit to the fate he unconsciously seeks to put himself out of his misery: death itself. The fact that Vollin's residence can be turned into a self-contained fortress by sealing it off from the world by steel shutters can be seen as symbolising for him a tomb, as well as the single-minded pursuit, cut off from society and its constraints, of his drives. Significantly, he finds what he was looking for in the form of a torture reserved for others: he is trapped and crushed to death in a room whose walls and ceiling close in on him, very much like a form of premature burial. That *Crespi* was inspired by Poe's story of that name is eloquent testimony to the obsessive nature of the theme of death in horror.

Mad Love will allow us to extend the discussion in an attempt to answer the question asked above concerning Frankenstein and Moreau. The opening sequence, where wealthy surgeon Dr Gogol attends the representation of a Grand Guignol play – a young woman is tortured on a rack by her husband for loving another man – is notable for its condensation of pain, terror and pleasure, the co-presence of sadism and masochism. By having the wife cry out in a way that condenses pain and orgasm, the film makes the woman a typical victim, while also admitting the problematic nature of female sexuality. It also represents the inherent human need to go beyond the pleasure principle with its attendant con-stancy. Gogol, his eyes closed in ecstasy, is clearly having an orgasm, but passivity and not seeing suggest on his part both masochism and a disavowal of the senses of a fetishistic nature concerning the female body. His infatuation with the young woman and his later admission he has had no sexual experience only reinforce the Oedipal dimension of the opening where Gogol unconsciously occupies at least three subjective positions through multiple identifications. He is the absent lover of the play, a fantasy enabling him to live out what he cannot attain in reality. He is a child present at the primal scene, mistaking the cries of pleasure for those of pain; in this scenario the victim represents the mother. He is also in the position of the woman, both enjoying pleasure and punishing himself for his incestuous desire. This last position is masochistic and fits badly with Gogol's megalomania and his opinion of how society sees him. His fame makes him a man of decision and character, training young doctors as surgeons. Nor can his social standing accommodate such humiliations as torture, passivity and guilt. These are later projected into the outside world in their inverted form: he tries to control the woman, exploits her pianist husband whose hands he has saved after an accident, and generally indulges in childish but vicious acts of sadism.

The incest theme is paramount in *Dr X* and I insist on it because of Berenstein's rejection of the notion in favour of a 'queer' reading that I accept, but with reservations. (Berenstein 1996: 124–8) It is evident that one scene is shot in such a way that it hints at 'unnatural' acts between men under a sheet. An earlier scene, however, is ambiguous in another way. Xavier's daughter enters his library looking for him, looks off-screen right and utters a gasp of horror. Cut to Xavier on a ladder, reading, and looking back at her in surprise. Now there is no reason for her reaction, as she expected him to be there. Moreover, he is alone. What is of interest, however, is that the room is in darkness, except for a small light by which Xavier is consulting a volume. We are in the presence of yet another primal scene and one that can be interpreted in the light of infantile bisexuality: Joanna's entry into the library has triggered off not an unconscious incestuous desire with her father as object, but the unconscious memory of such a desire with her mother as object. I offer this as a complementary reading to Berenstein's, not an alternative, as her remarks about homosocial relations between men are incisive. I would argue that incest becomes even more taboo when it takes the form of a daughter insisting on the role of her relationship to the mother instead of submitting to patriarchy and accepting the appropriate male, the better to inscribe herself into a self-perpetuating social situation where the woman is submissive. This reading is easy to defend in a film where Joanna falls for a nincompoop of a reporter, especially as this love interest clearly exists in order to save her from predatory males, of whom her father is one. What *Dr X* shows on the mode of disavowal is that 'unnatural' acts between men are no more unnatural than a young woman devoting herself to finding a husband.

Igor, the sculptor in the better known *Mystery of the Wax Museum*, is deprived of his artistic rights by his associate, a businessman who burns down the Wax Museum because Igor is more interested in art than in bringing in the public. Igor survives but is hideously burned, a fact we learn only at the end when his face is revealed as a mask. A decade later he has set up another Museum in Paris, but the waxworks are real people he has killed and plunged into wax in order to attain verisimilitude. This calls for a dual interpretation. On the one hand the insane Igor, craving immortality, has projected his death drive onto others who die in his place, at the same time ensuring his fame, and lasting for ever. On the other hand, his action is akin to that of his former partner: a striving for success and satisfaction, with the economic dimension displaced onto the artistic. Igor becomes a victim, not of a greedy man, but of an economic system which he then interiorises and transforms in his deranged mind into its artistic equivalent. He obtains the unconscious satisfaction of his death drive by plunging into a vat of molten wax.

We have come some way to answering our deferred question by indicating the social and economic dimensions pertaining to horror films; the characters are men of independent means undertaking experiments or business activities as if these go without saying, as if their social standing as men gives them every right. I explicitly compared Frankenstein to Moreau in *Island of Lost Souls*, so let us return to him. His 'House of Pain', where he carries out vivisection on live animals to transform them into humans, is more cruel than Frankenstein making a body from parts of dead people, but it is uncertain spectators will see this as more horrible: the dead are sacrosanct and society has always justified torturing animals to further medical knowledge. I suggest we look elsewhere. Frankenstein is a capitalist exploiter of labour, Moreau a colonialist with a steady supply of slave labour. The difference lies in the fact that the class and economic discourse is more conscious in *Lost Souls*, where the creatures call themselves 'things' and Moreau's striving for total hegemony leaves us in no doubt as to his desire to play God in more ways than one. In *Frankenstein*, the illusion remains that the hero has no desire to lord it over all Creation. In other words, his individualism can be contained within the capitalist discourse of science existing as a form of progress: audiences can identify with his desire to better himself through knowledge as this does not clash with society's interests in general. They reject him because what he is doing is *morally* wrong. There is, however, no way of identifying with Moreau who is pure egoism and cruelty. In that sense he is a more 'perfect' capitalist than Frankenstein. Moreau is the signifier of the true, untrammelled drives of capitalism, hence his being uniquely unsympathetic, this quality being separated off from the class and economic aspects of his experiments and presented as an individual failing. He cares for nobody but himself, and this is far too close to the truth of the system he symbolises to be tolerated. Moreau is the return of the repressed of the most ruthless aspects of capitalism, another Hyde perhaps. This is the film's 'political unconscious' making its effects felt and it is to politics that we shall turn to conclude.

iii) THE POLITICS OF HORROR

Hollywood is better known for its horror of politics; what one critic has written about German silent cinema applies there too:

> ... being chosen by fate or chance for social success is itself a distorted version of a class-struggle, insofar as a personal, individual solution is offered by the film, while the question of the whole class or group is blocked off and suppressed. Social rise is thus a version of the class-struggle that denies the existence of the struggle. (Elsaesser 1989: 26)

In *King Kong* Ann's social mobility is assured through marriage: thanks to men she will survive the Depression. The reality of class antagonism is manifest in an inverted form in Kong's attack on the New Yorkers packed like sardines into the subway train, whereas their exploiters have the leisure of admiring Kong, whose attack on them is thus the return of the repressed in terms of class. In the inane *Son of Kong* Denham refers scornfully to the striking seaman as 'the Soviet'. *Dr Cyclops* shows that no detail is innocent. After the characters, three American scientists, an American guide and Pedro the peasant, have been shrunk by Thorkel, we see them dressed in the latter's handkerchiefs, which are draped around them like togas, all except Pedro who wears his like a loin-cloth; it would never do to place him on the same class level as the Americans, although he later dies saving them. *The Devil Doll*, however, foregrounds the iniquity of the economic system by making its villains bankers, who prosper as a result of stealing and framing a colleague, a striking metaphor for capitalist expropriation and exploitation.

Given the reactionary nature of *Son of Kong* and *Dr Cyclops* and the ambiguities of *King Kong*, it is interesting to reflect on Schoedsack's other horror film of the decade, *The Most Dangerous Game*. Since the scriptwriter collaborated on *Kong* and *Son*, we can legitimately ask how the film came to convey so clear an anti-Fascist statement: Zaroff is a

White Russian who dresses like Mussolini and who hunts people rather than animals on his remote island. The film dates from 1932 and *The Invisible Man* of the following year contains a scene where the scientist shows his aim is to have the world grovel at his feet. That Rigas (*Man Made Monster*) should rave in a similar fashion is no surprise; the film was made in 1941. We can tentatively attribute *Game*'s radicalism to co-director Irving Pichel, a leading left-winger who almost found himself blacklisted in 1947. A scene on board ship early in the film shows big-game hunter Rainsford in conversation with the other men in a context which explicitly assimilates their discussions about hunting animals — in Third World countries — to debates between businessmen in a boardroom. Thus the film makes an implicit link between big business and Fascism.

The presence of the Third World is sufficiently insistent during the decade to merit our attention. We see just to what extent a class and economic point of view can be represented in a text in an ideological form (*Kong, Dr Cyclops*) and an accurate political one (*Game*). Rainsford and Denham are chips off the old block and the former's killing of Zaroff in order to sail off into the sunset with the heroine is simply Hollywood's imaginary solution to the real contradictions the film has put in place. A Western presence in those countries whose underdevelopment has been carefully maintained is never innocent and a film like *The Mummy* functions according to ideological norms. The same cannot be said of another film whose blatant racism and multiple contradictions taken together produced a fascinating result: *The Mask of Fu Manchu*. Much has been made of the way Fu Manchu is represented as a homosexual: he lisps and wears a long robe. This tells us more about the film and it critics than about China, but it is relevant to note that an Asian group protested against the re-issue of the film in 1972 on the grounds that the character is 'an ugly, evil homosexual'. (Benshoff 1997: 58) That this is considered worse than the film's racism is a reminder of how real power relations are displaced so as to stigmatise the other, the condensatory signifier of the West's desire to repress its own predatory past and present and induce its indigenous victims to turn against those who are in the same situation as themselves. This was the thrust of my remarks on scapegoating in *Frankenstein, Bride of Frankenstein* and *The Devil Commands*.

Other factors at work prove even more revealing. On several occasions we see coolies looking aggressively at the film's heroes; wherever there is a dark doorway or alley, there you will find a wily Oriental. I suggest we interpret this in the same terms as the relationship between woman and monster in Linda Williams' article quoted in Chapter 1: 'when the coolie looks' becomes a method of categorising him as menacing, monstrous other. We are dealing with the fear of the woman's 'lack' or difference displaced onto the other as signifier of difference, including racial difference. The frequency of such shots suggests a literal repetition compulsion: the acting out of a desire/fear that cannot speak its name, and hence of castration anxiety. This is overdetermined historically. It is as if the coolies were the foreigners threatening the inhabitants of the country, which naturalises the British presence but also reveals the political unconscious. It is precisely because they considered they had a right to colonise that the British were in China, having triggered off the Opium Wars in order to divide and conquer. We have the full meaning of Marx's definition of religion as 'the opium of the people'. This 'threat' is thus real on one level; it translates the paranoia of the colonialist towards those exploited in their own land. The portrayal of Fu Manchu as a sadist and a homosexual is an integral part of this discourse.

Why is he dangerous? Because he is so intelligent. When Fu Manchu refers to the various degrees he holds from British and American universities, his interlocutor Sir Lionel becomes sarcastic, a sign of the quandary the film has created for itself. This it 'solves' at the end. Fu Manchu safely dispatched, Nayland Smith and the others are on board ship returning to Britain and decide to throw overboard the sword of Genghis Khan coveted by the Chinaman so as to control the world. Suddenly a gong, symbol of Fu Manchu's China, is heard. The characters turn in horror, but it is only a waiter announcing dinner. The sequence shows the power of the word − mention a name and the person returns − and of sound; it can hide something malevolent. This unconscious manifestation of the superstitions of the civilised West is displaced when Nayland Smith asks the waiter (= coolie) if he has doctorates. The bemused man assures him he has not and, as everyone laughs, Smith shakes his hand: the Oriental is acceptable as long as he is not only ignorant but admits it and considers it normal. However, such racist representations were not limited to Orientals but formed part of two particular aspects of the Hollywood horror film of the 30s: the representation of peasants and the fact that the leading actors were Europeans. Let us consider these in turn.

The contempt shown for the peasants by the Baron in *Frankenstein* seems to have been shared by Hollywood: either carefree and forever dancing, or cowardly, superstitious and vindictive, they represent class prejudice and Hollywood's view of the rest of the world. The situation is somewhat different in *The Black Room*. Faced with a curse which says that the younger brother of the family will kill the elder in the Black Room, the head of the family adopts a simple solution: wall up the room so that nobody will enter and the curse will fail. Not having read Freud, the deluded aristocrat is unaware not only that he is super-stititious, but that an Oedipal drama is being evoked in the curse, one that does not fail to materialise when the evil Gregor kills his saintly twin brother so as to rule despotically over the locals. That they rise up and demand justice — refused by those who are meant to defend them — is worth nothing as they are organised and designate someone to lead them, almost like a trade union. However, the film is in no way radical; they were perfectly happy to be ruled by Anton, so the question of class and feudal abuse is shunted off into a siding in favour of a question of individual evil and decadence. Nevertheless, the attempt to repress knowledge in favour of belief by walling up the room triggers off a return of the repressed of history, inasmuch as the film shows peasants as refusing to accept abuse as natural.

If we turn to the question of the use of European actors in the 30s, the formula 'racial stereotypes' would be more precise, especially as neither Karloff nor Lugosi were used in a way derogatory to Britain or Hungary. Furthermore, Hollywood cashed in on the celebrity of Peter Lorre after *M* by using him in *Mad Love*. Things are, however, more complex when dealing with Lionel Atwill, Colin Clive and Charles Laughton: all three are represented in ways connoting homosexuality. I refer readers back to my discussions of 'unnatural acts' in *Dr X*, the behaviour of Frankenstein in *Frankenstein* and his relations with Pretorius in *Bride of Frankenstein*. In *The Old Dark House* the Laughton character is travelling with a young woman in whom he shows no sexual interest whatsosever; she even insists on this in a discussion with a clearly 'straight' male character. It is here, however, that 'queer' readings risk being reductive, especially when they invoke extratextual elements: Laughton was known to be homosexual, so appearing in a film made by Hollywood's one openly gay director could only mean that the 'queer' elements were intentional

(Ernest Thesiger, who plays Pretorius, has a decidedly 'feminine' role in the film). But what if we displace this dubious notion of intentionality onto Hollywood's stereotypical way of portraying all things British? What if we see it as a way of ideologically downgrading Europe's culture in favour of America's, the intellectual in favour of the 'frontier spirit'. This is manifest in Atwill's performance in *Dr X*, one of the four horror movies he made in 1932–3 (the others being *The Vampire Bat*, *Mystery of the Wax Museum* and *Murders in the Zoo*). In it he wears a fur coat and spats, yet it is meant to be 1932. Atwill's pronounced English accent hardly fits in with the film, but it does create links of a fantasmatic nature with the representation of England in American popular discourse: the country of Oscar Wilde, effete aristocrats and decadence in general (this ideology is systematically represented throughout *Dracula's Daughter*, which takes place in England). Is it not significant that American actors should play the role of British scientist Dr Jekyll in both films and that both of them are 'virile' and 'vigorous' in comparison with their English counterparts?

I raise these questions because something else is at stake: the notion of history, repressed in favour of the individual with his private desires, true to Hollywood ideology. This surely is one explanation of the use of isolated laboratories, houses and castles perched on clifftops, and remote islands. The tactic is at one and the same time a way of placing class and the collectivity in parentheses and is also an indication that the mad doctor, by cutting himself off from all human contact, is acting as an individual hostile to the common good. This is again a moral argument which in turn represents an ideological tension between the capitalist notion of individual success, the uses to which science should be put and the forms success is allowed to take. It also represents an ideological contradiction where the mad doctor rejects the rights of others, which is negative, and protests against the reductive representations of science and knowledge, the mediocrity to which capitalism condemns the average person from whom the mad doctor feels alienated. Perhaps the film that comes closest to representing this is *The Raven*, where Vollin has turned his home into a literal fortress, a self-contained world with a dungeon and steel shutters which turn the residence into a watertight compartment outside history.

The Black Cat refers explicitly to history, while at the same time disavowing this in favour of a love story. The character of Vitus

Werdegast functions as the common factor of two separate elements of the script: the honeymooning couple Peter and Joan and Werdegast's plan to destroy Poelzig. The three of them find themselves in Poelzig's home after the bus they have taken to reach their final destination (they meet on a train) crashes in a storm. Werdegast's desire for revenge stems from having spent fifteen years in a Russian gaol after the War; Poelzig had betrayed the troops under his command to the Russians for personal gain. His desire is overdetermined by the fact that Poelzig stole his wife from him and, after her death, married Werdegast's daughter. And just in case that was not enough to make Poelzig unsympathetic, he is a Satanist too! We can see at work here the need to individualise Poelzig, but the background of the War turns Werdegast's determination to kill him into a collective affair with class implications: an officer betraying his troops smacks of the capitalist closing a factory or sacking workers to increase overall profits. At the end Werdegast blows up Poelzig and his home but is shot by Peter who mistakenly thinks he has harmed Joan when he was in fact trying to save her. This fact is crucial: eliminate Werdegast so that only the couple are left alive and able to continue their journey. That Peter is a novelist is also central to the overall project: unexploited since the opening, this element duly returns to suppress all others. *The Black Cat* manages thus to privilege fiction over reality, just as Hollywood privileges the couple over the collective, especially when history, class and politics are at stake. The couple continue their journey as if the events, hardly banal, that have taken place were a mere parenthesis in their honeymoon, whereas in reality the events are a tribute to history as a Master Narrative and the couple simply a pair of actors on a stage. The bland Peter (another David Manners role) fades into insignificance alongside the unholy power generated by the confrontation between Poelzig and Werdegast: the former refers to them as 'the living dead'. The implicit political message of this exceptional film will become increasingly explicit over the decades, culminating in the work of George Romero. This is already the case with *I Walked with a Zombie*, a discussion of which is central to the next chapter.

3

VAL LEWTON PRODUCTIONS

⤛∽⤚

The title of this chapter is to be taken literally: the films produced between 1942 and 1946 by Val Lewton. I am therefore interested less in who contributed what to which film than in how meaning is produced and how the films address the spectator. In rejecting the notion that Lewton was the unique intellectual driving force behind the nine movies concerned, I shall show that, whereas it is possible to demonstrate a coherent approach to film-making on the part of Jacques Tourneur, such is not the case with the films directed by Mark Robson and Robert Wise. This in turn is not an attempt to transform Tourneur into an *auteur* at the expense of the other directors but to circumscribe and analyse the nature of Tourneur's specific contribution. In short, I wish to create a theoretical tension that will enable us to go beyond the dubious concept of intention towards that of the production of meaning for and by the spectator, something that is always in excess of what the director/producer/scriptwriter claimed they were doing. To attribute one element of a film to its producer, another to its director, a third to the writer and yet others to the director of photography, set designer and editor is to assume that each element has always a fixed meaning brought to the text by an individual, that one shot is a metaphor for something else – eternity or death, tolerance or racism, a phallic symbol or whatever – and that by adding up these imaginary quantities one emerges triumphantly with the finished movie.

Lest the reader find this esoteric, let us take some data. Tourneur's films – *Cat People, I Walked with a Zombie, The Leopard Man* – were all edited by Robson who went on to direct *The Seventh Victim, The Ghost Ship, Isle of the Dead* and *Bedlam*. Wise, who later directed *The Body*

40

Snatcher, was brought in to take over direction of *Curse of the Cat People* as Gunther von Fritsch was running over schedule. Whether Wise simply shot what was left to shoot or started over from scratch is immaterial; the film's interest and coherence lie in the script. This is not to neglect its other qualities but to draw attention both to the implications of the script and the lack of similarity between *Curse* and *Body Snatcher*, just as there is a lack of similarity between the films edited by Robson and those he directed. In short, I want to incite the reader to grasp what the films directed by Tourneur achieve that is exemplary.

When *The Ghost Ship* was shown recently on French cable TV, it was presented as an example of Lewton's genius, of his method of suggesting rather than showing. It is significant of the incomprehension surrounding these films that there is nothing in the film that suggests rather than shows in the special sense that Tourneur imparted to the terms. There are, however, instances where Robson's understated direction communicates to the spectator information which cannot be immediately given a single meaning. Take the scene where a crewman is engaged in ensuring that the anchor chain is stowed properly in the space designed for it; he is inside the hold controlling the chain as it is slipped in by other crew members. This crewman has committed a mortal sin in the eyes of the authoritarian Captain by making a complaint in the name of the crew. The film informs the audience by a simple shot that the door of the hold is open so that the man can emerge. There then follows a shot where the Captain, who is inspecting operations, notices the open door, closes and locks it. We cannot deduce from this that he did it deliberately so that the object of his vindictiveness would be crushed by the chain. Given the information we have of the Captain's psychology, it can be interpreted as an unconscious gesture determined by his obsession for order. It is only later that we learn the truth: he has committed murder. Here, we just hesitate.

This, however, is quite a different matter from the hesitation produced by the Tourneur films, or rather the forms hesitation takes. The opening shot of *The Ghost Ship* gives us a clue to this crucial difference. As the credits appear, we can distinguish the vague form of a ship starting to emerge from the fog. This may summon up the idea of a ship that is returning from the past, a literal ghost, but the script quickly makes clear that the title is to be interpreted symbolically in the sense of a ship dogged by death because of the attitude of its Captain. In retrospect the only hesitation is over how the hero is going to convince the other crew members that the man is a psychotic. This is therefore a typical Hollywood product, as are all the films directed by Robson and Wise, be they supernatural or not. The decisive difference operated by the three Tourneur films is that in retrospect the hesitation remains. We are in the domain theorised by Tzvetan Todorov: the *fantastique*, where we cannot decide between a rational and a supernatural explanation. If the most celebrated literary manifestation is *The Turn of the Screw*, cinema finds its equivalent in *Cat People* and *Zombie*. If I have not mentioned *The Leopard Man*, there is a reason and I propose to start with this film.

i) THE CONTRIBUTION OF JACQUES TOURNEUR

The title itself is ambiguous. Three men fit the description: the agent who enters with a leopard to explain how it can help his client steal the show from a rival; the man who earns his living from exhibiting animals, notably a leopard; and a zoologist called upon to give his opinion over the killings that follow the escape of the leopard. This hesitation, which has nothing supernatural, is due to the film's attempt to offer a psychological interpretation which presents the zoologist's illness as lycanthropy, except that he never takes animal form. This is also what distinguishes *Leopard* from *Cat* which is *fantastique* in Todorov's sense.

What is the story of *Leopard*? A leopard escapes and three people, a girl and two women, are murdered in a way that suggests the animal was responsible. The agent, held morally responsible as it was his stunt that resulted in the creature getting loose, starts to have doubts, as we are told that the leopard is frightened and would not attack unless forced to, which is never the case. The increasingly erratic behaviour of the zoologist draws attention to him and he confesses; he is shot down by the fiancé of the last victim. I wish to propose an alternative reading which argues that the film is a reflection on fear and the representation of women that implies anxiety on the part of the spectator, directly implicated from the first shot.

This shot is of an open door leading into an empty room. The camera tracks forward slowly, to the accompaniment of a strange clicking sound. Then a woman, dancing and waving castanets, suddenly enters the frame and the source of the noise is located. Why were we not shown the women dancing in her dressing room to start with, especially as she is a central character and the second murder victim? To answer this question is to enter into the textual system of *Leopard*, for the film is built around a number of absences and the excess of meaning produced by the spectator in an attempt to find meaning in them. These absences are both literal — black spaces connoting danger — and metaphorical: the representation of women as source of anxiety. This is a complex issue which finds its most extended representation and analysis in *Zombie*.

The dancer is presented as a vain and fortune-seeking woman and the fact that she is first seen dancing for her own pleasure seems to render her narcissistic. But of course she is dancing for us, transformed by our regard and that of the camera into an object of desire. The spectators deny their place in this system of vision and representation, which Tourneur underscores in the night-club sequence. We see a reflection of the dancer in a fountain before she starts her act, thus subtly indicating that a woman is not the subject of but is subjected to representation, a mere image for others. Suddenly she stops and looks off-screen; cut to the heroine, framed in a doorway and leading a black panther. A link is drawn between the two women by the framing and by the fact that the heroine is also represented as a spectacle and functions as an image inasmuch as she is completely in shadow. Superficially, they are sisters under the skin, but in reality both are victims of a male discourse that fetishises the female body the better to ward off castration anxiety. At one point the zoologist tells the agent that people are like a ball spinning on a jet of water: they have no choice, nor are they responsible. This absolves the agent of all guilt concerning the death of little Teresa following the leopard's escape and, retrospectively, is an attempt on the part of the zoologist to plead insanity. As only women are represented as the object of the gaze and are also murder victims, *Leopard* is accusing men and their cultural artefacts of hypocrisy when they deny any responsibility for the plight of women.

This is rendered more complex with the murder of Teresa who is forced to go shopping by her mother at night; the implication is that this is a girl's job, not a boy's. The terrified child makes her way slowly through the darkness. Cut to her look as she stops. Cut to a passage between a tree and a bush, which produces anxiety by the fact that we see nothing but know the leopard could be prowling the area. However, this shot, unnerving in itself, is transformed by the film's overall structure, in particular the opening shot. There it was not a question of darkness but of an enigmatic absence due to an incomprehensible sound, the entire shot turning on the presence/absence of a woman, standing in for the presence/absence of the phallus and therefore for male castration anxiety. This is repeated with the death of the young woman who is late for an assignation with her fiancé and is locked in a cemetery. Her terrified looks off-screen are overdetermined by shots of darkened alleys where the spectator adopts her point of view.

The last shot of the film — a darkened street as the heroine and her agent walk off together — is also seen from the spectator's point of view. The street is empty and the spectator is thus placed in relation to darkness and absence as in the previous examples. Although the truth is known — the leopard and the zoologist are dead and there is no danger — the shot nevertheless takes up what we have seen, apparently for no reason. The reason, however, is not hard to find and we can locate it in the zoologist's fear of darkness. His fascination with the female form is accompanied by a feeling of power over such frail bodies. I would suggest we are seeing at work the primal scene, the child's curiosity over its parents' activities at night leading to a feeling of guilt and, later, a repression of sexual difference in an attempt to ward off castration anxiety. There is nothing like strange noises and vague movements to trigger off anxiety when no source can be pinpointed. Tormented by the sight of Teresa's body, the zoologist feels constrained to kill and it is here that the question of the darkness of the primal scene becomes operative. The child's guilt at spying on its parents is also guilt at the desire to remove one parent in order to enjoy the favours of the other. Teresa's mangled body thus drives the zoologist, unconsciously reliving his guilt, to destroy the other women in an attempt to defend his physical and psychic integrity by eliminating those whose bodies inspire dread, guilt and the fear of punishment. In this reading the leopard killed Teresa and the zoologist killed the creature after tracking it into the hills. Too late, for the cycle of fear and guilt and the need to visit on the female body the lack threatening his own has been set in motion.

Yet this conclusion is not sufficient. It could be argued that the zoologist's entire existence is based on an event, real or imaginary, from early childhood that has left indelible traumatic traces. In that case there are two possibilities: either the zoologist killed the little girl and remembered nothing of the event (hence my evoking lycanthropy); or else he killed the woman only as a result of what the sight of Teresa's body implied unconsciously. The fact that Teresa sees the leopard watching her and is pursued by it does not mean that it killed her, any more than a moving branch over the head of the women killed in the cemetery signifies the animal's presence. The film places us therefore in such a way that we find ourselves faced with a variant of the *fantastique*: a rational explanation (it was the leopard) or a psychoanalytical one (the zoologist is a psychotic). I have tried to go through the various theoretical stages to demonstrate what kinds of problems are raised by the articulation of the various elements at work but also by the evolution of the character of the zoologist. The spectator can only hesitate.

Coming a year after *Cat*, *Leopard* is instructive in that it makes explicit the fact that the marks of the creature's claws on the bodies could have been made by the assassin to fool the police. This takes up the question of the heroine's torn robe after the scene in the swimming pool in *Cat*: are they caused by Irena wielding some cutting instrument or the claws of the transformed Irena? Here we enter the *fantastique* proper where we cannot choose between the supernatural (Irena is telling the truth) and reason (we and the character are imagining it). However, *Cat* poses a number of problems. At certain points we are given information, such as growling, that obviously opts for the supernatural interpretation; at others it is impossible to decide. I will suggest a reason for this, linked to the textual unconscious and therefore determined by cultural forces coding the film's makers as a collective social unit. Firstly, we need to ascertain what is meant to be occurring in the film.

Irena, a young Serbian immigrant, is convinced that she has come under a curse that turns the females of her village into 'cat people'. Oliver, the man who befriends and falls in love with her, dismisses this as superstitious nonsense and is supported by his colleague Alice, secretly in love with him. Just as sceptical is Dr Judd, the psychiatrist Irena consults unwillingly to please Oliver, by now her husband (he is presented as a very tolerant and understanding man; he endures the absence of sexual relations in order to give Irena confidence). Already a form of hesitation is at work on the spectator's part: between a belief that people know who they are — the ideology of ego psychology that is part and parcel of Hollywood's representation of mental illness — and a rejection, like Oliver's, of anything as outrageous as such a curse. Also at work, however, is another form of hesitation, intimately linked to that involved in the *fantastique* but determined by the extratextual, namely the need to prove that Judd is not only a sexual profiteer but that his medecine is wrong and dangerous because he is patently a Freudian. We are dealing with a conflict between the conscious project of the text and the textual unconscious and it is this that I wish to address here.

Cat has two sides to its unconscious project: to prove Judd wrong in order to dismiss psychoanalysis; and to tame 'dangerous' female sexuality by having it submit not to medicine but to the 'American way of life' represented by the (depressingly) average Oliver (the choice of bland Kent Smith is perfect). The conscious project is therefore clear: lead the audience to accept that Irena really does turn into a leopard. This latter project almost succeeds and is certainly the one that critics have chosen. Almost, but not quite. The ending of the film reintroduces precisely those hesitations that Tourneur so brilliantly creates and that are meant to give way to a supernatural reading.

From the very outset the cat is presented as a symbol of evil. From a Freudian standpoint we must remember that the unconscious represents literally what the conscious mind sees as figural, so Irena is unconsciously coded by values of a very precise nature which are far from being simply Serbian. If the legend has woven a web of guilt around women, Oliver reinforces this by making Irena feel guilty about dropping litter in the zoo, a fact overdetermined by the script's repressive recourse to religion. The zoo keeper quotes the Bible at Irena who falls for this primary source of the propagation of guilt in the West and of the link between female sexuality and evil. Here, however, the film subverts its own project; the keeper is singing 'nothing else to do' as he carries out his monotonous job of sweeping, symbol of a social and psychic alienation that has led him, not to reflect on his condition, but to seek imaginary truths.

Everywhere she turns Irena is confronted with the hypocrisy of American standards; alienation is the order of the day. Attention has been drawn to a possible lesbian dimension to the encounter in the restaurant where the woman says 'my sister' to Irena, whose session with Judd under hypnosis seems to lend credence to this: she refers to women's 'corrupt passions'. This is certainly ambiguous, but inasmuch as 'passion' is represented as dangerous – Alice, the all-American woman, is anything but passionate! – the addition of 'corrupt' is significant. Whereas male friendships are ennobling, female ones are subject to scrutiny and suspicion. It is hardly surprising that Oliver and Alice treat Irena as a child, telling her that they will meet her later while visiting a museum in order to be together. Oliver reveals Irena's secret to Alice, while Judd invites Irena not to tell her husband anything. Although this can be seen as an invitation to adultery, it is also a case of privileging secrecy and deceit and thus inscribing Irena into the circuit of male desire of which she is the object. Thus, when Irena says she prefers panthers to lions as 'they scream as a woman does', we are surely entitled to see this as the unconscious linguistic manifestation of her desire for sexual ecstasy, denied her by a conflation of Serbian legend and Christian repression. The fact that the film presents Irena as refusing sexuality simply represses all social and cultural determinations other than superstition. Irena alone is responsible for her morbid fantasies. There is an interesting parallel here with Rogen in *Supernatural* (Chapter 2), seen as dangerous precisely because of her sexuality.

'Corrupt passions' could also refer to jealousy and revenge, which brings us to the film's justly famous set-pieces: the pursuit of Alice along the street and the terrorising of her in the darkened swimming pool. We know that Irena is following Alice, but the fact that her footsteps suddenly cease does not mean her shoes have suddenly become paws. As the noise of the wind seems to be turning into a feline growl, the hiss of the bus's brakes makes any identification impossible. The scene at the pool, however, leans clearly towards the supernatural. Although we see nothing, we can hear growls which, despite any rational explanation one can find for the torn robe, takes precedence. A shot of Irena tearing a couch with her nails (= claws) also argues in favour of the supernatural interpretation which the film wants us to choose over the rational one of a young woman tormented by desire and collapsing under the weight of repressive ideologies. Surely Irena here, like the freaks at the end of *Freaks*, is identifying unconsciously with the image everyone has of her and behaves accordingly. What then of the ending?

Irena's attack on Judd after he has kissed her is filmed so that no image is clear, even if her strength suggests something inhuman. What follows is extremely complex; all we know is that Irena has been stabbed by Judd and that he is dead. It is presented thus:

Shot 1: Irena opens the cage of the panther.
Shot 2: the animal knocks her over as it escapes.
Shot 3: Irena is lying recumbent, her fingers clawing the ground.
Shot 4: the animal jumps over a wall and is run over.

Shot 5: the drivers of the vehicle are seen looking at an object in the road.
Shot 6: Oliver and Alice come across Irena.
Shot 7: 'She never lied to us', says Oliver as Alice turns away weeping.

I would argue that both the thrust of the film and the tradition of which it is part — the werewolf film — argue against a supernatural interpretation and leave us with a hesitation that persists after the end. On the one hand, both Oliver and Alice are by now convinced that Irena has turned into a panther and killed Judd, whereas the spectator must be more wary, given the evidence, or lack of it. On the other hand, what is lying on the ground: Irena the woman or Irena the panther? I ask this question because it is customary for the werewolf to return to human form at death and Irena is always seen as her normal human self after a supposed transformation. But the shot of Irena's hand with fingers resembling claws could also be interpreted as her acting in the *image* of what society tells her she is, even at the moment of death. In other words, Irena's unconscious determines her behaviour because it is the unconscious desire of society to write her off as a victim of supernatural forces in order not to have to admit that her neurotic state is due to a combination of factors she cannot understand, let alone control. In which case Judd was right to interpret Irena's case in the light of Freud's theory of the Oedipus complex, but wrong to see this in purely individual terms in the hope of exploiting her condition sexually. His lack of ethics can only lead spectators to doubt the sincerity of both his theories and his treatment. If the conscious project of *Cat* is repressive, the unconscious project is surely feminist. *Zombie* raises these and other questions in such a way that the *fantastique* ending is also a political one.

The script of *Zombie* demonstrates an uncanny understanding of the political unconscious and ideology as discourse. As the nurse who has been hired to look after Jessica, the sick wife of West Indies plantation owner Paul Holland, is being driven from the boat to the family mansion, she enters into a discussion with the elderly black driver who evokes for her the suffering of the slaves whose labour brought wealth to the whites. The nurse, however, can only see beauty around her, beauty of the kind constructed by colonial discourse for the benefit of those who live off the fruits of slave-labour. For her, the slaves were brought to a beautiful place, to which the man replies 'if you say so, Miss'. It would be difficult to represent and sum up social and economic blindness more cogently. That the nurse looks without seeing makes her another sort of zombie: the Third World is exotic, a place where she can live out her fantasies. When she sees the house of the Holland family, her reaction is significant: 'From the gate it seemed strangely dreamlike; the garden had a life of its own'. Thus she shows her own alienation, exteriorised and turned into its positive opposite in the form of a garden which exists in its own right, a manifestation of the fact that she is no more a free agent socially and economically than the slaves of the past and blacks today.

This blindness is not limited to the nurse or to women (an important point, as we shall see). The doctor attributes Jessica's illness to a purely physiological source and claims she can neither think nor act alone, which is contradicted by the scene where the nurse is approached by Jessica in the dark tower. It is impossible to know whether there is any hostility in her behaviour, but we can surely claim that she shows a desire for contact, something denied her by all the family. She is their skeleton in the cupboard (we learn later that she attempted to seduce Holland's half-brother Wesley). Present here is the symbolic debt, with Jessica returning to claim her due to be treated as a human being, whereas she is assimilated to native zombies and to the figurehead in the garden, symbol of exploitation and murder on the part of colonialists, past and present.

Holland would seem to be a man of knowledge, attempting to lead the nurse out of her benighted way of thinking, but the possibility that this be interpreted in the traditional way — women attain self-awareness through men — is quickly scotched. Holland reveals his repressive hand in all its social and sexual complexity when he rebukes the nurse for interfering in family matters: hers is the female role of caring, his the traditional one of capitalist employer (which assimilates her to the blacks under his control). It is crucial to note that the mother, Mrs Rand, is the condensation of the nurse and Holland: she both cares for the natives by running the dispensary — Christian charity is economically determined — and also exercises control over their minds. Both she and Holland have the same narrative and ideological functions, but her case is more complex. As a woman she has found it in her Oedipal interest to ally herself with the forces of economic and psychic repression, the better to maintain some control over her younger son Wesley. In a patriarchal capitalist society the woman's only function is to bear and rear children, something Mrs Rand cannot accept.

In a desperate attempt to have some role beyond that of child-rearing, Mrs Rand had asked the voodoo god to make Jessica a zombie to prevent her from destroying the family and hence the mother's control over her sons. The doctor tells her this is only her imagination, for to become a zombie one has to die first. Tourneur cuts to Mrs Rand and we see the look of utter despair on her face. The truth of her unconscious desire concerning her sons has been revealed to her by the other's discourse and she leaves, shattered. This weakening of the mother's control via the deconstruction of the nature of her desire, which she is forced to renounce, brings to the surface the hostilities that have plagued the family for so long, all turning on Jessica and the possibility that Holland drove her mad to get his revenge for her seducing his brother. However, we have previously learned that Jessica fell into a coma prior to her mental paralysis, a state conducive to transformation into a zombie. The doctor is unaware of this, so the questions remain and the film moves into the realm of the *fantastique*.

Let us take stock of the situation. If Jessica has been turned into a zombie at Mrs Rand's request, then she enters the circuit of desire comprising the mother and her two sons, with Jessica playing the role of 'the other woman'. At the same time Mrs Rand's Christianity is in conflict with superstition: she believes in the strength of voodoo, even if she claims to use the natives' belief in it for medical purposes, a clear case of disavowal. The film is just as much about a fight over who controls whom for reasons of power (sexual, social and economic), which we must not lose sight of when considering the extraordinary ending. The scene is set by the nurse when she takes Jessica to see if the witch-doctor can cure her. Although Mrs Rand is there to make sure Jessica is removed before anything can be done, the victim's presence is enough for the natives to consider she is theirs and, with the aid of a doll, they try to coax her back. This use of a doll refers back to what a servant told the nurse earlier: when dressing Jessica after her collapse into mental paralysis, she had the impression of dressing a doll, so Jessica has always fulfilled the function of an object to be exploited by the various members of the family. In this way *Zombie* links up the family to social and economic power and exploitation, the implications of which we are about to witness.

It is Tourneur's direction that concerns us here. We see the witch-doctor beckoning to the doll, then starting to pull it towards him on a string. Cut to Jessica emerging from the house and approaching the main gate where she stops as it is locked. The juxtaposition of the shot of the witch-doctor practising voodoo and Jessica attempting to leave the house clearly encourages the interpretation that he controls her. The supernatural is privileged. However, Freud remarked on several occasions that the unconscious of one person was able to enter into contact with that of another person without the thought becoming conscious. This would explain telepathy and is summed up by the familiar expression 'great minds think alike'. What I am arguing here is that Holland's unconscious desire is to rid himself of Jessica; being in love with the nurse is libidinal compensation for relinquishing control over his 'doll'. I would further argue that it is the mother who has exercised the firmest control up to this point, dominating both her sons. To have a doll is to be childish. It is also to be feminised. Holland is therefore exercising his phallic rights in the sexual sphere instead of in the purely economic one, which can no longer fulfil this compensatory role. The nurse has given him a more open outlook on life, although he has sought to control her way of thinking. That Holland is not conscious of what is happening can be seen when he cries out 'Jessica!'. Is it a command to stay or to leave?

Jessica is led back inside, but the witch-doctor continues to call her and this time Wesley opens the gate and lets her out, acting on what he has just said to the nurse: he wants to deliver Jessica from her suffering. Or is he too under the sway of voodoo? Once again Tourneur's direction places the spectator before an alternative: the witch-doctor plunges a needle into the doll; cut to Wes stabbing Jessica with one of the arrows he has removed from the figurehead. Wes is therefore refusing to renounce his desire for Jessica, even if this entails his dying too; he picks up her body and walks into the sea to drown. Thus the arrow that signifies the suffering and oppression of the slaves is used by a subject of colonialism to free himself and the woman he loves from the oppression of Holland, but also from that of the mother. A weak and cowardly man, Wes can accept separation from the women he loves — his mother and Jessica — only through death, thus turning both Jessica and himself into literal victims, akin to those the exploitation of whose labour has allowed the whites to live in luxury for years. The *fantastique* here takes on a distinctly political edge, inasmuch as the film has made

explicit the role of superstitition within the white community. The
parallels set up between Jessica and the voodoo doll on the one hand,
Jessica and a native woman dancing under the influence of voodoo on
the other and overdetermined by the role of superstition within the
white community indicate that religion/voodoo as fetish and colonial
wealth as fetish merge. The 'reason' of the whites is based on superstition and the 'superstition' of the natives a defence against the negative
and repressive effects of such displays of reason.

ii) THE OTHER LEWTON PRODUCTIONS

Zombie is the highpoint of Lewton's productions and a landmark in the
horror film. Its exceptional textual density is due to Tourneur's
collaboration with director of photography Roy Hunt and to their
exploitation of all the subtleties and ambiguities of the brillant script by
Curt Siodmak, the leading specialist of horror, fantasy and science-fiction
in the 40s and 50s. Just to what extent Tourneur's direction is chiefly
responsible can be seen from the ludicrous attempts by Mark Robson to
instil suspense and anxiety into the mundane script of *Victim*, the only
outright flop of the series. The victim of the title, Jacqueline, has just left
a meeting of Satanists where she has been told to commit suicide as a
punishment for having mentioned the sect to non-members. We are
treated to a shot of an empty street, which is totally devoid of any
menace, suspense and anxiety for us for two reasons: there has been no
suggestion (a crucial notion in the three Tourneur films) of anything
awaiting the character and the characters, particularly the Satanists,
totally lack any degree of elaboration likely to interest us in them.
Suddenly there is a crash and Jacqueline jumps and turns round. Cut to a
dog raiding a dustbin! This would be laughable, were it not so pathetic.
Robson then displays his complete ignorance of what was at stake in *Cat
People* by coming up with his own version of the scene in the street with
the hiss of the brakes of the bus: Jacqueline is almost run over by a car
whose tyres screech.

Robson copes better with the story of *Isle of the Dead*, although there
is no real motivation behind the way the central character, the Greek
colonel played by Karloff, suddenly moves from scepticism concerning
legends of vampiric spirits to a belief in them. Basically, the film wants us
to believe in such spirits and thus has the only interesting character in

the film change his mind. However, Robson manages to create a genuine feeling of fear and anxiety in the final section following the burying alive of one of the characters. Everyone assumes she too has died of the plague, but we know that she is subject to catalepsy; the only characters who know are dead. There is a slow track forward into the black rectangle formed by the open door of her tomb as her faint white figure emerges, but the dimension of uncertainty omnipresent in Tourneur is absent here: we are dealing with stylistic effects to create atmosphere and nothing more, however effective they are.

The other films of the series, *Bedlam* and *Body Snatcher*, are of interest for other reasons. In its very modest way *Bedlam* is a political film turning on the repressive treatment of poverty and the sadistic treatment of the inmates of the asylum by the Karloff character (very much in keeping with that of certain 'mad doctors' of the 30s). When he says, prior to being walled up alive by the inmates, 'what this world thinks, I must think; what this world does, I must do', his fear indicates that he is speaking the truth. He is thus carrying out the desires of the ruling Tory aristocracy who have the poor and their enemies declared mad and interned the better to suppress any move towards social reform. *Body Snatcher* contains a 'mad doctor' who resorts to grave-robbing to obtain specimens to experiment on. Just as interesting as the film's concern for the fate of the poor and the unprotected is its evocation of psychoanalysis. Dr McFarland's aggressive bedside manner traumatises the little girl confined to a wheelchair, for he has failed to appreciate the extent to which a subject can prefer certitude to its absence. Thus she refuses to walk, not because his operation has failed, but because she needs some form of reassurance. Being crippled is a symptom, something she can live with in the face of the anxiety produced by the doctor's aggressivity. McFarland understands this unconsciously when he says angrily to his young assistant who tries to reassure the girl, 'she won't walk'. By this he unconsciously means 'refuses'; she cannot replace the known (paralysis) by the unknown (what will happen when she tries to rise from her wheelchair?).

This dimension of child psychology is at the centre of the most interesting film of the series after the Tourneur films, *Curse of the Cat People*, although its concerns are radically different from those of *Cat People*. The excellent script makes explicit something that *Cat* only hinted at: the ideology of the American way of life. Here its double standards are deconstructed in a way that highlights just how superstitious adults remain. Oliver and Alice are married and have a little daughter, Amy, who is rejected by her schoolmates because of her tendency to retreat into a fantasy world excluding other people. She is rebuked by her father for believing that wishes come true, but is told that certain wishes will come true: when you wish on blowing out the candles on your birthday cake, for example. Amy has been told that such wishes are secret, then is forced to say what she wished for, as this is a special occasion. An excellent way to turn a normal child into a neurotic. What the film is suggesting is not that the parents are liars but that they unconsciously wish to regress to childhood to shirk their responsibilities. This brings us back to *Cat* and the role played by Oliver and Alice in Irena's death: whether they like it or not, by treating her as a child and hiding things from her they brought grist to her mill and helped turn her into what legend told her she was.

It is therefore significant that Irena returns in *Curse* as Amy's playmate and here lies the *fantastique* element, for Irena comes into Amy's life before Amy knows consciously of her existence (she discovers photos of Irena and Oliver together and wants to know about her). Two interpretations are possible: the supernatural one which asks us to believe that Irena really has returned from the dead to find in Amy the love and understanding she did not find when alive; and the rational or psychoanalytical one where Amy's desire for a playmate who understands her is the unconscious manifestation of her father's desire for an idyllic existence with Irena that would exclude the latter's neuroses. In that case Oliver and Alice's marriage is a 'second best' for Oliver and his aggressive attitude towards his daughter hints both at her not being wanted and, especially, an overwhelming feeling of guilt on his part concerning Irena.

The script encourages this interpretation via the old lady who welcomes Amy into her house, despite the hostility displayed by the menacing young woman living with her. She turns out to be the daughter of the old lady who refuses to recognise her, claiming that her daughter died when very young, when she was Amy's age, in fact. Thus interesting and revealing parallels are set up which turn on parental desire and repression. Just as Oliver refuses to recognise that Amy is still a young child, the old lady refuses to recognise her daughter and looks for an ideal replacement. Oliver punishes Amy for carrying out what he unconsciously desires concerning a relationship with Irena free from the weight of legend and prejudice, but also for reminding him of the repressive way he treated Irena. There is a repetition compulsion in Oliver that suggests an inherently repressive and patriarchal streak in this very typical American male. By denying that the young woman is her daughter, the lady can have her cake and eat it: she can blame her for everything, accuse her of wanting to get rid of her (an unconscious reversal of the truth) and be free of parental responsibility by transforming her daughter into the hired help. We find here the same social and psychic structures revealed by our analysis of *Zombie*. Like Mrs Rand, the old lady wants to exert total control over her family as it is all she has. At the same time she has refused the ideological implications of being a housewife to the point of denying the reality of her daughter's existence and has thus become psychotic. *Curse* is denouncing patriarchy through the representation of the father figure and what can befall a woman who refuses an all-male order, yet who cannot face up to the consequences of her independence.

Thus the female victims in *Leopard*, Irena, Jessica and Mrs Rand, mother and daughter and Amy, all meet the fate of the female in a male-dominated capitalist society. It is a theme we shall find occurring again and again.

4

NUCLEAR AND OTHER HORRORS

It is common practice when discussing the films of the 50s to evoke the Cold War, the Bomb and the 'Red Scare'. The cultural and political articulation of these three component parts of post-war America had the most serious consequences as far as Hollywood was concerned: black-listing. As a result of the condemnation of the 'Hollywood Ten' in 1947 and the role played by Senator Joseph McCarthy from 1951, several hundred Hollywood artists found themselves deprived of their livelihood. Although this led to an overall intellectual impoverishment, particularly when it came to openly discussing negative aspects of American society, I would argue that it is being politically correct to assume that the decade was less interesting and inventive than the 30s and 40s. This goes on the assumption that an explicit commitment to social justice makes a movie superior to one that eschews that explicitness. To simplify a complex matter, such an approach to the 50s represses any notion of unconscious desire, of how genuine collective anxieties are represented in the films of the period. Thus *The Alligator People* argues for the curative use of radiation and shows the disastrous results of a lack of stringent control, while indicating that the well-meaning scientist proved inadequate to the task. For once, the panacea does not lie in military hands.

The Brain Eaters is a virtual textbook working-out of themes to be broached in this chapter. It starts off by presenting an ambitious Senator who aims to embarrass the Government and whose assistant reminds him of the usefulness of threatening an investigation, which corresponds perfectly to the behaviour of McCarthy and his aide Roy Cohn. Soon, however, the Senator has joined forces with those fighting to discover the truth behind the taking over of a small town by parasites, which corresponds equally perfectly to McCarthy's description of Communist subversion. Similarly, the fact that the parasites wish to eliminate strife can be seen as an attack on those who refused to countenance Cold War ideology, while also representing the importance of peace for the American public. The device implanted in the necks of victims looks back to *Invaders from Mars*, much of which is nothing but a glorification of the military, and ahead to *The Hidden*. Like *Invasion of the Body Snatchers*, *The Brain Eaters* captures the climate of paranoia by showing telegraphists and telephone operators who obey their new masters. The film also contains a remarkable scene where the spectators adopt the point of view of a parasite making its way to where the sleeping victim is lying in bed. This both sums up the split subject positions created by the paranoia of the time and looks ahead to the use of such shots in slasher movies.

One book that makes a determined effort to negotiate all the incoherencies and contradictions inherent to the period and its films is Mark Jancovich's sophisticated *Rational Fears*. He shows how certain unconscious prejudices concerning the Army, science and the average citizen had led critics to hail as courageous and progressive such a film as *The Day the Earth Stood Still*, whereas its message is fascistic: what the Earth needs is to be policed by aliens to control mankind's worst instincts and save the Universe from destruction, a position which blames everything on the stupidity of the man in the street in order to inflict even greater oppression and terrors on everyone. It would be possible to read the film as a McCarthyist tract justifying the abandonment of civil liberties for patriotic reasons. This is the sort of problem one faces when criticism decides to transform every element of a film into something else, as if each element had a fixed meaning that could be traced to a single source. The film thus becomes an extended metaphor and ceases to have any aesthetic autonomy.

It is not a matter of suggesting an alternative reading but of attempting to pinpoint elements that translate anxieties other than those considered to be paramount: the Bomb and Communist subversion. Thus much has been made of *The Thing from Another World* as a warning against Soviet aggression — 'Keep watching the skies!' — and as a tribute to the vigilance of the military and the need for discipline to protect the human race from scientific irresponsibility. This is obviously a double-edged weapon and brings closer to the surface a genuine anxiety concerning nuclear war; after all, scientists invented the Bomb! Militarism, anti-intellectual prejudice and anticommunism were component factors of the concerns of film's producer Howard Hawks, a member of the right-wing organisation at the origins of blacklisting in the 40s, the Motion Picture Alliance for the Preservation of American Ideals. We need, however, to refuse to force the film into such a mould and to look more closely at the alien's status: it is not just an 'intellectual carrot' but an intergalactic vampire. That its purpose is to turn 'the human race into food' and that it reproduces itself without procreation brings together two crucial dimensions of the genre that we shall encounter elsewhere. The alien is a hermaphrodite, thus condensing an unconscious fear of female sexuality and the concomitant fantasy of male bonding. It is also a signifier of capitalist ideology, which strives to hide all traces of labour in favour of the end product, then discarding the worker once he or she has carried out an allotted task. The links with *Dracula* and *Frankenstein* are patent.

I have raised the question in this form in an attempt to make the point about aspects of a film exceeding the reductive cause-effect formula, where one system is transposed into another, a denial of the unconscious dimension of ideology and the aesthetic forms it assumes. To illustrate my argument, I shall examine *Them!*, *Invasion of the Body Snatchers*, *Creature from the Black Lagoon* and the less well-known *I Bury the Living* and *The Monolith Monsters*.

i) FIVE CASE STUDIES

Them! presents the struggle of scientists and the military against ants mutated by radiation. At one point the expert Dr Medford evokes the social organisation of ant life, the way they make war on other species and enslave their prisoners. It would be difficult to find a clearer reference to a Communist takeover, with an implicit reference to the 'underground' activities of Hollywood 'Reds'. And just as nobody proved Hollywood was producing Communist propaganda, so nobody in the film provides any evidence that humanity is about to be eliminated: Medford just says this and it is taken for granted. There is no question that *Them!* is a profoundly reactionary movie, but other elements suggest that its real anxieties have nothing to do with Communism, the latent content hiding the unconscious. Thus the film is forced to admit, via the characters of Medford, the policeman and the FBI agent, that the constant presence of Medford's daughter Pat, a scientist like her father, is indispensable at key moments such as the search through the ants' underground nest, despite the claim that it is not a task for a woman. We find here the condensation of certain more real post-war anxieties than a Communist takeover: the demand of women to continue to have the right to work; the feeling by men that their position in society was threatened by active, independent women; the whole vexed question of unemployment and the clash between the sexes, where class solidarity was weakened.

It is in this context that the film's unconscious project must be unmasked. I do not wish to eliminate its Cold War message which is explicit. Martial law is declared to protect Los Angeles from the ants: the population must do what it is told. The parallel with *The Day the Earth Stood Still* is too clear to be a coincidence. The film is therefore an apology for the suppression of civil liberties, without any consultation of Americans, if the authorities and their experts deem it necessary. However sinister this is, it is not the source of the film's anxiety. The answer is to be found in the character of the policeman who discovers the little girl in the desert. Why is so unimportant a person in the social hierarchy given such prominence? Why does it go without saying that he should accompany the scientists and the FBI on their search? Why should he be the one to lead the search through the drains at the end to find the children trapped by the ants? This is illogical, given his modest status (a New Mexico patrolman), his inability to determine strategy and the fact he does not represent the State as the FBI man does. Both the way the final scenes are shot and the policeman's death suggest a plausible answer.

The fascistic discourse is passed off as acting in people's best interests and one aspect of the film adheres to the 'enlightened' and 'moderate' ideology underpinning this. Society must evolve and cannot be left to ignorant couples unaware of technological advances and the wisdom of federal law. In the drains the FBI agent, for no reason as far as the manifest content of the script goes, is shot alone, thus turning him into someone more important than he is. Pat is no longer indispensable as she was earlier and we see her waiting outside, along with the mother of the children, whose husband has been killed. *Them!* is presenting Pat as the perfect future wife of the FBI agent; the symbols of science and national security unite to create a new 'nuclear' family in place of the traditional one. The policeman is unmarried and can be dispensed with;

the film sacrifices him in a spurious attempt to valorise him as hero. It is significant that the dead husband was looking for a second job to make ends meet, and such an evocation of social hardship must be displaced so as not to foreground contradiction. Pat will be wife and mother in the future, the FBI man father and guarantor of the country's security against all enemies. This was also part and parcel of the discourse of anti-Communist liberals at the time.

Them! adopts a contradictory approach to women, hardly surprising in a Hollywood movie, although this has historical roots. The title is in red, the film in black and white. This undoubtedly corresponds to its anti-Red dimension, but a certain semantic excess is produced beyond the simplistic metaphor. Since there exists a species called the 'red ant', there is a transfer from the *letter* of the text to the *body* of the text, which in psychoanalysis is called a 'symptom' and refers to the state of hysteria. Male hysteria stems from male anxiety faced with the possibility of not being 'virile' enough, of being feminised. We return therefore to the themes raised above: active women 'threatening' unemployed men or men with a resolutely sexist and patriarchal view of gender relations. This is precisely what *Them!* treats us to.

Invasion of the Body Snatchers has always been interpreted in two ways: as part of the anti-Communist thrust, where the aliens threaten freedom and the American way of life like the Soviets and their Hollywood 'allies'; and as a humanist attempt to warn Americans of the way they have allowed themselves to be conditioned by an uncaring, emotionally arid society. The problem with this second interpretation is that it is ambiguous: do these threats to free thought come from outside or within? Superficially, things seem to point to the former, with the doctor hero saying how everything 'looked normal' on his return home, admitting 'I feel almost like a stranger in my own country'. A psychiatrist refers to 'a malignant disease spreading throughout the whole country'. Such are the paranoid trappings of anticommunism. It is this overwhelming feeling of anxiety in the film that suggests a conscious discourse is hiding an unconscious one.

Three aspects of the film suggest things are moving in quite a different direction. Firstly, the notion that the person taken over lacks something, that 'little something' that makes him or her what they are. This is explicit in the discussion between the doctor and the woman convinced her Uncle Ira is not her uncle. Secondly, the fact that people no longer go out to restaurants indicates a fear of contagion as well as an indifference to others, in which case we are in the realm of the genuine paranoia experienced in post-1947 Hollywood where people kept out of the way of those blacklisted or suspected of 'subversive' activites, for fear of being suspected themselves. In other words, 'contagion'. Thirdly, the psychiatrist evokes people being 'worried about what's going on in the world', which hints at anxiety about one's own society and nuclear warfare and not simply about dangerous enemies. Significantly, after the person has been taken over, he or she becomes the spokesperson of the alien ideology. 'People with nothing but problems' will find them all solved 'in an untroubled world'. In other words, everyone will be the same. If this is an accusation levelled at the fate of people in the Soviet Union, it has other ramifications that we shall see returning elsewhere.

A fascinating and potentially subversive element of the film is the parallel drawn between the character of the psychiatrist who is taken over and the psychiatrist in the opening scene who listens to the hero's story. Inasmuch as the latter is considered mad, he functions here in relation to the psychiatrist and the police as he does at the end in relation to his friends who have been taken over: the outsider to be neutralised. Thus the film represents psychiatry as functioning as a form of social normalisation. The character of Uncle Ira can help us here. The niece's doubts over his identity turn on the question of subjectivity, that unconscious aspect of the individual that makes him or her a desiring subject, in other words, what lends the individual an identity, without which he or she feels incapable of desiring since desire is determined by social values, advertising, ideology and so on. The psychiatrist, once taken over, represents ego psychology, whose purpose is to encourage people to adapt and to submit to what is 'best' for the community. The supposed 'faceless anonymity' of the individual under Communism is closer to home than comfort: it is that of the average American reduced to a consumer of goods which are basically the same, a worker deprived of his identity in the production process by the expropriation of the product of his labour, the systematic alienation — psychic and social — visited on society's members in an attempt to prevent any genuine collective consciousness and activity. Paranoia is not just a question of feeling persecuted but a discourse which can allow for no conflicts or imperfections. It is the discourse of the psychiatrist-as-alien, symbol of a society under the domination of one force: money. People are not individuals but objects to be manipulated for profit. What makes *Body Snatchers* so terrifying is precisely the total elimination of any traces of individual desire, hence of subjectivity, once the takeover is complete. Let us not forget that, in capitalist jargon, a 'takeover' or 'merger' threatens the livelihood of workers and produces alienation. In *Body Snatchers* humans and aliens 'merge'.

Creature from the Black Lagoon turns on this notion of the commodification of people and desire, where what people desire is both private and determined by values beyond their control. Significantly, the Creature, supposedly a throwback to the time when creatures were aquatic or had adapted to an existence on land, is both amphibian and humanoid. It is represented as being sexually attracted to the heroine, who logically should not attract it as she is human. That the Creature has desires must be seen in the context of the film's insistence on evolution and the fact that time appears to have stopped in this South American lagoon. It is human in a way the film cannot openly manifest as it is the locus of a Utopian urge: to escape a world based on money and exploitation (of nature or of one human by another) and to return to some Utopian, if imaginary, earlier existence where no such exploitation existed. The Creature is compared to the hero by the fact that bubbles signal the presence of both under the water, a parallel of some consequence in a film which denounces the way research depends on private funding.

The hero, a marine biologist, is such a case: whether on land or under the sea his desire is alienated. For the man who provides the funds, there is nothing to show for this research, which we can interpret in economic terms; the hero's labour has produced nothing, so there is nothing to exchange for that all-purpose commodity, money. We should not, therefore, be surprised that the hero says of the capitalist that he has 'taken credit' for important findings: the money lent must yield profit, produce something 'of interest', as it were. The fund-raiser is after a trophy and behaves in an absolutist fashion, like Count Zaroff on his island. The Creature, in turn, lives in its private world, one cut off from the anxieties of contemporary times, another King Kong. It too falls – illogically – for a woman. Its cavern functions somewhat like Kong's domain, but is also a womb to which the hero can retreat for protection and sustenance. Here, too, we should not be surprised that the heroine is nothing but a sexual object for the film, as this particular manifestation of phallocentrism enables the male characters to feel in control and deny their unconscious affinities with the Creature. This is typical of mercantile capitalism: each person is always another's social and economic victim. Similarly, the deaths of the natives are unimportant; only the loss of a scientist is a waste of ability, a loss of labour difficult to replace. The natives are only fit to be sacrificed once they have carried out their tasks — in this they resemble the crewmen killed in *King Kong* — but one of them is superior: the owner of the boat. He shows the good taste of a male moviegoer by calling it 'Rita', a reference to Rita Hayworth and an unconscious justification of the commodification of *Creature*'s heroine. This striking movie perfectly captures the ideological values of the 50s and the insistent attempts to escape them.

Seemingly a tale of supernatural possession, *I Bury the Living* is a reflection on what can lead people to believe they are possessed. As such it turns on social and psychic alienation and also insists on questions of class in its handling of the hero, a businessman called Kraft, and the elderly caretaker of the cemetery. Kraft is asked by his peers to assume responsibility for the cemetery as part of the services a man in his social position is expected to render to the community. Kraft's office in the cemetery sports a chart showing the position of every grave; some are occupied, others bought by those wishing to rest there for eternity. A black pin indicates someone's final resting place, a white pin a grave awaiting its owner. Implicitly, the film shows that the community makes money from death, and it is from the notion of invisible forces determining our existences that the film derives its genuinely uncanny power.

By mistake Kraft places a black pin into the chart, thus designating as already dead someone who is simply the owner of the plot of land (the parallel between the family plot and real estate is present without being stressed). Soon after he is informed that the person has died. What appears to be an unfortunate coincidence promptly happens again and Kraft comes to believe he has the power of life and death over people. Unlike the mad doctor, however, who revels in such a belief, Kraft is seized by uncontrollable anxiety. This is not helped by a colleague who thinks he is joking and remarks that this will enable the businessman to wipe out all competition. This observation in bad taste takes us to the heart of the matter.

Two of the characters are a young couple who have just married. Before they can inherit the money left to the husband by his dead father, his will stipulates they must purchase a plot. Thus a wealthy business-

Figure 3 The Creature defends its home against intruders. *Creature from the Black Lagoon.* Copyright © 2002 by Universal Studios. Courtesy of Universal Studios Publishing Rights, a Division of Universal Studios Licensing, Inc. All rights reserved.

man shows his determination to rule over the lives of his family from beyond the grave, a form of economic possession of a decidedly patriarchal nature. The young couple are 'dispossessed' of their right to choose where they want to be buried, which excludes the right to be cremated. What we are dealing with here is 'the invisible hand of the market' in the dematerialised shape of a dead capitalist who, thanks to the legal and economic power invested in his will, functions as if he were still alive and controlling people's lives by economic power.

Things come to a head when the hero agrees to put a black pin in the place on the chart corresponding to the plot belonging to a colleague in Paris on business. He too dies but the police unmask the caretaker as the murderer of the various victims. He had been driven mad by the fact of being retired against his will, although the community continues to pay him. As he claims responsibility for all the deaths, however, it is clear that something is seriously wrong: how did he get rid of the last victim without going to Paris? This element is the key to the film's real interest and its representation of how ideology holds sway over our lives. We are surely entitled to dismiss his claim of being a mass murderer and attribute it instead to insanity, the most extreme form of social and psychic alienation. Deprived of the right to work and having no control over the decision, no say in his own life, the caretaker is the perfect stand-in for the worker robbed of the fruits of his labour by the capitalist who pays him what he deems fit. The caretaker has become paranoid, one of the traits of which is acute megalomania. Thus his belief that he killed all the victims is determined by a need to possess a power denied him throughout his life. That the businessman hero can possibly believe in some supernatural force because of the coincidental deaths only shows that anyone, irrespective of class, can submit to obscurantism. This is easier than analysing the nature of the economic 'forces' determining our lives, forces that are determined by men (rather than by women; significantly the inheritance was the husband's) acting according to values they underpin by their actions but which they in no way determine consciously and individually.

The Monolith Monsters has an aspect of *déjà vu*. The meteor recalls *It Came from Outer Space*, directed in 1953 by Jack Arnold, who wrote the story on which the script is based. The opening commentary describes meteors as an 'invasion', thus evoking *Invaders from Mars* (1953) and the whole paranoid 'Communist conspiracy' theory. However, this element of the film is due to the way it represents, not anxiety, but what produces it. If the film in no way communicates the horror that *Body Snatchers* does, it does find the perfect image to represent the commodification of people under capitalism; the victims who come into contact with the meteor are turned into stone. The entire film proves Freud's theory of the unconscious which can represent an idea by its opposite, a fear as a desire. This explains a contradiction contained within the script and explained away by pseudo-science. Whereas the fragments from the meteor grow, topple over, smash into fragments, then grow again, the body of the first victim — water starts the process off and salt water ends it — is described by the doctor as 'welded into a solid mass'. My argument is that this is a representation by its opposite of the Marxist theory of the 'fragmentation' of the workers arising from Taylorisation, whereby work is 'fragmented' into its component parts, each of which is treated separately by individual workers (the construction of a car, for example). The purpose is to prevent worker control over the production process, the result that alienation mentioned earlier: social, inasmuch as this organisation of labour blocks off any genuine contact between workers who are turned into annexes of machines and psychic, inasmuch as it prevents any coherence of personal identity. Objects are exchanged in a way that sets up between them precisely those social relations denied the workers. Thus the bodies turned to stone stand in for labour under capital, the formula cited representing this via the notion of a desire to form a collective unit. We would expect the stone bodies to be smashed to pieces.

Other elements of *Monolith* insist on this political dimension. Thus the meteor fragments drain all substance from their victims, an image that conjures up vampirism, precisely the image Marx used to describe capital sucking the life blood from workers to replenish itself, before discarding them. We have noticed this in *The Thing*, but the image occurs in all versions of *Body Snatchers* where the empty pod becomes a human, the human an empty pod that dissolves into dust and is consigned to the rubbish bin, an eloquent representation of the current neoliberal attitude to history itself. However, *Monolith* is also prophetic about certain forces in American society that have continued to develop. Shots of the giant monoliths approaching the town bear an uncanny resemblance to skyscrapers and anticipate discussions of the destruction of downtown Los Angeles and working-class areas in favour of skyscrapers housing banks and insurance offices, symbols of modern capitalism and its drive to knock buildings down and put ever taller ones in their place. Inasmuch as the monoliths threaten a small Californian town of the kind shown in *Body Snatchers*, the political analysis co-exists with the reactionary rejection of big cities for peaceful and supposedly unproblematic rural life. The contradictions traversing American society in the 50s find a unique outlet.

It is therefore intriguing to notice that a clip from *Monolith* – the sequence where the monoliths advance by rising up, crashing down, then rising up again – is included in *They Live* in a context which goes beyond mere coincidence: dispossessed people inhabiting a shanty-town near Los Angeles are watching the movie on TV. I draw attention to this because, in the background and dominating the scene, is none other than downtown Los Angeles, whose skyscrapers figure prominently throughout the film; we are even treated to a low-angle shot of the Wells Fargo building, very much a 'monolith' in appearance. Since the aliens control banks, big business and TV and an explicit link is made in the script between them and free-enterprise multinational corporations, the insight of *Monolith* — the film represents unconscious anxieties concerning the evolution of society — is prescient indeed.

At one point in *Monolith* the owner of the town's newspaper calls a delivery boy over and tells him to round up all children possessing bikes in order to inform everyone of the danger. The boy at once asks how much they will be paid, upon which the Sheriff orders him to jump to it. As the boy rides off, the two men deplore that kids always want to be paid. This banal scene speaks volumes and introduces another element. If the boy demands payment, this is surely understandable, especially as he has no idea what the urgency is. He is asked to do a job and, inscribed as he is into the logic of a system that exchanges labour for money, expects due payment. At the same time the attitude of the men is that of the small entrepreneur who expects his workers to be at his beck and call, to do overtime without complaining. The scene also brings into focus the place and function of young people in the 50s, particularly their purchasing power and their tastes in matters cultural. Thus that silly cult movie *The Blob* has endless, tedious scenes where young adults fight with one another, argue with the police and bicker about sex. The film is also 'enlivened' by a rock song. It is in this context that we shall turn to *I was a Teenage Werewolf, I was a Teenage Frankenstein* and their companion piece *How to Make a Monster*.

ii) FORCES AND SOURCES OF REPRESSION

Despite the outrageous titles, neither *Werewolf* nor *Frankenstein* is exploitative in its analysis of the theme of young people and their supposed sexual obsessions. The setting of *Werewolf* may be the appropriately named Rockdale High School, but apart from one musical number in the 'dive' opened by the central character Tony, the film turns out to be a sober and highly intelligent analysis of various social problems. The neglect of such films, or their transformation into cult movies, is one of the more deplorable results of the critical tendency to downgrade the 50s and of the ever-present prejudice against such 'debased' cultural artefacts as horror movies. Let us take such films seriously, without treating them like cult objects, that religious dimension of fandom that is a perfect manifestation of the fetishism that accompanies commodification.

Werewolf is a subtle attack on the ideology of success, as defined by the female Principal of the school and the parents of the hero's girlfriend. Her mother wants her to date another boy who is 'the druggist's son' and her father tells the hero Tony to be interested 'in the right sort of things', adding that he 'should bow to authority'. The Principal is anxious that Tony succeed academically because this will enhance the school's reputation; good grades and behaviour are paramount, never the boy's desire. Here the woman is wrong only inasmuch as she is conveying a purely mercantile and class-related view of intellectual activity, devoid of the pleasure it can bring to the individual pupil. Both *Werewolf* and *Frankenstein* denounce the dimension of exploitation of knowledge and people for personal self-aggrandisement, thus implicitly criticising the ideology of the individual shorn of any social and cultural ties. If *Werewolf* is a remake of *Rebel Without a Cause*, there are clearly causes for Tony's condition. The film is particularly interesting in the way it foregrounds a taboo subject: class.

If the girl is from a middle-class background, Tony's father is working class and works on the nightshift. This enables the script to elaborate a sophisticated analysis of the social and psychic causes for Tony's aggressivity, which gets out of hand to the point that he is forced to consult a psychiatrist. The father tells his son that it is sometimes necessary to accept the other's point of view and gives the example of how he was forced to obey his foreman who had criticised his way of working. Thus *Werewolf* neatly introduces the repression of the working class and, crucially, the notion of responsibility as a constraint where the subject overcomes purely selfish and narcissistic drives in order to respect the other. This is part of what Lacan called the 'Symbolic Order': the social and unconscious dimension of language, the overcoming of the Oedipus complex and the acceptance of castration, the ability to put oneself in the other's place and respect his or her desire. Significantly, the father deplores his wife's death. Thus the mother is not seen as a bad influence on the son, wanting to prevent him from growing up, but as an integral part of family life. She would have counterbalanced society's patriarchal ideology, something the father wants to do but seldom can, given his inferior class status. The girl's mother, however, merely echoes the father and becomes 'her master's voice' the better to force the girl into a class mould. A druggist, of course, owns his own shop and Tony points out sarcastically that his girlfriend's father wants him to earn money when not at school, so that he will learn that knowledge is just a step on the way to social climbing.

The full extent of *Werewolf*'s subversion of capitalist patriarchy can be gauged from the representation of the psychiatrist, Dr Brandon, who uses his position to exploit Tony as a guinea-pig (he makes this explicit in a discussion with his assistant). Brandon's theory is that humanity is on the road to self-destruction and that the only solution is to get it to regress to its primitive urges, wipe the slate clean and start again. Brandon may be a mad scientist in the best tradition, but his remarks betray the anxiety that is the insistent sub-text of the films analysed above. Behind his theories, however, lies a profound truth concerning society. In wanting to release Tony's primitive urges (turning him into a werewolf in the process) so that he can become his 'real self', Brandon becomes the signifier of a particular discourse which has already made innumerable victims. He wants people to express desires without constraint, which is both infantile (the child demands instant satisfaction of its needs and desires) and inherent to capitalism: never mind the other fellow, just work hard, make money and get what you want. This is the ideology of the girl's father and one Tony's father, out of a certain class consciousness, denounces.

Werewolf is therefore deconstructing ego-psychology, the ideology of adjustment, a word in everyone's mouth, including Tony's; he has been brainwashed into believing this is the only way out. For Brandon, punctuality is a symptom of adjustment, where the patient bows to authority, submitting to the Law of the father, real or imaginary. He sees himself as a sort of natural authority, given his knowledge and status, and thus stands in for the foreman Tony's father must obey on occasion and the social big Other of capitalist values unconsciously represented by the girl's father. Particularly significant is Brandon's contempt for his assistant, a quiet, worried man whose passivity does not prevent him from questioning Brandon's methods. Brandon calls him 'an old woman' which the other does not consider an insult. Here we touch on a crucial dimension of the text: gender as a social function, a means of class and sexual repression. This can be seen in the assistant's adoption of a stance identical to Tony's father's, refusing to be exclusively masculine and dominating. He condenses within his subjective being the paternal and maternal and strives to allow the two to co-exist. This is precisely what Tony wants to do but cannot and brings us back to the theme of hysteria, which is the boy's problem. It is noteworthy that the father fulfils paternal and maternal functions: he works and looks after the house, thus providing Tony with an ego ideal that is non-sexist and opposed to society's values.

Tony is told to control his violent temper and Brandon functions socially to help him to do just that. What causes his aggressiveness? The answer is complex, but it should be noted that it is the sound of the school bell that causes the first transformation. I would suggest it is the signifier of authority, at once forcing Tony to submit to excessive discipline and to Brandon's medicine and his revolt against both. I shall repeat here what I said in Chapter 1. The werewolf is the co-existence of the masculine and the feminine within each subject, given the bisexuality inherent in each of us since the pre-Oedipal period. What is a natural anatomical difference – the presence/absence of the penis – is trans- formed into a social opposition: male versus female, with the latter coming off second best. An awareness of the interdependence of the masculine and the feminine is what Tony's father and the assistant have assimilated, which makes them unusual in patriarchy. Any male assum- ing the existence and validity of the feminine within himself is looked upon as lacking virility, of being feminised, even 'effeminate', in other words, homosexual, which is Tony's 'problem'.

The film provides an answer to the question concerning his violence. *Werewolf* opens with a fight between Tony and a classmate. Tony claims the other started it by slapping him on the shoulder from behind, to which the boy retorts that it was a friendly slap. Even if this image did not proliferate throughout not only *Werewolf*, but also *Frankenstein* and *Monster*, it would be necessary to address it carefully. The hand on the shoulder is a sign of friendship but also connotes male bonding, which excludes women. This ideology sits uneasily with another discourse of patriarchy: physical contact between two men connotes homosexuality. Tony is caught unconsciously between conflicting ideological inter- pretations of a gesture that is coded socially. He is anxious to be friends with his male classmate but refuses to privilege that relationship. As an 'average' American boy he considers close friendships as suspect. At the same time he has come under the positive influence of his father whose progressive class and gender attitude is a minority one. Being slapped on the shoulder is thus the signifier of the contradiction he is living out. It is not that he feels the boy was making advances ('from behind' shows the linguistic signifier translating a supposedly homosexual position), but that he is afraid of not being masculine enough, should he adopt the feminine position transmitted by the father. It is revealing that Tony should repeat this act at the 'dive' where he approaches his best friend from behind and puts his arm round his shoulder. The context explains an apparent incoherence in the film's discourse which is perfectly coherent from a psychoanalytical standpoint. On the one hand, the 'dive' is frequented by boys and girls who interact outside certain repressive social constraints imposed by their parents, a space where Tony can experience for his friend an affection he no longer needs to stigmatise. On the other hand, the school setting forbids such manifestations of friendship as they clash with the ideology of the active male, the passive female and social success.

Werewolf is remarkable in the way it foregrounds the social construction of sexuality, desire and gender, while trouncing the notion that difference is purely physical. *Frankenstein* takes up many of these concepts and, by concentrating on the mad doctor, succeeds in being a more overtly political movie but less elaborate in the domain of adolescence. Made the same year but with different scriptwriters, the films complement one another perfectly, with the deliberately hysterical character of the former giving way to the austere, almost clinical approach of the latter. It makes up for this via visual horror – Frankenstein feeding dead bodies, then his fiancée, to a crocodile he keeps beneath his laboratory (a reference to *Murders in the Zoo*) – and grim humour; the film abounds in the use of figural expressions employing 'eat' and 'chew'. It is indeed the dialogue that permits a political reading. Basically, Dr Frankenstein takes up the theories elaborated by Brandon concerning the superior social and intellectual function of the devoted scientist but is even more callous. The idea that people exist simply to be exploited as a form of raw material for the doctor's scalpel underscores what we have seen in *Monolith* and *Werewolf*: human beings are turned into objects, commodified for the social advancement and financial success of others. The drive to make money and the drive to succeed with an experiment are inescapably linked under capitalism. Psychoanalysis has taught us that drives permit no hesitation or obstacle. The perfect manifestation of this in horror is Leatherface in *The Texas Chainsaw Massacre* (see Chapter 6). What must be stressed here is the way Frankenstein talks of his creation, a young man whose body he has made whole by grafting on limbs from the bodies of athletes killed in a plane crash. 'What a waste!' exclaims Frankenstein, thus turning the victims into something to be exploited for gain. Because of the crimes committed by his creation, Frankenstein decides to return to England. Transporting the boy poses no problem; just as he has 'assembled' him, he will now 'disassemble' him. The linguistic link with 'the assembly line' could hardly be more clear, with the boy reduced to a car or its spare parts, not to mention the concomitant class element present in the image.

The choice of athletes is significant. It is a manifestation of the need for perfection which evokes both paranoia (Frankenstein cannot admit error in anyone) and fetishism. They in turn introduce the second element, far more insistent here, of homosexuality. This time, however, there is ample textual evidence for its existence, but its negative representation is an integral part of the overall political project of a rejection of patriarchal capitalism. When his creation cries, Frankenstein sneers 'it seems we have a sensitive teenager', a refusal of the feminine both because it is alien to patriarchy and because he is unconsciously repelled by women. Consciously, he despises them as inferior, which itself is part of the ideology the film is denouncing. He praises his fiancée's 'initiative', adding 'it sets you apart from other women'. The logic of financial success and its concomitant logic of female inferiority are perfectly expressed. That Frankenstein is in love with his creation – which the film shows in a striking scene where the boy, now with a handsome new face, admires himself in a mirror, thus condensing a condemnation of the fetishisation of teenagers for mercantile reasons, of male narcissism and Frankenstein's love of physical beauty – becomes manifest through a remark made by his fiancée to the effect that she has made efforts to find out what his experiments are: 'I felt you wouldn't want to marry a puppet, someone who'd obey you blindly'. This is precisely what Frankenstein wants from the boy. The truth of his desire is revealed to the audience via the other's discourse.

Frankenstein also seems to be in love with his assistant, an older man resembling the character in *Werewolf*. Thus when the man leaves town to buy equipment, Frankenstein says to his fiancée 'I miss him – I mean as my assistant'. If the script is trying to present him as homosexual, then it has succeeded, but I suggest we may be dealing with exactly the same question as that broached by *Werewolf*. Frankenstein is not homosexual in the sense of physically desiring sex with another man, however often he places his hand on the legs or shoulders of his creation. He is a 'typical' male in the social sense: women are so inferior intellectually that they can only fulfil the function of home help. Frankenstein 'loves' his assistant because the man submits to his authority and does his dirty work, whereas the fiancée is independent and active. She thus threatens his being at its most sensitive point: she has the phallus. The castration symbolism of severed limbs and a crocodile eating them is clear. I would privilege this reading over the one of manifest homosexuality, not to deny the latter but to insist upon the ideological forces at work.

It is precisely because the homosexual sub-text becomes a patent theme in *How to Make a Monster* that the film is more one-dimensional than its companion pieces. This is unfortunate, as it contains interesting reflections on film-making. Pete has been working for a studio for twenty-five years, in charge of the make-up for monster movies, and *Monster* uses the monsters from *Werewolf* and *Frankenstein*, brought together in a new film, destined to be the studio's last. New studio heads consider that such movies no longer correspond to what audiences want: musicals and films for teenagers are what matter. Pete rejects this interpretation and it is worth reflecting on the film's prescience. Indeed, *Monster* is a genuine historical document; it arrives towards the end of certain tendencies in the genre, which proves the bosses right. At the same time there was simply a reorientation of horror circa 1960, then again at the end of the decade, and again at the end of the 70s. We shall consider the matter throughout Part II and in the conclusion, but the film's makers – the script was written by the scriptwriter of *Frankenstein* in collaboration with producer Cohen, with the same director – clearly wish audiences to think about what is said and shown. The director in the film insists on the fight between the werewolf and Frankenstein's monster – a throwback to the tendency in the 40s to bring together characters from different movies – being done in one shot, a reference to the limited budgets. If there is an element of (self-)parody in *Monster*, the film is nevertheless quite serious. Pete plans to murder the new bosses and uses a new foundation cream which he applies to the boys playing the werewolf and the monster as it contains an ingredient which functions like a drug, enabling Pete to hypnotise them and send them out to kill. Pete is thus a variant of the mad doctor.

The murder of one studio head is perpetrated by the boy made up as Frankenstein's monster. He escapes by running along the street, knocking over a black woman who screams blue murder. This is not without significance; she was returning home from the cinema. Although the police believe her tale of a monster, there is a reference here to both of the earlier films. In *Frankenstein* the monster gets out of the doctor's house, kills a young woman and terrifies witnesses. In *Werewolf* Brandon the psychiatrist dismisses as hallucinations witnesses' descriptions of the killer; he would have to see the monster with his own eyes to believe it. The merging of fact and fiction does not go very far but is worthy of note as it is a constant theme in modern horror, particularly in the shock tactic consisting of revealing a scene as a nightmare. A non-horror film, *Deliverance*, first had recourse to this device, since used frequently, as we shall see in Part II. Although a very different sort of film, *Monster* does anticipate *Wes Craven's New Nightmare* and *Scream 3*.

The problem with the homosexual theme stems from two factors. It is seen in individual terms, with Pete as the ageing 'bitch', whereas both Tony and Frankenstein are analysed in remarkably complex and subtle ways for such 'debased' films, and Pete's increasing madness can only reinforce prejudices. There is, however, an aspect we must not neglect: Pete's devotion to his trade, to the notion of a job well done. This can be compared favourably with the current obsession with special effects as a necessary adjunct, existing solely to turn films into spectacles. There is something touchingly parental about Pete's love, transferred from his craft to the boys he makes up (interestingly, this confusion of fact and fiction, taken literally, leads to psychosis, which is Pete's fate). One striking scene has him terminating the werewolf make-up, then crossing the studio from his office to the shooting stage. He walks arm in arm with the boy, touching his cheek affectionately. At that moment a scantily clad female extra crosses their path and the boy glances surreptitiously in her direction. Here *Monster* manages to intimate Pete's homosexuality and his hold over the boy, without laughing at him. His treatment of his assistant, however, ever the passive male, prevents the film from pursuing the progressive line taken by *Werewolf* and *Frankenstein*.

iii) CORMAN AND OTHER PHENOMENA

Roger Corman is important because of his output in the decade 1955–64 (he directed forty-two films, of which twenty-four are horror, fantasy and science-fiction) and the opportunities he gave to many of his collaborators (Bogdanovich, Coppola, Scorsese) to launch independent and successful careers. I shall concentrate here on *The Wasp Woman, A Bucket of Blood, The Little Shop of Horrors* and *House of Usher*, but it is necessary first to give some notion of the range of Corman's films and the themes used, especially in the light of the contributions of his scriptwriters whose work Corman directed with a greater or lesser demonstration of talent. Thus we find the scientist whose hubris destroys him: *The Undead, The Man with the X-Ray Eyes*; alien invasions: *It Conquered the World, Not of this Earth*, the latter also linked to the theme of vampirism via the alien's need for new blood; giant mutations: *Attack of the Crab Monsters*; nuclear destruction: *Teenage Caveman, The Day the World Ended*. The last of these is a suitable point of reference to the way Corman worked with a team. A mixture of horror, science-fiction and *film noir* (two of the characters are a hoodlum and a stripper), *The Day the World Ended* evokes the evolution of humanity after a nuclear war in the shape of a character who can eat only contaminated animals and who runs through the woods at night in search of nourishment. A discussion between two characters evokes cannibalism as the next stage, so the film both refers to the theme of the werewolf and looks ahead to Romero's *Living Dead* trilogy. Unusual inasmuch as it does not evoke the dangers of war but the consequences, it is nevertheless ideologically traditional in its treatment of sexuality; thus the father dies in order to leave his daughter to the virile hero, a patriarchal logic quite unnecessary except within the Biblical context the film evokes and adheres to.

Different writers, different ideologies. Both Leo Gordon (*Wasp*) and Charles B. Griffith (*Bucket, Shop*) introduce radical elements into their contributions: an awareness of female dissatisfaction with patriarchy for the former; class and economics for the latter. The eponymous central character of *Wasp* is a woman of forty who has spent eighteen years building up her company, which markets beauty products, and making money. Her desire to return to the age of twenty-two can therefore be interpreted, not in the usual male terms of the woman wanting to please the opposite sex, but as an unconscious rejection of the patriarchal world based on female submission and profit. Beeswax is at the base of the products and the workers are in a constant state of competition to see who can turn in the most wax in a month. Thus they allow themselves to be exploited by the company, just as the bees work without realising they are doing so. The film gives new meaning to the expression 'as busy as a bee'. The heroine's obsession with ageing is meant to be a female concern, but a closer look at the theme reveals other factors at work. Movies systematically downgrade older actresses until they are forced into grotesque parodies of themselves (see *Whatever Happened to Baby Jane?*). Ageing can therefore be seen as a predominantly male obsession, the spectacle of the female body approaching death and decay evoking long-repressed fears of the female body as locus of castration, a fear that remains after the subject has realised his Oedipus complex and accepted death for what it is. A perfect manifestation of this in horror is the beautiful woman in the bathroom in *The Shining* who abruptly turns into a decaying hag as she comes too close to the male character.

The heroine is punished by being turned into a wasp because of what her status implies for men in a context both sexual and economic. Two members of her research team toss a coin to see who will pay for a meal, the secretary present being thus invited. It is men who take decisions, which suggests on the characters' part an unconscious resentment of a female boss. The active woman is a threat and becomes literally dangerous. This is an appropriate place to consider a theme that is common to a number of low-budget movies which appeared at the end of the 50s: women's plight in a context of general masculine fear and contempt. Thus in *I Married a Monster from Outer Space* men are portrayed as drones who hang about bars drinking and being objectionable to women. Of particular interest as feminist texts are the two films directed by Nathan Juran under the pseudonym of Nathan Hertz: *Brain from the Planet Arous* and *Attack of the 50-Foot Woman*.

In *Arous* the heroine is treated as a virtual slave by her fiancé and his friend and, like the film, seems to take it for granted. Living in the shadow of her father, she becomes a mother figure and the men can do without her except when she is called upon to prepare meals. The Oedipal implications of this are patent, but what happens when the evil brain Gor takes over the body of the fiancé is revealing: he becomes

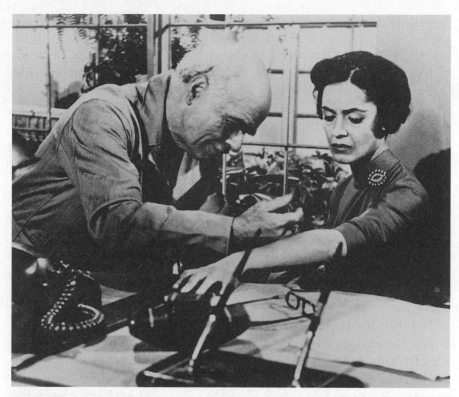

Figure 4 Age after beauty – and before monstrosity. *The Wasp Woman*. Copyright © 1959 The Film Group/Santa Cruz – Roger Corman.

aggressive towards her, which suggests unconscious male resentment as well as an 'alien' influence. To combat Gor, the good brain Vol takes over the family dog but, seen only by the spectators, leaves its body once Gor has been destroyed. When the heroine tries to explain to her fiancé what has happened, he laughs and refers disparagingly to her 'female imagination'. He assumes he conquered the alien all alone, which is sufficiently denied by the film to hint at conflicting representations of women structuring the text and persistent anxiety over the social role of men who need women to be passive.

The future fifty-foot woman rushes furiously from a bar where her husband is making love to his mistress. He has returned to his wife after a separation as 'community property' means both must agree to a divorce and she refuses to share the money, which is hers. 'A man doesn't stand a chance', he claims, but the mistress has a solution: the wife's notorious alcoholism and a stay in an asylum will provide the means to get rid of her. Meantime, she has been threatened by a space invader in the form of a giant hand (a feminist recycling of the encounter between Ann Darrow and the ape in *King Kong*?) and this alien contact will result in her growing and growing. Given the opening sequence in the bar we are entitled to interpret this as a representation of the limited possibilities open to women under patriarchy and of unconscious male fears concerning women who have money and a degree of independence. The transformation indicates both that a woman functions as the property of men, much as if she were a child, and that as a giant she stands in for the mother men need to protect them from the responsibilities of life and its drawbacks. For the woman marriage and motherhood are the only social functions and it is revealing that, once again, psychiatry is the scheming husband's accomplice by assuming the victim is still an alcoholic and ripe for a straitjacket. The law plays a similar role: the husband bribes a policeman to lie about his wife's behaviour.

The dialogue is explicit on the 'dangers' involved when women have some control over their destinies. The mistress argues that, once they have the wife removed, the husband 'will be in the driver's seat' and they will be wealthy. This is a remarkable example of language functioning literally and figuratively, inasmuch as the wife is driving her car when the spaceship lands. And the notion of removing her points to the pre-Oedipal desire of the child for the parent of the opposite sex, where 'remove' = 'kill'. This nicely places both husband and mistress in the position of dependent children, a situation that cannot go unchallenged. Thus the last line of the film is 'she finally got Harry all to herself'. It is spoken by the doctor after she has killed the mistress and been electrocuted along with her husband. The ironic reference to the three deaths is surely suggestive. This is the behaviour of the possessive mother who refuses to let her children leave home and devours them (I use the word 'devour' figuratively, but later horror applies it literally as cannibalism, as we shall see in Part II). Unfortunately for the manifest content of the film, this notion is the basis of a capitalist society which represses the social in favour of the individual within the family unit where selfishness is erected into a virtue for purely economic reasons. Moreover, the woman's size symbolises the horror of the feminine and shows how elements are overdetermined in the unconscious. Her dimensions betray both a male fear – the woman has the phallus – and the con-comitant need to fetishise women so that she is the phallus the male desires and can obtain by turning her into an object (of fascination), a sort of 'trophy', like the heads adorning the walls of Count Zaroff's den, for his acting in the appropriate virile fashion.

The scripts of *Bucket* and *Shop* concentrate instead on class and economics. In the former the hero Walter hangs out in beatnik bars where he tends to be the object of jokes, given his limited intelligence and the fact that his marginal status is due not to choice but to social oppression. His accidental killing of a cat leads him to cover it with clay and to pass the result off as a work of art. Unfortunately for Walter, a fan slips him drugs in appreciation and he is followed home by a suspicious policeman whom he also kills accidentally, covering up his tracks as with the cat. What Griffith does in his most subtle script is to set up a parallel between Walter's somewhat infantile behaviour and the economic system which temporarily transforms him from victim into artist. Like young children, Walter takes literally what he hears and falls under the influence of the poetic declarations spoken by beatniks in the bar. The formula 'repetition is death' – Freud is hovering in the background here – makes Walter assume that he must be inventive and show initiative, which he does with the cat and the policeman. The link between the death drive and the drive to make money and be socially successful is patent, with the film insisting on the fact that, in order to survive in the artistic/economic jungle, Walter must turn into a murderer; he actually makes things happen, rather than react passively. As such he shows that such success can only come into being at the expense of others/rivals. His secret made public, Walter commits suicide.

All the elements of this very black comedy are taken up and extended in *Shop*. Seymour works in a florist's on Skid Row and creates a hybrid plant which he discovers thrives on blood. The film sets up a parallel between the plant and Seymour's boss, ever ready to exploit his naive employee. Marx's comparison of a capitalist to a vampire is once again taken literally, for Seymour is forced by his boss to make sure that the plant survives so that he can make money out of its uniqueness. Thus Seymour's labour is doubly exploited; he 'invents' the plant but his boss profits from it; Seymour has to relinquish a part of his 'life's blood' to keep the thing alive. Indeed his boss contemplates opening a new shop in Beverly Hills and it is here that the highly unusual – for a Hollywood film – shots of Seymour wandering among winos and tramps, like Walter only a step from this himself, take on their full resonance.

Another interesting parallel between the two movies is the theme of art. People come to see the plant and the film satirises the contemplative nature of gazing at paintings, that aspect of art appreciation which Lukacs linked to fetishism as it effaces all traces of labour in favour of beauty as an ahistorical end in itself. This link between plant and paintings is stressed by the former being the only one of its kind. In the art world this leads to vast fortunes being paid for a Picasso or a Van Gogh, implicitly criticised in the film by the fact that Seymour's creativity is handsomely rewarded: his boss grants him a two-dollar payrise. A further, revealing parallel between *Shop* and *Bucket* is to be seen in the plant's starting to talk. It insists on being fed ever more regularly, screaming 'more!' Thus the plant becomes a vampiric and insatiable child feeding off the body of 'mother' Seymour. This in turn underscores the active, patriarchal role of his boss, leaving Seymour with the task of nourishing the plant, then depriving him of all rights over his own creation. *Shop* both denounces capitalist exploitation and over-determines this by showing how proletarian men and women are equally exploited through Seymour functioning as a condensation of both. The final bitter irony lies in the plant becoming autonomous, hypnotising him in order to be fed. By having Seymour go out to look for suitable human fodder, *Shop* anticipates Romero and the modern horror film with the theme of cannibalism as signifier of capitalist exploitation and the consumer society. This autonomy, where the product of labour is felt to live a life of its own by the alienated worker, is taken to its logical conclusion: in an attempt to kill the plant – which has grown to be bigger than the average person, a throwback to *50-Foot Woman* and an indication of the hero's maternal status – Seymour is promptly eaten and the film closes with the thing shouting 'feed me!' The cycle of vampirism, consumerism and exploitation must continue.

House of Usher is a pivotal film, coming as it does at a time when major changes were operating in Hollywood in the realm of horror. *Usher* really does give the impression of a director engaging totally with his material, rather than illustrating someone else's scripts. More pertinent, however, are the film's central theme and its ramifications: incest, family values and the repression of women by neurotic or intolerant patriarchs, for these form the backbone of many horror films to come, and certainly the most important and influential ones. Through his use of the wide screen to create the sense of a vast space closing in on characters and audience alike and his direction of Vincent Price in one of his great roles, Corman succeeds in creating an overwhelming atmosphere of guilt and repressed desire. Thus Roderick Usher has his sister buried despite his knowledge that she is alive as a form of displacement for his own incestuous attachment to her. The woman is turned into a victim, sacrificed to the man's deranged sense of his own importance and that of the family. Like its exact contemporary *Psycho*, *House of Usher* ushers in the modern horror film, at least in its themes. Hitchcock's film will enable us to take the matter further.

Part II

MODERN HORROR

5

THE CHANGING FACE OF HORROR

One word can sum up the shift from classic horror to modern horror: *Psycho*. The very title foregrounds psychoanalytical elements of *House of Usher* and the film insists on their ramifications: sexuality and death in the context of the social function of the family, patriarchy and money. Dominant in much contemporary horror is the family and *Psycho* goes to the heart of the matter; it is less a question of 'home is where the heart is' than of 'hearths of darkness' (Tony Williams, 1996). What, then, does Hitchcock's movie show us? The element that needs to be stressed, precisely because it is so easy to overlook, is that we are dealing with the modern, everyday world, not with one situated in the past. Gone are the mad scientists, the remote islands and settings, the dangers of invasion and radiation. Gone too is the need to placate the censors: the shower sequence and the murder of Arbogast create a new approach to horror.

However, this is not the only important feature of *Psycho*. It is rather the link between sexuality and death in a precise family context that deserves to be foregrounded, as the very opening of the film makes clear. The camera zooms in slowly until the window of the hotel corresponds to the screen frame; momentarily we are faced with a black rectangle which slowly transforms into the shot of a bedroom where we observe a woman lying on a bed and a man, a towel in his hands, standing and looking at her recumbent form. There is something uncanny about the shot: the immobile woman seems to be dead, the man her possible murderer. This link between sex and death is one that will be recreated again and again over the coming years; it condenses the roles of victims and serial killers, just as the murder in the shower condenses those of victims and slashers. What follows is just as important: the role of mother, whose picture must be turned to the wall so that the couple can exercise their rights as sexual beings. However, lest we be tempted to construe this as yet another conservative attack on the mother, let us not forget the role of the father and his phallic weapon: money. The true 'villain' of *Psycho* is not Mrs Bates but the Texan millionaire. It is he who uses his fortune to impose his desire both on his daughter and her future husband and on Marion. It is he who, having tried to seduce Marion, inverts the situation by accusing her of making a play for him. Or, rather, this is how Marion imagines the situation in Phoenix during her drive through the night. She assumes unconsciously the ideology of patriarchy, where only the male has the right to decide and make money and where the woman must submit and limit herself to having and bringing up children. At the very point where Marion imagines the millionaire as wanting to replace the money with her flesh, she gives an enigmatic smile, the same smile we witness on the face of Norman at the end of the film, now completely psychotic and dominated by his mother, as the superimposition of her skull indicates. Submitting to capitalist patriarchy is akin to a living death for the woman and the only alternative for her is to keep her son jealously to herself, thus depriving him of his phallic rights as she was deprived of certain rights once married.

Just as Norman is possessed by his mother, so Marion is possessed by the ideology of the respective functions of men and women in a society determined by an exclusively masculine discourse. I do not use the word 'possessed' idly. The woman is possessed by the man both sexually and as a commodity, and possession by the Devil is a central theme of contemporary horror and is a major concern of this chapter. I suggest we try to strip it of its obscurantist and reactionary coating to probe the causes. To do so I shall look first at one of the key works of the genre, a film that is thematically rooted within the modern horror film but whose self-conscious approach to the image, representation and the spectator shows a commitment more in keeping with the modernist temperament that formed Tourneur and Hitchcock: *Rosemary's Baby*.

i) THE MODERN *FANTASTIQUE*

Polanski's film partakes of the same logic that informs the ending of *I Walked with a Zombie*: there is not a shred of textual evidence that Rosemary was impregnated by the Devil and that the child she bears is not the fruit of her union with Guy. The critical readiness to assume that Rosemary is not only a victim of Satanists but also of Satan and that the last shot of her looking into the child's crib shows that she has accepted the situation is revealing; it indicates that the need to believe is stronger than the desire to analyse, which certainly helps explain why films like *The Exorcist*, *The Omen* and *Audrey Rose* are taken seriously as reflections on that hoary old chestnut, the fight between 'good' and 'evil'. Such an approach is strictly ahistorical and needs to be deconstructed.

Rosemary's Baby is a film about sexual repression, religion and unresolved incestuous desire. It is significant that, when Rosemary decides to act independently instead of following the instructions of Satanists Roman and Minnie Castavet, she throws a party open only to 'the under sixties' and invites her old friends, excluding the Castavets and theirs. By so doing she is attempting to overcome her submission to parental figures, to eliminate them from the lives of her husband Guy and herself, but she cannot eliminate the traces of early childhood influences. This is patent in the sequence which is presented as a dream but also as the beginning of Rosemary's alleged seduction by Satan. The fact that she has objected to the strange taste of Minnie's chocolate mousse and later has attacks of vertigo and nausea can be put down to hysteria or to the presence of some hallucinogenic drug. Given the hallucinatory status of dream images, the film places us in the position of not being able to decide whether Rosemary is the victim of a plot or simply imagining everything. Thus the images present Rosemary as floating on an ocean, then being raised up towards religious paintings in a church. The change in environment to an apartment where we see characters such as Dr Sapirstein in no way proves she is actually being raped by Satan but that she is the centre of a ritual mounted by people who believe in Satan and base their lives on this, just as Christians base theirs on the existence of God.

The presence of an image of Hutch, Rosemary's best friend, must be taken as just that: an image. It clearly suggests an incestuous attachment to the father via a father figure, which allows us to see Satan with his piercing eyes as the representation of the object of Rosemary's unconscious desire. This is overdetermined by images of sado-masochism in the film, with Rosemary being held down by the Satanists when making a last effort to escape just prior to the birth of her child. During the party her girlfriends are horrified by her appearance; she is haggard and emaciated as a result of taking the brew prepared for her by the Castavets instead of the medicine prescribed. One woman refers to Sapirstein as a 'sadist', another says to Rosemary 'you can't go on suffering'. Thus the film subtly introduces the masochistic component of religious belief which, when articulated with the incest theme, predisposes the heroine to a state of submission and belief in father figures.

Here Roman Castavet is more than a match for Hutch, who can only bring the arguments of a rationalist to bear on the case. Castavet is more knowledgeable of the way the psyche functions. Near the opening of the film Rosemary meets Terry, a future victim, who shows her a good-luck charm. There is nothing quite like exploiting everyday superstitions and social alienation to control a person's mind, which the Castavets do. Thus Minnie gives Rosemary the charm and, when she says she cannot accept it, replies 'you already have'. From the point of view of the Satanists, this means the recipient is coming under the influence of Satan, but we are entitled to see it as an instance of the subject submitting unconsciously to an ideology sufficiently powerful to 'go without saying'.

A more social and political dimension can be suggested if we remember how Guy got his acting job: the actor chosen woke up one morning to find himself blind. Guy's need to be a success is quickly understood and exploited by the Castavets. They offer to help him with magic and he goes along with this because of his acceptance of the ideology at the basis of capitalist society: the success of one person or firm can come about only through the failure or collapse of another. Guy refuses to see a coincidence when he comes across one because he wants to believe, just as Rosemary has always needed to believe in God and the Castavets in Satan. In so believing they expose themselves as insane and paranoid, the opinion Rosemary has of them when she says to Dr Hill (the doctor she has consulted in an attempt to overcome the control of Sapirstein) 'maybe all of this is a coincidence'.

Surely this is why Polanski does not show us the baby. Rosemary looks down enigmatically into the cradle and the Satanists sigh with relief: she has accepted Satan is its father. Rosemary can no longer fight and has found it easier to believe than to apply knowledge. Polanski deliberately prevents us from identifying with her at this point, unlike at other moments when he has recourse to subjective point-of-view shots. This alone should have made us sceptical and realise that what we are seeing is a persecuted young woman accepting the tasks of the dutiful mother and their attendant ideology. The fact that Rosemary asks 'what have you done to its eyes?' when she first sees the baby only further underlines the impact of the traumatic images of the dream/hallucination sequence earlier. And the reply – 'he has his father's eyes' – is just another way of making sure that the woman will continue to submit to patriarchy. For during the 'rape' sequence the alternating shots of Guy and of Satan having sex with Rosemary insist on the piercing eyes of both: whether one accepts the supernatural reading or prefers a rational one, Rosemary will be under constant surveillance.

ii) 'POSSESSION' MOVIES

Rosemary is possessed not only in the sexual sense but also in the economic one: she is alienated as part of the male's panoply of goods and chattels. Social and psychic alienation will be a persistent theme in this and the following chapters and I propose to lay the groundwork via the more common themes of Satanic possession, reincarnation and tele-kinesis. Let us start with *The Exorcist*.

It is essential to cut through the obscurantist trappings and the sensational special effects and draw attention to issues stressed by certain critics, rightly anxious to highlight the social and political significance of the very real anxieties the film exploits (in every sense of the word). What, then, are its main concerns? One is to equate the East with mystery, sexuality (the statue with the erect penis) and the Devil, the West with necessary abstinence, purity, holiness and godliness. Everything from sexual licence and obscenity to mere ugliness are the Devil's work. However, this obscurantist ploy is constantly undermined by elements that are as much out of control as Regan's body, which is hardly surprising: the body is the site of desires that cannot say their name but which can become manifest in the most unusual ways. The appearance of 'help me' on Regan's body, to which we shall return, is an eloquent example of the discourse of the unconscious.

Basically, the film exalts sacrifice and self-abnegation: Regan's mother looks after her daughter alone, Father Karras his mother. Although the film has the merit of underlining what happens when poverty prevents proper medical care, its real interest lies in the problems posed by giving pride of place to father figures belonging to the Church and therefore celibates. The script finds itself in a double bind. On the one hand it

implicitly denounces Regan's father for deserting the family; on the other
it clearly indicates that the possession of Regan starts when she is alone
while her mother is busy with her career as an actress. Behind this family
drama lies a particular discourse: the mother should be at home looking
after her daughter. This, however, would deprive the mother of her
right to a profession, an approach the film dare not adopt openly for fear
of becoming controversial instead of merely causing a scandal because an
apparently demure pubescent girl starts shouting obscenities, masturbat-
ing and showing her sex. The text's 'message' is surely clear: bring girls
up properly – away from drunken, debauched males like Burke, the film
director – and you may prevent them from becoming feminists. Unfortunately for this reactionary project, *The Exorcist* tends to move precisely
in that direction.

This move is implied but certainly not intended. The film presents an
image of men that hardly militates in favour of marriage and children.
Although Regan seems to be in favour of her mother marrying Burke, he
is not represented as someone likely to be willing to play surrogate father
to a girl at a difficult stage of her life. The two priests, furthermore, are
celibates. Thus the intense love that binds mother and daughter and
whose incestuous nature is patent can be interpreted as a form of defence,
faced with the father's desertion. It is here that the question of hysteria
arises, with Regan unconsciously punishing herself for being too
'possessive', yet having no other option. If the Devil that possesses
her kills Burke, it is because Regan cannot bear the idea of a second man
behaving like her father, which is understandable, given the world in
which Burke moves. The 'help me' on her body is therefore the manifestation of hysteria, the guilt-ridden daughter addressing an appeal to society
and its adult representatives to help her find a solution to conflicting
desires: the pre-Oedipal one of keeping her mother for herself and the
adolescent one of growing up sexually and enabling her mother to fulfil
that function, while having a career and a sex life. Thus the controversial
scene where Regan urinates on the carpet in front of party guests can be
seen as both a regression to childhood in order to draw the attention of
a mother who is insufficiently present, and a demand to be included in her
mother's activities as a girl approaching womanhood and inviting respect
for that reason. The ending of the film is downbeat: it suggests that none
of these very real questions has found an answer. That Regan remembers
nothing of her ordeal is the film's conscious resolution of its internal

contradictions, the most important of which is the desire to conclude as if the possession were a simple question of Satanic evil, rather than the return of the repressed.

This reading is not completely satisfactory. One cannot help but be struck by the fact that Satan's male voice is provided by an actress. I suggest we take this literally and see Satan as condensing father and mother, indicating that Regan needs both parents to become adult, but that she also needs to separate herself from both. Her real father has abandoned her, her real mother is both over-possessive and insufficiently present. Both are 'bad parents', which is where Satan comes in: a symbol of a refusal on their part to help the child realise her Oedipus complex, become emotionally independent and occupy the social position of a non-neurotic young woman. The 'help me' is thus both Regan calling on Karras to be the 'good' father and Satan as bad father/mother calling on the priest to maintain Regan in a state of sexual ignorance or celibacy. Freud pointed out how climbing stairs in a dream symbolised the sex act. That Karras should plunge down a flight of steps thus symbolises the negation of such an act. But his sacrifice is in vain: Regan forgets everything, which can be interpreted as a positive sign of leaving negative parental influences behind her.

Yet another reading is possible, however, and I raise the issue only to show how the tensions and contradictions within the film can produce multiple and necessarily complementary or conflicting interpretations. Why should we go on the assumption that the 'help me' is a call from Regan? What if we interpret it as a call from Satan to Merrin and Karras, as one 'male' to another? In that case, Satan is addressing them, not as priests, but as symbolic representatives of repressive patriarchy, asking them to lend a hand in maintaining both children and women in their place. The idea of a holy – or an unholy – pact being made between Satan and a priest is a most attractive one and certainly far from the conscious preoccupations of Blatty and Friedkin, but one we would be advised not to neglect, given the peculiar status of *The Exorcist* in modern society. The fact that Regan's body is 'burned' by holy water that is only tap water suggests the possession is a 'game' played between Satan and Karras. It is therefore all the more regrettable that critics, blinded by their refusal to see, should have dismissed *The Heretic*, with its 'deliberate assault on the horror film's traditional boundaries' and its criticism of 'the violent masculinity shown by Karras towards Regan in *The Exorcist*'.

(Tony Williams 1996: 128) Seldom mentioned except to be scorned, *The Heretic* merits a revival and Williams' analysis is invaluable. Another neglected film, *Alice, Sweet Alice* (aka *Communion*) is also a welcome departure from the pro-religion stance of *The Exorcist* in the way it locates the potentially murderous effects of a massive repression of sexuality within the family and Christian ideology.

I see nothing to redeem *The Omen* whose crassness and incompetence I can only take at its face value: objectionable. Here the severe father and all-powerful, all-knowing male hides from his wife the truth about the death of their child at birth and substitutes another in its place, as if the mother had no say in the matter. Something might have been made of the theme of punishment, with the child of Satan venting on the father the results of the guilt he comes to feel, but the 'good/evil' opposition is the only criterion adopted. The follow-up, *Damien: The Omen 2*, has at least the merit of being competently made and of not taking spectators for idiots.

Audrey Rose is a most interesting and intelligent movie, even if it goes out of its way to disavow at the end all the ambiguities it has created. Wise goes for understatement (having learned his lesson after the unsubtle special effects of that overrated movie *The Haunting*), which renders the nightmare or 'possession' scenes all the more effective and frightening. The story turns on the fate that befalls little Ivy, who becomes the site of the reincarnation of Audrey Rose, a girl of the same age who died several years earlier when trapped in a blazing car after a crash. The father, played by Anthony Hopkins, tries to convince Ivy's parents that she is Audrey reincarnated; he even kidnaps Ivy, whom he considers his own daughter. If the husband refuses to accept these claims, the wife gradually comes to believe them. We have a striking parallel with *Rosemary's Baby*, with Audrey's father playing the role of the Castavets, Ivy's father that of Rosemary and her mother that of Guy. By that I mean that it is a question of imposing one's beliefs on others and succeeding or failing, according to the willingness of the subject to accept what is patent nonsense. I could not agree more with Tony Williams when he calls Audrey's father 'demented' (Williams 1996: 278), although I prefer the term 'psychotic': he has completely withdrawn from everyday reality and is living in a fantasy world where he does not hesitate to destroy a family by being responsible for Ivy's death.

Both story and direction strive to force the spectator to go along with this obscurantist ploy. Hopkins' elegant diction and quiet manner function to make us sympathise: it is easy to understand why he was chosen to play Hannibal Lecter. The father, on the other hand, is portrayed as having a closed mind. In a society less given over to religious fervour, this would be a point in his favour and the film has a hard time convincing us, given the dangerous behaviour of Audrey's father. At the outset Ivy's mother says of one of her daughter's friends 'girls like Jill just like to fantasise', but remains incapable of applying that insight to Ivy, let alone herself and the insane father. What is disreputable about the film — although this has a precise significance — is the way Ivy is stripped of her identity, her mother accepting such sadistic treatment. Audrey's father raves on about a 'vast cosmic drama' and the film complacently includes shots of India, as if his years there lend credence to such claims. Yet the trial, which concentrates on his look, can easily be interpreted as suggesting that he is fantasising, rather than remembering. All such doubts are meant to be eliminated when the mother, now a convert to religious fanaticism, writes to Audrey's father in India to say that Ivy was denied peace and fulfilment while alive. It would be difficult to find a clearer example of disavowal, with the mother blaming everything and everyone except the person really responsible for Ivy's suffering and death. Shots of photos of Ivy at differing stages of childhood, including a recent photo the spectators have seen several times, contradict this: she was clearly a happy child, until the unfortunate day a religious maniac confused fantasy and reality to the point where it became necessary for him to sacrifice another little girl in order to find his own identity and peace of mind.

Audrey Rose is interesting as the statement of a recurrent pathology: an anxiety over social and psychic alienation finding an imaginary solution in religion. A salutary rejoinder to this is *The Rapture*, an attack on sects and charlatans and the way the economically exploited and psychologically fragile risk mental or physical destruction. That social alienation will lead inevitably to psychic alienation is neatly represented at the opening where an office space is divided into cubicles, each with a woman and her headphone and computer. A colleague arrives to take over from the heroine, thus summing up their function: so much merchandise, each capable of being exchanged for the other. Hardly surprising, then, that the heroine and a male friend spend their time looking for sexual kicks as an attempt to overcome alienation which only increases as the subject abandons all control over his or her existence in the name of supposedly liberating experiences: the ideology of 'free choice' transforms the person into a sort of automaton, abandoning the self to drives that can only be destructive.

Sexual encounters take place in an airport hotel, a perfect symbol for social alienation and aimless movement. Later in the film it is the call of the desert where the heroine will hear God's voice. In the meantime the heroine has had a child whom she sacrifices in an attempt to save her from hell on earth; seeing life as a punishment for sins, she punishes her daughter. Thus *The Rapture* deconstructs the ideology of submission defended in *Audrey Rose* by highlighting just how easy it is to impose one's will on another: the daughter goes along with her mother's delirium and is in no position, psychologically or socially, to defend herself. Other children are less passive, as we shall see, but the theme of alienation is treated with intelligence in *Christine* which plays on the various meaning of 'possession(s)'.

Christine is about the fetishisation of that ultimate symbol of modern society, the car, and hovers between conservative nostalgia and a progressive criticism of male values in relation to the female. At one level the film is a protest against assembly-line cars and the notion of waste and it is interesting to note that the feminised car enables the hero Arnie to overcome his timidity and introversion. However, he soon transforms into exactly the same kind of male as the youths who torment him and destroy the car. The film defends female values against 'football virility', sexism and the reduction of girls to sexual objects. As the car was made in the 50s, it also implies that female values favour quality and endurance in contrast to masculine values which fetishise the ephemeral. It would therefore be inaccurate to see the car as symbolising only nostalgia. It foregrounds rather contemporary alienation, both social and sexual, and insists on the need to preserve the past. The spectacular transformation of the car from a wreck to a splendid 'new' vehicle certainly suggests nostalgic wishful thinking, but also the importance of the notion of quality that contemporary society tends to consider as old-fashioned. *Christine* is claiming that the past must 'possess' the present, but the historical dimension tends to disappear behind the discourse of individualism and the importance of possessions as a validation of this ideology.

iii) THE CHILD STRIKES BACK

What is positive about *Carrie* and *Firestarter* is the insistence on sexuality as normal: it is precise social factors that lead to Carrie's horror over menstruating in the shower and to the repression of any notion of infantile sexuality on the part of the characters of *Firestarter*. If we take blood as the privileged element in De Palma's film, then it must be construed as a signifier circulating literally and metaphorically. Carrie's religious bigot of a mother is spreading the Gospel 'through Christ's blood', which introduces the crucial themes of suffering and atonement. Carrie must atone for her mother's past sin — enjoying sex! — and suffer in her stead. As her classmates persecute her, we can interpret her devastating use of her telekinetic powers as both a visiting of the Apocalypse on a guilty humanity (taking her mother's ravings literally) and as a pointed rejection of the whole ethos of Christian suffering. Attributing her misery to her mother, she crucifies her then gets her revenge. As sexuality is not repressed in the society represented in the film — on the contrary, sex is a regular activity — then we must see Carrie herself as the return of the repressed. What might that mean?

We could do worse than reflect on the character of the gym mistress. She is clearly maternal in the way she protects — or thinks she is protecting — Carrie and therefore seems to function as the 'good' mother as opposed to the 'bad' mother. Just how good she is, however, is a moot point. Her efforts to encourage Carrie to see herself as pretty — and she does a sterling job in transforming the ugly duckling into a swan for the Prom Night — are not exactly disinterested. Miss Collins is surely unconsciously submitting herself to an image of what constitutes female beauty within a masculine discourse. By making Carrie conform to that image, she is ultimately using the heroine as a way of reinforcing her own narcissism. This in turn helps explain an aspect of *Carrie* William Paul has stressed: the film insists on the gym mistress's thighs via the very tight shorts she wears. (Paul 1994: 362) If we interpret this as a 'come hither' sign, then Miss Collins is conforming to the discourse of the Other: dressing and making herself up in a way that transforms her into an object of the male gaze, yet another commodity. Is this not what Carrie is during the Prom Night, the newly transformed girl worthy of admiration, an object of beauty, where beauty may be only skin deep, as it certainly is in the case of her tormentor Chris?

This line of reasoning gives a further twist to the already complex shock ending. Carrie's friend Sue approaches Carrie's grave after everything is over and a hand suddenly reaches out and grabs hers. This, however, is 'only' a nightmare; in reality Sue's mother is trying to comfort her. We should not allow the shock to numb our faculties: a nightmare is a manifestation of a desire that the subject cannot accept coming uncomfortably to the surface, like the hand from beyond the grave. As Paul points out (Paul 1994: 368), is the hand Carrie's or her mother's, inasmuch as we are shown Sue and her mother in what follows? In that case *Carrie* is drawing parallels between the various mothers and maternal figures, suggesting that they are a negative and destructive force. Rather than see this as pure misogyny, we should interpret it as the manifestation of Sue's fears unconsciously determined by Carrie's: all that girls have to look forward to under patriarchy – significantly the headmaster cannot remember Carrie's name, a striking instance of the repression of the female – is conforming to mother's image, itself determined by male desire and its attendant discourse. Moreover, the totally negative religious influence of Carrie's mother lives on socially for the unfortunate Sue. The nightmare thus translates a terrible fear on Sue's part: like Carrie, she will end up dead and buried.

Firestarter broaches the great repressed: sexuality in children. The heroine, Charlie, is much younger than Regan and at a point where pre-Oedipal drives are turning into desire through the realisation of the Oedipus complex. Thus at the outset she has no control over her telekinetic powers which function if she dislikes someone, a situation we can transcribe into Freudian terms: both a case of giving vent to drives to obtain immediate satisfaction (= pre-Oedipal) and having an unconscious which can become manifest at any moment because it is outside the subject's conscious knowledge (= post-Oedipal). This needs to be stressed as Charlie makes a promise to her father never to use her power again, a clear case of renouncing satisfaction in favour of social constraints. Thus, when she agrees to break her promise to please one of the villains (anxious to exploit her powers for political reasons), her special strength functions in reverse: instead of setting a forest on fire, she starts to heat up herself. This is a succinct and effective representation of the unconscious dimension of guilt returning to punish the subject, and the function of the father at once places Charlie's power in a framework of infantile sexuality. This is made abundantly clear through the figure of a doctor who sees in Charlie and her father the 'greatest threat' the nation has ever had. That he evokes both child and parent stresses the place and function of desire as an unconscious phenomenon: the child's desire is mediated by the father's. For the doctor the power is linked to the pituitary gland and is most active at adolescence. Thus he is both mouthing society's fear of teenage sexuality and repressing any notion of children having a libido. For the government agents, the best way to get Charlie to cooperate is to ply her with presents, reducing the child to a consumer subjected to economic forces. This ideology of the family as both a private and an economic unit constantly adapting itself to the market is taken up, in various guises, in much contemporary horror.

iv) FAMILY VALUES

At one point in *Dolls* the doll-maker remarks that 'being a parent is a privilege, not a right'. This evokes the question of parental responsibility and children's rights. Sandwiched between the extreme gore of *Re-animator* and the extreme nastiness of *From Beyond* (both of which are rare modern instances of the 'mad scientist' movie), *Dolls* risks sinking without trace, which would be to neglect a subtle and adult movie. The tone is set quickly when a pair of rich, bitchy adults, reluctantly dragging the man's little daughter in tow, get bogged down after a storm and have to take refuge in an old dark house in the country. The woman, anxious to punish the girl for simply existing, throws her teddy into the undergrowth. Cut to the girl, furious, looking off-screen intently. Cut to a giant teddy lurching from the bushes, then turning into a monster that throws the man aside and chews the woman's face off, to the girl's delight. Cut back to the girl who was imagining it all. Throughout the film the doll-maker and his wife act out such desires and turn them into reality.

The fact that the girl identifies so intensely with her teddy is testimony to the identity problem she suffers as a result of being rejected by her father and stepmother. Reduced to excess baggage, she needs to assert herself and the elderly couple do this in her stead. He is opposed to mass-produced dolls that deny difference, which brings us back to the theme of children as consumers, trained from an early age to want only what the market offers; each and every toy is conceived to be exchanged for any other toy, the whole question of a child's desire and identity being elided

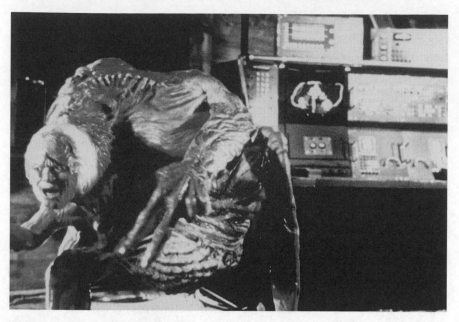

Figure 5 The mad scientist transformed: modern horror. *From Beyond*. Copyright © 1986 Taryn Productions/Empire Productions – Brian Yuzna.

in favour of profit. The film thus takes up via toys what we have seen at work in *Christine*. That the girl should be treated as a toy by her parents sums up the values transmitted to children by adults. The film is careful to open out the problem in more social terms. Two young women, also stranded, dismiss the dolls as old-fashioned as they do not correspond to the current fabrication of toys, whereas the hero Ralph has kept alive his boy's love of toys instead of simply repressing his childhood memories in the name of growing up and being 'modern'. Thus the film becomes an extended allegory of an inversion of conservative family values, where children are either fetishised or repressed and parents unconsciously act out society's economic values, based on endless consumption and the repetition of the same. By having Ralph tell stories about dolls coming to life, the film explicitly represents commodification, where objects take on a life of their own and people are reduced to simple adjuncts of them as consumers. It is significant, too, that the girl leaves her teddy with the old couple at the end of the film, an act which is a symbol both of her growing up – thanks to them she has learned to overcome an excessive attachment symbolising her own reduction to the function of a toy – and of their recognising her genuine needs as a child.

A striking example of the ability of contemporary horror to raise important questions and then repress them is the unsatisfactory *Cujo*. It soon becomes apparent that the little boy's fear of monsters stems from unconscious fears about his future in a household where the parents are drifting apart, the wife having an affair. We can also read his terror faced with doors opening by themselves as the primal scene, in this case the possibility that he has witnessed his mother and her lover in bed. In this context the transformation of lovable Cujo into a rabid monster is the literal exteriorisation of family tensions and hatreds, also manifest in the working-class family to whom the dog belongs. This in turn brings class antagonism into the picture, but like so much else this is not exploited. The film ends in such a way that it is patent the mother must be punished ideologically for having an affair which has threatened the family, although the attitude of the husband – absorbed in business deals – hardly inspires confidence. Having saved her son's life and killed Cujo, she then literally hands the boy over to the father who comes to rescue them but who turns out to be superfluous. The assertion is that a woman's role is to have children and behave in a way that reinforces the husband's phallic rights, the interest lying in the fact that his rights are as much economic as sexual and that the mother is the 'hero'. In this light Cujo's single-minded attacks on her and her car suggest the animal is the projection of the male's murderous unconscious desire, much as in *Forbidden Planet*.

The refusal to recognise the needs and desires of the other is at the centre of *The Stepfather*, whose main character demands perfection and kills when disappointed by the failings of his adopted family. As he is careful about his appearance and always says the right thing at the right time, he runs little risk of being found out. In his own words, as a realtor, 'what I sell is the American dream'. It would be a mistake, however, to assume the film is criticising the family, rather than a certain repressive and Reaganian version of it. The 'disappointment' the stepfather is forever evoking stems precisely from a problematic childhood; his insistence on 'tradition' clearly shows how he needs a repressive, obsessional order to mask the encroaching breakdown of his very being. When he reacts to his daughter Stephanie being with her boyfriend, he evokes as an excuse the rough time he had as a child and asks her not to grow up too quickly.

This betrays an unrealised Oedipal complex and the absence of the father, for which he compensates by being overbearing and tyrannical. When we see him watching with envy and longing the signs of warmth and tenderness between members of a family he spies on, it becomes clear that it is the lack of a positive family background that has made him a killer, which suggests the film is defending such a family as a bulwark against neurosis and madness. *The Stepfather* is less a radical film than one which attempts to walk the tightrope between a fatherless family likely to produce psychosis and a repressive patriarchal family reproducing the same pathology.

Both *Parents* and *Mother's Day* are variants on this, the former deliberately solemn and tongue-in-cheek, the latter outrageous. *Parents* is explicit about the transmission of repressive, phallocentric, patriarchal values: 'I grew up to be a big, strong man, just like my dad', says the father to his son, who is expected to keep up the tradition. For the father

Figure 6   A murder a day makes mother's day. Mother at work in *Mother's Day*. Copyright © 1980 Duty Productions/TROMA – Charles Kaufman, Michael Kravitz.

the need to fit in means seizing opportunities, which in turn suggests that any success in a (literally) cut-throat world can only be at the expense of others. The political dimension of this is explicit: the father works in a plant that produces defoliants for destroying the Third World. Such destructive tendencies, however, can come closer to home: by robbing corpses of organs for experiments, the father represents consumerism pushed to its limits, a notion we shall return to in detail in the next chapter. The desire for order manifest in *Parents* is patent in *Mother's Day* where the mother gets her sons to wipe their feet on a mat. House training, where the sons are maintained in a position of infantile dependence, is an example of an unconscious submission to the values of a society that the mother seemingly has no time for: she encourages her moronic sons, grotesque parodies of hillbillies, to give free rein to their drives. In so doing, however, she only reproduces in an extreme form the ideology of success based on the other as an economic rival to be eliminated. Thus the ferocious maternal superego – the film harks back to *Psycho*, the only difference being that the mother is very much alive – heeds no law, legal or paternal, in its determination to control the sons. However, the way they all act out films and TV shows suggests their behaviour is determined by an identification with characters and situations who cannot but be the relay of 'normal' social and family values.

Serial Mom cunningly encourages the spectator to identify with the 'typical' family, then sets up a distance by having the mother behave in a truly obsessive fashion: pursuing a fly around her kitchen at breakfast to maintain order everywhere and at all times. The effectiveness of the film stems from portraying adolescents indulging in such activities as watching pornographic and horror films. Normally proscribed, these viewing habits are now considered the done thing. Thus the heroine triumphs during the trial – a farcical parody where everyone, including the judge, behaves according to the narrative constraints of TV programmes – precisely because she knows how to turn the tables: one of her victims is transformed into the villain because she does not recycle her rubbish. The politically correct becomes the only criterion for everyday actions and for the very legal process itself. Committing murder in order to prevent the slightest deviation from the politically or socially correct thus becomes the epitome of normality. Life in the middle-class suburbs must be sanitised and protected at all costs, a concept that has given rise to a particular sub-genre of horror.

v) REAL-ESTATE VALUES

Superficially *The Amityville Horror* brings together elements from earlier films: the haunted house (*The Haunting*) and demonic possession (*The Exorcist*). Thus the young man who slaughters all the members of his family claims he heard voices, which experience also befalls the priest who, as a close friend of the heroine (a devout Catholic), comes to bless the house. That the hero bears an uncanny physical resemblance to the murderer suggests reincarnation. There, however, the resemblances end and the film is not simply an exploitative follow-up. Unfortunately the new and genuinely interesting elements of the script are in no way followed through (with one exception) and give the impression of having been dragged in complacently. For instance, whenever the priest tries to intervene, he is either driven from the house or prevented from contacting the wife by some invisible force. The film shows the complete inability of religion and the Church to combat the malevolent spirit. Moreover, there is a suggestion that the priest is neurotic: he becomes aggressive and hysterical when rebuked by his superiors for claiming the house is evil. When he tries to conduct a form of exorcism in his church by invoking Christ, he collapses and discovers he has been struck blind. Cannot we see here a manifestation of hysteria as in *The Exorcist*, his blindness resulting from his refusal to accept a desire to which he cannot give conscious recognition?

An equally vague doubt surrounds the case of the husband who becomes increasingly surly, detached and aggressive for no apparent reason and which we put down to the influence of the house. There exist, however, points of convergence with *The Shining*, which Kubrick was shooting when *Amityville* appeared: the husband breaks down a door with an axe and the little daughter has an imaginary friend. The husband is, in fact, partly rejected by the children, who are not his and who call him 'George', a fact he resents as it deprives him of his paternal status. He too shows signs of hysteria: his going around trembling and complaining of the cold can be seen as the literal manifestation of the expression 'left out in the cold', which is how he feels the children treat him. Once again, however, this is not followed through: the script is heterogeneous to the point of general confusion. It is not surprising that the one interesting element is a throwaway remark that shifts *Amityville* into the realm of 'real-estate' horror. We learn the house was built on grounds where there once stood the dwelling of a Satanist driven out of Salem. More to the point is that the land used to belong to an Indian tribe given over to sombre religious practices. This changes matters considerably.

This parallel between a Satanist and Indian religion is of a racist and obscurantist nature typical of mainstream Hollywood, but it is of interest in the present context. The couple buy the house because they get it cheap, which means that their gain is another's loss. Moreover, the wife is anxious to be an owner; the members of her family have always been tenants. The film foregrounds the theme of private property, a right obtained over the dead bodies of the Indians as far as the North American continent is concerned. 'Getting a house on the cheap' implies the antagonism inherent to a capitalist economy with its aggressive and destructive ideology of 'the survival of the fittest'. That the family is literally driven from their home which they abandon is a striking example of the return of the repressed of history. *The Shining* makes this theme explicit.

During the family's drive up to the Overlook, mention is made of the Donner party: settlers at the time of the Gold Rush, they were snowed in and resorted to cannibalism so that some could survive. Once again we see 'the survival of the fittest' in a precise economic situation: 'get rich quick', or at least a belief in its possibility. To this must be added the information about the hotel given by the representative of its owners: it is located on an Indian burial ground and the builders had to 'repel a few Indian attacks'. We can see at work here, in the name of 'progress' and profit, a form of alienation: that of territorial rights and the inalienable right (especially in a Christian society) to sleep undisturbed for the rest of eternity. This is a right not respected in the case of Indians, or whenever profit can be made from real-estate development. Other forms of alienation are manifest in *The Shining*. The company representative warns Jack of 'isolation and solitude' and 'cabin fever', which seem to be opposites that exclude each other. The former indicates a possible nervous breakdown when alone, the latter when confined with other people. In fact they are the twin and indissociable results of an individualistic society which, by pitting neighbour against neighbour in the name of 'keeping up with the Joneses', succeeds only in creating a fragmentation of the social that exposes the subject to aggressive forces he or she can turn against the other at any moment. Such alienation has precise psychic repercussions and it is hardly coincidental that Amy in *Amityville* and Danny in *The Shining* have imaginary friends, symbols at once of their need for companionship and of their sense of estrangement in a society for whom such companionship and its attendant 'warmth' (compare the theme of 'coldness' in *Amityville*) are irrelevant as having no exchange value on the economic market. The living are transformed into the living dead and the only thing that is warm is the flesh devoured by the reluctant cannibals, as we see in Chapter 2.

Enough has been written on the family and madness in *The Shining* to warrant turning to a film that deserves some attention here: *Poltergeist*. The film has suffered from one of those ingrained prejudices of *auteur* theory: unable to decide whether the film was that of writer/producer Spielberg or of director Hooper, critics chose to see it as incoherent. Certainly the bright optimism of the former and the dark pessimism of the latter seem to be ill-suited companions. However, things are far less schematic, and the opening shot of the apparently carefree community contains the seeds of the horrors to be unleashed on the typical conservative family. That the film opens in bright sunshine and closes during the night should give us reason to pause, despite – or because of – the dry humour of the last shot where the father pushes out onto the balcony of the hotel (the family have been forced to leave their home which is destroyed soon after) the TV set, symbol of all their problems. Or so it would seem.

There is plenty of evidence for anyone anxious to give a classic Freudian reading of the family: the juxtaposition in two shots of a poster of Darth Vader (*Star Wars*) in the children's bedroom and of the husband reading a book on Reagan, where the 'dark father/bad father' is implicitly linked to the President as father-figure, looks ahead to Freddy Krueger; the fact that the children want to sleep in their parents' bed; the little girl drawn into the TV who is heard later shouting 'stay away! leave me alone!', as if addressing, precisely, Freddy. Other elements are more unusual and more disturbing, particularly in light of the complacent remark of the clairvoyant to the effect that the house has been 'cleansed'. Her speech is eminently Reaganian: the family as the seat of all values, with religion and economic survival their primary concerns. What this implies we must now try to elucidate, especially as the spirits return even more implacably after the 'cleansing'.

One of the horrors the family has to contend with is the gnarled tree outside the house which suddenly comes to life, bursts into the bedroom and carries off the son. We learn that the tree was there before the estate was built; the father is a real-estate agent employed by the building company now contemplating further expansion. It is here that the opening shot comes in: it starts at the top of a low hill overlooking the estate, then pans down slowly. Of interest is the hill, for it is here that the head of the company offers to build the hero a new house with a splendid view to thank him for being their most successful agent. It is also here that he learns that the estate he helped build is located on a graveyard, although he is assured it was relocated. His boss sees no problem: it was 'not an ancient burial ground, just people'. This remark at once evokes Indian graveyards and suggests that, once dead, people have no exchange value for capitalism, except that supposedly hallowed ground is exchanged for profit in the name of 'family values'. As with *Amityville*, however, the past as repressed returns in the magnificent sequence in the swimming pool the family is building: bodies suddenly surge up from the depths of the muddy water, surrounding the wife like the living dead from a Romero movie.

I do not make this comparison simply because it is visually imposed by Hooper. There is a clear parallel between the dead – whose bodies, of course, have not been relocated; the cynical gesture has been to leave them there, on the grounds that they are past caring – and the various objects of the film, such as chairs, tables and – significantly – a steak, that suddenly start moving about, as if endowed with a life of their own. We find therefore a perfect representation of reification and commodification, with dead people exploited for profit (think of Frankenstein's experiments) and living people reduced to unthinking consumers and transformed into ways of making money. The home for the company is just a number of dollars made from a transaction, but the film suggests otherwise. The clairvoyant makes a remark to the effect that the dead want a home but cannot have one any more. This is not to be seen as a truism but as a profound truth. Even one's final resting place, considered as sacrosanct by believers and non-believers alike, is not one's 'home' as from the moment several acres of land can be reduced to a certain sum per square foot. It is in this context that we must interpret the last shot as both witty and profound. By pushing the TV out onto the hotel balcony, the father is being superstitious, as if this set too will come and claim his daughter. But this attempt to enter into contact with the living was carried out in the precise circumstances of the violation of privacy as an individual right of every subject, even after death.

Ultimately, then, there is nothing surprising or even supernatural in what society is wont to call 'haunted houses'. As from the moment we accept that, unconsciously, people are deeply affected by their surroundings, a belief in such dwellings and their attendant ghosts and evil spirits is quite rational. In a reified society, things – and there is no 'thing' more personal and familiar than one's home – become the signifiers of dehumanised social relations and take on human characteristics both as a libidinal compensation for the subject and as a sign of his or her alienation. Anxiety stems from the familiar suddenly taking on an unfamiliar aspect, from a feeling of being under the influence of forces one can neither comprehend nor control. What neo-liberals like to call 'the invisible hand of the market' is therefore to be taken literally in the case of such films. However, I would not suggest that the effects of *Poltergeist* are progressive, although I do react against the reading of the film as simply Reaganian. The fact that the spirits become visible *for the spectators* encourages us to take them and the characters' superstitious beliefs at their face value, whereas it could be claimed in the case of their absence that they are hallucinations and the product of the characters' neuroses, with the film putting a certain distance between us and them.

Both *Wolfen* and *Candyman* contain elements that move in the same direction. In the former the wolves are the spirits of long-dead Indians and avenge the real-estate exploitation of their sacred burying grounds. The fact that their victims are not only the capitalists who have made money in such ventures but also assorted derelicts and winos has, I would suggest, two separate meanings, both political. Firstly, the spirits represent the return of the repressed of history. Secondly, they act out the unconscious of bourgeois society, eliminating those 'dregs' and 'leftovers' of capitalist indifference and inhumanity so that people can go about their business (literally) without having to concern themselves with its tragic and inevitable victims. Hence the eponymous central character of *Candyman* is doomed to shed innocent blood; apart from the heroine, his victims are poor blacks, symbols of that racism and dispossession that characterised the torture and murder of Candyman and now relegate the blacks of Chicago to slums and a wasteland existence. It is as if they do not exist – which, for capitalist realtors, is precisely the case – and Candyman, like the wolves, enacts the purely destructive forces structuring social relations where only profit matters and where profit is made at the expense of the poor, black or white. This vision of contemporary society has also been rendered in an openly satirical form.

Society and *The Dark Backward* approach real-estate values from opposite extremes: the wealth and luxury of Beverly Hills and the utter squalor and degradation the poor live in. The young hero of *Society* suddenly realises that his family and friends are literally inhuman, not in the sense of being aliens, but economically; in the extraordinary finale they take over the bodies of those chosen to assuage their depraved and sadistic tastes. The young man's psychiatrist is an ego psychologist with a vengeance. There are those who make the rules and those who follow them: 'it depends what you're born to'. Adapting is therefore the order of the day, with the police there to back up money with force and murder if necessary, removing a friend of the hero's who has understood how things work. *The Dark Backward* adopts a similarly literal approach; one of the main settings is a rubbish dump where literal debris stand in for human debris. It is hardly surprising, then, that the poor should live off rotting leftovers, much as the wolves did human leftovers. Both food and the human body are reduced to objects of consumption. Immensely fat prostitutes spend their time eating, their bodies transformed into objects of and for consumption. Similarly, when the hero Marty grows a third arm, he turns himself into a spectacle for visual consumption, his physical defect and his new status as a freak allowing him to exchange not his talent, but his very body, for money. The human subject is literally reified and this is brilliantly suggested in a stage act where a woman uses five dwarfs as a xylophone. The film's most remarkable twist lies in the ending. Marty's third arm disappears as suddenly as it appeared, thus depriving him of his livelihood. He understands what must be done and succeeds where he had failed before: by telling jokes about his third arm. Nobody believes him but he brings the roof down. If *Society* rubs our noses in our unspoken desire to get rich any way, then *The Dark Backward* rubs our noses in the most repulsive squalor in order to show us what we refuse to see. The two films are the outrageous satirical versions of *Wolfen* and *Candyman* respectively.

The 'Burbs is a satire on suburbia. The object of curiosity in a tidy and right-thinking suburb is an old dark house where odd things happen. Curiosity soon becomes suspicion, firstly because the house's occupants are never visible during the day, then because it looks untidy and rundown, which triggers off a fear that prices will drop (a subtle reference to excessive debt in American society). The parallel drawn between yuppie success and the fact that the Bruce Dern character dresses up in his Green Beret uniform to lead a 'search and destroy' investigation of the house makes the film's political slant clear, especially given Dern's devotion to the American flag. This is an insistent part of Dante's work, as we shall see in the next chapter, as are constant references to other movies. Here the bright lights in the basement look back to the landing of the aliens in *Invaders from Mars*. As it stands, however, the film fails because it ends by showing that there was indeed something nasty going on in the basement, whereas the brunt of the satire had always been born by the warped values of suburbia and its denizens, their paranoid reaction to the other as locus of differences not to be tolerated.

Even a ghost story like *The Fog* turns on the function of land and money. The ghosts that return to haunt and murder the inhabitants of the seaside town are those of lepers murdered one hundred years before to prevent them from establishing a colony along the coast from Antonio Bay. Crucially, this enabled the townspeople to steal from the lepers' leader money that could be used for a church, an anti-religious element of the film that finds a parallel in the desecration of Indian burial grounds for profit. The town has embarked on the renovation of its graveyard — a case of fetishising the dead — as a sign that it is proud of its past, but in so doing it is honouring a past that is a lie. When one of the characters refers to those in the past 'who struggled and sacrificed to make Antonio Bay what it is today', the film denounces a travesty of history and society in the name of mercantile values that place money and social status before people. Another form of exploitation of the dead is taking place: instead of the ground being exploited for building projects, the dead are fetishised in order to displace the issue and to centre attention onto a 'noble' act that masks past murder.

vi) OLD FRIENDS, NEW FACES

The eclipse of the mad scientist in contemporary horror — one finds him insistently only in Cronenberg — is accompanied by that of other figures from the Golden Age, such as the Mummy and the Wolfman. It is regrettable that special effects should attract so much attention; the spectacular transformation scene in *An American Werewolf in London* must not be allowed to hide the pathos of the situation and our sympathy for the victim. The notion of a character afflicted through no fault of his own is central to *The Beast Within* but takes on a marked family perspective. Not only is the boy and future beast the product of the rape of a woman by some creature, but the father of the girl who tries to help the boy has killed his wife and her lover and calls her his 'baby', counting on the fact that the judge is his cousin to avoid justice being done. Such repressive male figures are much in evidence in the one form of the genre that is alive and kicking: the vampire film.

The variety of stylistic approaches is patent in the three versions of *Dracula* (Curtis, Badham, Coppola). The portentous vies with the pretentious, with tiresome self-consciousness triumphing with Coppola, although there is at least some substance to the film, unlike coffee-table junk like *The Hunger*, with its opportunistic representation of lesbianism passing itself off as chic social comment. More to the point is the gender ambiguity in the Badham version where three men are needed to over-power Lucy, condensing both the desire to control female sexuality and the sense that this is no longer possible. In the remarkably atmospheric *Count Yorga, Vampire* the last male survivor is caught out by assuming that his wife is merely under the vampire's influence, that his presence and the destruction of the Count suffice. This belief in inherent male superi-ority is a form of superstition the film attacks; the hero's vampirisation is punishment by the woman for not taking her into his confidence. Van Helsing adopts such an approach to the family in Curtis's *Dracula*.

Family values and gender relations run through those films that posit the existence of vampires in everyday settings. Attention has been drawn to the gay sub-text of *Fright Night*; the boy seems more fascinated by the handsome neighbour than interested in his girlfriend. His best friend is clearly homosexually attached to him and the seduction of the friend by the vampire is presented in explicit homosexual terms, the older man initiating the adolescent. We can interpret the scene where the vampir-ised girlfriend turns on the hero as punishment for his neglect of her, a situation at work in *From Dusk to Dawn*. Whereas the Tarantino character is incapable of attacking his elder brother even when vampirised and can only reiterate his love for him, the Harvey Keitel character rounds on his son when his own transformation is complete. Why? Because the son had refused to obey his injunction to kill him and must pay the penalty for not submitting to paternal law. Significantly the character is a Protestant pastor and 'stern father' whom the daughter obeyed at once!

Thanks to a cleverly devised script, *The Lost Boys* manages to overcome the mannered direction and the inability to decide whether humour or horror should dominate; the film should have been directed by Joe Dante. Thus the local businessman first suspected by the younger son and the two adolescents dedicated to fighting vampirism in the name of 'the American way' is indeed the head vampire. It is difficult to decide whether the film — which portrays a coastal resort in California as being invaded by aimless, unemployed teenagers — is being satirical, critical or simply prejudiced in its representation of current social values. What is abundantly clear is the patriarchal function of the head vampire. His intention is to vampirise the mother who has settled in the resort with her two sons after her divorce. 'Boys need a mother and discipline', he informs her, and suggests 'it will be so much better if you don't fight', thus insisting on his masculine prerogatives. Although he considers that his boys 'misbehaved' by attempting to transform the elder son into a vampire, we can surely assume that it is the father who transmitted 'vampire family values' to his children. The twist at the end comes through the character of the mother's own father who arrives in the nick of time, like the cavalry, to dispatch the 'bad father' and assert himself. He knew all along about the vampires and was just biding his time. As he is a man of tradition out of sympathy with modern society, the film seems to be championing a return to past values but the tension between script and direction precludes any clear formulation on the subject.

The Lost Boys also introduces the theme of a character — the girl the elder brother falls for — fighting her need to suck blood, which is at the centre of the overrated *Near Dark*, another irritatingly self-conscious movie. The fact that the girl overcomes her sadness over her need for blood and her original refusal to vampirise the boy she likes when he forces his sexual attentions on her required a less solemn, pseudo-existential approach. The film's complacent attitude to violence suggests Bigelow is self-conscious when making an 'arty' use of the camera, but not when it comes to reflecting on the best way to represent a family or a person at odds with society. A film deserving of more attention is *Vampire's Kiss* where the hero, after being attacked by a bat, informs his psychiatrist that his fight with the creature increased his desire. Soon after he is bitten by a young vamp, Rachel, who informs him 'you chose me', thus moving the film into the classic territory of male fears of impotence faced with an active woman and an unconscious desire to be dominated. The film turns on this conflict within the hero, whose need to be actively phallocentric and passively masochistic are represented strikingly. Thus he pursues and sadistically persecutes a young woman named Alva at his place of work – significantly she is in a position of social inferiority – as a form of libidinal compensation for the way Rachel stalks him and controls his sex life. She is both sadistic and dominating, thus enacting what he unconsciously desires from a woman. That he should be intimately convinced Rachel has vampirised him and begins to behave like a vampire, to the point of refusing to go out during the day, can thus be seen as a psychotic symptom for his inability to admit his sexual needs; he can thus consider himself a victim of the very kind of woman he is anxious to be enslaved to.

Both *Vamp* and *Graveyard Shift* concern characters who move in the sleazy night world of New York and its strip joints. Whereas the former turns on such a club run by vampires (anticipating the better known *From Dusk to Dawn*), the latter moves out into far more complex and sophisticated territory. *Graveyard Shift* is both a homage to *Taxi Driver* in its mood and bleakness and a genuinely different vampire movie. Thus the vampire taxi driver enters unconsciously into contact with women about to die: one wants to commit suicide, another has terminal cancer. The subtlety and novelty of *Graveyard Shift* – arguably the most remarkable and unusual vampire movie since *Black Sunday* (Mario Bava, 1960) – stems from the parallels and contrasts set up between various male and female characters. Just as the heroine's husband is a 'lady killer' who metaphorically takes the life of the woman he pursues, so the taxi driver literally brings life to the women he seduces. Likewise, women who are approached by men on the assumption that a stripper is what one could call 'easy prey' turn out to be predatory vampires who turn the tables on those for whom they are just sexual objects.

An example of how *not* to make a thoughtful modern vampire movie is *The Addiction*. Apart from a striking shot near the opening where the heroine crosses a dark New York street at night and is accosted, from the right of the screen, by a tall, elegant woman who promptly vampirises her, the film is a pseudo-philosophical tract about good and evil. If the tiresome and meaningless name-dropping is objectionable enough, this is nothing compared with the film's use of shots of Nazi concentration camps. Basically, the argument is as fatuous as it is reactionary; evil is inherent in humanity, which simply transforms genocide into just another manifestation of our inability to resist the evil in each of us. This nicely eliminates History and any attempt other than Catholic metaphysics to come to grips with horror. There was a time when this facile postmodern pessimism was not the dominant trend, either in cinema or in society, and the following chapter will analyse films that present alternatives to it.

6

DIRECTORS AND DIRECTIONS

⟡

The directors discussed here are George Romero, Wes Craven, Tobe Hooper, Larry Cohen and Joe Dante. If Brian De Palma and John Carpenter are absent, it is not only because their work is analysed elsewhere, but because of the lamentable quality of much of their output. Carpenter hasn't made a decent horror movie in nearly twenty years, as the execrable *Prince of Darkness* and *Ghosts of Mars* and the scarcely less atrocious *In the Mouth of Madness* and *Vampires* bear painful witness. The case of De Palma is perhaps even worse, inasmuch as he asks us to take him seriously, but *Phantom of the Paradise*, *The Fury* and *Raising Cain* lack any serious engagement with their material. Given the number of major films produced by the five directors mentioned, a choice was necessary. The films chosen for analysis testify to a certain homogeneity in theme and outlook conducive to the psychoanalytical and ideological approach to class, gender and politics I have adopted from the outset. I shall draw the strands together in the last section, on the one hand by reference to Vietnam, on the other by reference to pertinent remakes and variants.

i) GEORGE ROMERO

Critics have drawn attention to the flag fluttering in the foreground as Johnny and Barbara reach the cemetery in *Night of the Living Dead*. This 'naturalistic' detail shows to what extent we must be alert to apparent banalities. The *Living Dead* trilogy constitutes a full-scale criticism of American values, the films' interest stemming from the articulation of the different themes and the subtlety of their representation. An analysis of the cemetery sequence will clarify this.

It is significant that Johnny should ask his sister if there is any candy left, as his infantilism soon becomes apparent; he complains about the late hour they will return home, although it is he who got up late, showing a refusal to impose any discipline on himself. Resentful of Barbara's attitude — at once submissive to their mother and respectful of their dead father — he recalls a visit to the grave they made as children and re-enacts the way he frightened her at the time by jumping out from behind a tree. Spying a man walking among the graves, he acts like a little boy sadistically tormenting a sibling or chum by evoking the bogeyman: 'he's coming to get you, Barbara'. She is clearly more frightened than irritated, showing a belief in some childhood fear adults are meant to have overcome. Johnny continues the game by running away and the man promptly attacks Barbara. What is happening here?

Their grandfather berated young Johnny for this prank, thus function-ing as the stern father-figure replacing the dead father. I suggest we see the man (a zombie) as the manifestation of both father and grandfather, returning to punish children who do not submit to a repressive family structure where respect is imposed rather than deserved. Representing pure drive, he enacts Johnny's resentment, unhampered by any form of social constraint, just as Johnny will be responsible for Barbara's death later. If we see the living dead as people returning to collect the 'symbolic debt', some right they were denied in life, such as respect or their share of the family inheritance, then we can explain Barbara's collapse in the besieged house. It is not because she is a woman unable to withstand stress, but rather because she is a 'typical' woman under patriarchy, going through the motions of mourning and filial piety to the extent of assuming her 'share' of guilt over Johnny's attitude. Unconsciously she recognises in the zombies the Oedipal meaning of the scene in the cemetery and thus retreats into a private world. It is a form of autism indicating a regression to earliest childhood, a psychotic state.

The scene also helps explain the husband, the film's representative of the man in the cemetery as manifestation of the paternal superego, punishing relentlessly any deviation from the family norm, itself over-determined socially and economically. He takes his superiority for granted and from that point of view it is essential that the hero be black and the other characters a young unmarried couple. Moreover, his barricading himself in the basement can be seen as the equivalent of the paranoid 'real-estate' values analysed above. Indeed, he and the flag anticipate the Vietnam veteran in *The 'Burbs*. Although his wife stands up to him, she is nevertheless ready to count on the authorities who represent ideologically the husband she no longer respects. Moreover, she shares something with Barbara. Just as the latter tends to mother her brother, so the wife is over-protective towards her daughter, which does not help her when the girl returns from the dead to exact her own vengeance; the mother's superego is just as repressive as the patriarch's. In the same way the Sheriff and his men represent the legal dimension of paternal law. By enjoying the hunt like so many Count Zaroffs and by shooting the hero down without more ado, they both indicate the true mentality of the authorities — their sadism is a libidinal compensation for their public loss of control over the situation — and act out the unconscious desire of the father who has fought constantly with the hero and has been humiliated.

Dawn of the Dead takes up the various themes of *Night* and extends them into a more radical criticism by adding an explicitly economic dimension; eating human flesh is not a simple sign of 'zombieism' but a literal extension of everyday consumerism. Moreover, repression and its concomitant chaos prevail, whereas opposition to it takes a striking form from the opening. Romero brilliantly articulates race and class to show that even a national disaster is insufficient to overcome the conflicts and contradictions inherent in capitalism. Thus a doctor talks on TV about the need to move the contaminated out of private residences into communal shelters. As those concerned are blacks and Puerto Ricans, a racist soldier translates this into a privilege. Incapable of reasoning logically, he submits to resentment, misrecognises his own position as 'underdog' and attacks the idea of welfare. More pertinent is the attitude of the 'minorities' who refuse to relinquish their dead and thus trigger off repression. Faced with general incomprehension, a black priest states his parishioners 'still believe there's respect in dying'. In a society fragmented by economic and class rivalry and where each person is reduced to a means to produce goods for consumption, it is not surprising that only lip-service is paid to the dead. We have seen this ideology in *Poltergeist*. At this juncture *Dawn* introduces an extraordinary moment where a woman, recognising her zombie husband, rushes to prevent him from being killed and embraces him. Momentarily his face appears to

Figure 7   'Let us in!' Zombies as consumers. *Dawn of the Dead*. Copyright © 1978
The Laurel Group/Dawn Associates – Richard B. Rubinstein, Dario Argento.

show recognition, then he bends over and bites a lump of flesh out of her.
I suggest we interpret this as condensing the subject's role in capitalist
society when alive – a mere consumer – and the place of desire where,
even when beyond symbolic contact in love and language, a trace of
subjectivity survives, symbolising that if drives can be manipulated,
desire can resist. *Dawn* is making an extreme but rational statement here;
it is better to die as a family than live in a society that recognises the
family only as the locus of the eternal reproduction of the ideologies of
the division of (sexual) labour.

One witty scene sums up perfectly the complexity of Romero's
approach. A zombie falls into the fountain in the mall and picks up a
handful of coins there. Nothing explains better the fetishisation of
money than the superstition that throwing a coin in a fountain and
making a wish will bring wealth, health and happiness. The shot both
shows that money is now worthless and suggests the return of the
proletarian repressed, the worker demanding payment for the labour

that produced the goods many people do not have the wherewithal to purchase. Romero assimilates exploited labour to zombieism. What we take for a store dummy is really a zombie, which catches both the reduction of people to objects in a reified society and the unconsciously automatic quality of buying and spending; desire is determined by the discourse of capitalism and is no longer a private realm. Significantly, the male characters have to learn to go beyond this consumerist drive. Stephen, Fran's fiancé, is content with the mall: 'we've everything we need right here'. The repetition compulsion continues to function, both as far as consumption goes and in human relations, whereas Fran and Peter — again, a black character — see the need to overcome this logic. If Peter says 'let's get the stuff we need', shots of the other male characters jubilating over the possibility of taking what they want without paying, as if nobody had had to work to produce these goods, must be seen in relation to the sequence where they try to reach lorries in order to escape. The moment he gets behind the wheel, Roger reverts to infantile drives and behaves more like the bikers than a responsible adult, running zombies over gleefully as if it were a game. The looting of the mall by the bikers is thus the logical extension of the drive to possess instilled by an aggressive ideology of success. Looting is the return of the repressed of this logic, which is why looters are shot in real life; they are the living manifestation of the contradictions inherent to the system and therefore represent a possible challenge to it.

The escape of Fran and Peter heralds a potentially new society, whereas *Day of the Dead* is a movie where pessimism of the intelligence has triumphed over optimism of the will. I see it as a regression, insofar as it counts too much on a binary opposition: the progressive, active woman versus the repressive, fascist soldier. However, many elements show Romero remaining faithful to his radical critique. Logan the mad scientist wants to prove zombies 'can be domesticated, conditioned to behave as we want them to behave'. This is a neat representation of society's attitude towards children and capitalism's attitude towards labour, with children learning to take their place in the system of (re)production according to sex and class. Potentially liberating sources of knowledge such as medicine and science are turned into institutions for producing repression, channelling desire into drives such as those we have seen expressing themselves in the function of the mall in *Dawn*. By having Logan feed dead soldiers to his pet zombie Bub, *Day* is suggesting that the values of a consumer society are imposed unconsciously on children from an early age and that the private realm of desire must be eliminated in favour of drives where individual pleasure takes precedence over any potentially collective project.

ii) WES CRAVEN

I am concerned here with *Last House on the Left*, *The Hills Have Eyes*, *The People under the Stairs* and *The Serpent and the Rainbow*. *Last House* is refreshingly politically incorrect in its refusal to fetishise pop culture and youth, unlike the young heroine's father. The opening is remarkable in the way it represents a mother obliged to adopt a repressive, regressive and possessive attitude towards her teenage daughter to counteract the father's trendy and quasi-incestuous relationship to the girl. The use of framing – mother on the left of the screen alone, father and daughter together on the right – stresses the way a mother must allow her children to live their own lives and how a father can exploit this to have the daughter for himself. Thus Craven subtly renounces binary oppositions in favour of productive parallels: the complacent father gives his daughter a 'Ban the Bomb' necklace and turns into a butcher when he learns what has become of her. For him, allowing her to 'have a fling' goes hand in hand with an abandonment of all parental responsibility. Significantly, the mother, who must repress her opinions faced with patriarchal law, 'derepresses' during the final carnage. That the body of the woman whose throat she slits sinks beneath the surface of the family's swimming pool exactly as the murdered daughter sinks below the water of the lake is as precise and telling a comment as one could hope for on the parallels set up between the lifestyle of the bourgeois family and that of the murdering rapists.

A nice pun sums up Craven's insistence on class and its social ramifications. A friend of the heroine refers to her parents being in 'iron and steel', adding, 'she irons and he steals'. A less obvious pun is at work in *Hills*. When the mother of the family that gets lost in the desert is amused at their dog killing a poodle, should we not see here, in the context of a film that presents the father as riddled with class and racial prejudices and their attendant violence, a reference to the expression 'dog eat dog'? What must be stressed is that the two families – the one that lives in the hills and the stranded one that becomes its victim – are not on an equal footing. The aggressors are first and foremost victims and their victims turn out to be even more monstrous. A parallel exists between the 'hillbillies' and the family in *The Texas Chainsaw Massacre*. Just as Leatherface's family has been made redundant by technological progress, so here the community, cut off from social commerce, lives by stealing and exchanging objects for food; capitalism being an exchange economy, to have food you need either money or barter. This is no longer possible for them as the owner of the gas station who dealt with them is moving away for lack of customers. There is surely another parallel at work: between the 'hillbillies' and the Indians, whose lifestyle and livelihood were destroyed by the systematic elimination of the bison, their main source of food, clothing and lodgings.

It is perhaps the character of Doug who bears the brunt of Craven's criticism. As father of a new baby, he can be seen as literally reproducing family values which are inextricably linked to economic ones (a theme Craven shares with Romero and Hooper). When he comes across valuable material being thrown away, he complains about taxes, but is ready to steal it to 'open an Army surplus': first you denounce the way Big Government steals from you, then you take the product of another's labour to make individual profit, as opposed to the collective use made of taxes. The excessive nature of his pleasure as he hunts down and kills the family fits in perfectly with Lacan's comparison of surplus pleasure with surplus value. Neither is necessary to survive or even for the subject's well-being, but both enable him to exist at the other's expense in the drive towards individual 'freedom' and that 'self-expression' referred to in the context of the pop group. *Hills* is exemplary for its condemnation of the lack of restraint in contemporary society. Thus when one of the hillbillies tries to rape the girl they have captured, another stops him, but for the wrong reason: 'you wait until you're a man'. No question, then, of respecting the woman; the family excluded from society reproduces unconsciously the values perpetrated and perpetuated by that same society, with the female body the privileged site of repression and exploitation, sexual and economic.

If *People* is sometimes crude in the elaboration of its satire, the film deserves the closest attention as a late and rare manifestation of tendencies within horror that more or less disappeared with the rise of the 'slasher' movie. Its anti-Reaganian message, coming as it does at the time of the Gulf War, is a precious reminder of what we have lost over the last two decades in favour of game-playing and exploitative violence, where the genre tends to adopt the 'anything goes' ideology I have discussed. Craven makes his central theme simple to grasp the better to place it in a context of considerable complexity: a landlord allows the blocks of flats he owns and which are inhabited by blacks to decay so as to be able to replace them with luxury accommodation. Significantly he and his sister have not only barricaded themselves in but have also transformed their home into a booby trap in case of breaking and entering; 'real-estate' values once again. This has led to a literal regression: the sister refers to her brother as 'Daddy', a neat comment on male castration fantasies, dutifully submitted to by the woman. At the same time she assumes phallic power as a form of compensation for her secondary role; the brother is not allowed to shoot his gun outside, so life within is a parody of the world of the frontier. When he shoots Elroy, the black who has succeeded in breaking in, she shouts like a cowboy, enabling Craven to draw a parallel between the treatment of the Indian and the current fate of blacks. The street the blacks live on resembles the decaying neighbourhood portrayed in the contemporary *Candyman*.

Fantasies of castration and political repression come together in a remark made by the brother. The 'people' of the title are the couple's offspring who 'saw things they weren't supposed to' or 'heard too much'. In such a context psychoanalysis is indispensable for understanding the pathology of horror, but must be seen in a symbolic context – the social, economic and historical – to have a real, deconstructive thrust. The sexual dimension is patent: children anxious to know about sexuality, the role of the primal scene and the ensuing parental repression. If children should be seen and not heard – the formula is written on the wall of the little girl's bedroom – this is because they must be living proof of the couple's function of reproduction and denied all access to knowledge outside what is needed for them to fulfil that same function. Thus the father 'cut out the bad parts and put them in the cellar'. We are also entitled to see a parallel with the representation of the Gulf War where the media collaborated with the White House and the military, mindful of the 'errors' of showing the truth about what was happening in Vietnam, to present a sanitised and censored version of America's revenge for being humiliated by a Third World nation.

The basement where the 'rejects' are incarcerated is reminiscent of the house in *Texas*, with its bones and skeletons, but, rather than see this as enforced cannibalism, I would argue for another interpretation. Just as the family in the Hooper film turns to murder to survive, so the 'people' here resort to an 'unnatural' act for the same reason. They have in common being victims of the logic of capitalism and patriarchy – profit and the survival of the dominant family unit – with 'failures' being ruthlessly eliminated. In both *Texas* and *People* characters behave in a way that imitates predatory capitalism. Similarly, Craven renders homage to Romero, with the 'people' bursting through the walls like zombies. One can also interpret this metaphorically: the need to break out and not reinforce the vicious circle of exploitation, censorship and repression within the related realms of politics and the family. That the adolescent black hero and the girl form a couple at the end of the film reiterates the call for radical change made by *Dawn of the Dead.*

The Serpent and the Rainbow has been denounced for its racist treatment of voodoo and Haiti, but the remarkable analysis of the film by Tanya Krzywinska shows just how superficial and mistaken this attitude is. (Krzywinska 2000: 168–75) The tension existing between the film's attempt to deconstruct the ethnocentric position of the scientist hero Dr Alan and the commercial ending where he and the villain fight it out is to be found elsewhere. When the sadistic monster Peytraud (leader of the 'Tonton Macoutes') tells Alan that Haiti is not Grenada, he is representing a split political discourse. On the one hand, Haiti will not give in to America's call for democracy; on the other Haiti is an objective ally of the States inasmuch as there is no danger of Marxism as there is in Grenada, since Peytraud is an opponent of any form of liberation. This ambiguity, which I find ideologically productive, spreads out to the representation of America, particularly the role of Biocorp, a multinational anxious to exploit a voodoo medicine likely to save lives on the operating tables. Little is made of this by Craven, unlike the explicit attacks on such corporations by Cronenberg, as we shall see, but we are entitled to interpret this concern as economically motivated and also as a means of ensuring American control over an 'unruly' and 'unreliable' island. It is striking to note that it is the people of Haiti who rise up against the Duvalier regime and that Alan triumphs thanks to the spirits of the victims of Peytraud. In other words, Alan is the agent of the people rather than the reverse, which upsets the simplistic binary oppositions usually applied. It is by no means certain, however, that this element remains explicit at the end of the film.

iii) TOBE HOOPER

At one point in David Lynch's *Wild at Heart* Laura Dern, listening to the radio where the news is a list of violent deaths, cries, 'It's like *Night of the Living Dead*'. It would have been more pertinent to refer to *The Texas Chainsaw Massacre*, for an identical scene takes place after the opening credits, providing us with information we would be wise to heed: the collapse of a building in Atlanta, mutilated corpses found in Indiana, violence in South America, a baby found chained in the attic of its home. All this follows the discovery of grave robbing in Texas, at the site of

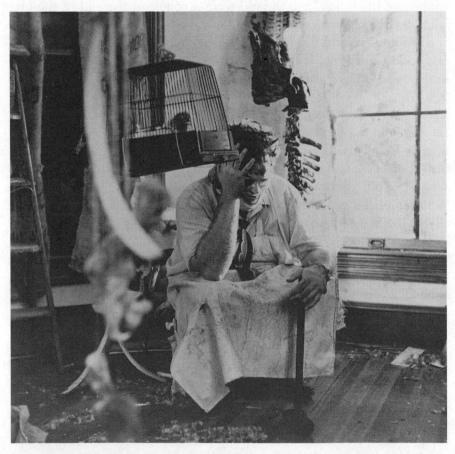

Figure 8 Little boy lost. Leatherface in *The Texas Chainsaw Massacre*. Copyright © 1974 Vortex Productions/Blue Dolphin – Tobe Hooper, Kim Henkel.

the action of the film. The choice of news items is not random and takes us to the heart of the movie.

Texas is a film about violence in all its manifestations. The fact that the builders can offer no explanation for the fatal accident in Atlanta suggests criminal negligence which in turn hints at cutting corners to increase profits. This is precisely the fate that befell Leatherface and his family, made redundant when the slaughterhouse became automated, technological progress enabling the owners to increase production and cut down the workforce. *Texas* is uncannily prescient of current trends, where 'restructuring' is a euphemism for mass unemployment to boost profits for everyone except those whose labour created the profits in the first place. The brilliance of the film lies in the means employed to represent the drive to economic success, the unconscious hold of the economy on all aspects of life and thought and the place of the family within this structure.

The unholy power of the film derives from Leatherface as the literal embodiment of drives, whose aim is immediate satisfaction in the most direct fashion. One is both impressed and horrified by the character's eruption from nowhere and his implacable pursuit of victims as he lets nothing stand in his way. As such he is not just the drive become flesh, but the drive as the basis of economics. To succeed you must eliminate your rivals, cut down on costs and make workers increasingly 'flexible'. Leatherface also shows just how the victims of this 'get rich quick' ideology accept its implicit values: he has interiorised them, made them his own, then projected them onto the outside world so as to transform any and every person he encounters into a rival to eliminate. And more: just as *Dawn of the Dead* makes the zombie the privileged signifier of capitalist consumerism, so *Texas* transforms the victims of Leatherface and his family into so much meat to be recycled and sold for profit.

Insofar as the youngsters who fall prey to the family belong to the economic class reponsible for unemployment, it is clear that the film is representing the return of the proletarian repressed. However, it would be insufficient to leave it there. *Texas* is equally concerned with the unconscious effects of ideology to which nobody is immune. Thus the family acts against its best interests by simply repeating the same infernal logic as that which victimized them. This crucial reflection on the film's part is brought tellingly home by the use of the theme of magic and horoscopes, a constant leitmotiv. A member of the family the youngsters pick up takes a photo of them. This must not be interpreted as simply a way of recognising them, a purely cognitivist approach which tells us nothing that is not patent. Rather it suggests a belief in magic, in the possibility of 'possessing' someone, which in turn must be seen as a form of control identical to that of possessing wealth or, by extension, the bodies of the workers whose labour is turned into surplus value. He is no more unbalanced than the girl who believes in the stars and their control over our lives. The stars correspond to what neoliberals call 'the invisible hand of the market' and fulfil the same function: a way of blinding people to the real social relations binding them. Thus economic forces become as natural as floods and earthquakes, things that merely exist independently of us and which we must accept, like the globalisation of the economy. The character of the young man presents the additional interest of condensing in his acts both a masochistic manifestation of his status as victim and a sadistic transferral of this onto the other. He cuts himself with a knife, thus inscribing onto his body both the now obsolete act of cutting up cattle manually and the fate of the workers: redundancies in the form of 'cuts'. At the same time, by slashing the arm of Franklin the cripple, he is doing much more than marking him out to be turned into an aggregate of body parts by Leatherface. He is also unconsciously acting out his family's deranged belief that they can keep the past alive by behaving like the owners of the slaughterhouse.

This view of the past is as deluded as the girl's belief in horoscopes; the misrecognition of one's place within an economy based on repression of every kind. Hardly surprising, then, that the young should show complete indifference to the past and family, just as the mad family has transformed the concept of the family into a fetish. At the same time the members of the family recognise both the lethal nature of the economic values they are grotesquely imitating and their own status as relics. The abundance of bones as symbols of death in the house, not to mention the grave-robbing with which *Texas* opens, are eloquent testimony to the power of the death drive, personified by Leatherface, that under-pins the film. The family barricaded in its ramshackle home is surely the most extreme and negative instance of those 'real-estate' values we have analysed elsewhere.

The theme of the past is central to *The Texas Chainsaw Massacre 2* in the use of the theme park representing Texan history. It is under this park that the family has taken shelter so as to be able to extend their culinary talents to the making of chilli from human flesh. Just as the park offers Texans an image of the past as they would like it to have been, so Sawyer, the head of the family, represents capitalist success as people want it to be: individual and 'clean'. Sawyer is a representative both of the ideology of success and consumerism and, in his social and psychic alienation, of the unconscious desire for an identity of a collective nature through keeping the past history of Texas alive. At the same time, by showing the park as a form of necropolis, *Texas 2* stresses that this particular view of the past, decidedly nationalistic, produces precisely the deadening effect that is at the origin of the family's alienation. Revealing is their taking refuge in catacombs under the park, symbolising both a cemetery and a level of reality even further removed than the vision purveyed by the park, the Disneyland of Texas.

The fact that the park no longer functions is surely an ironic comment by Hooper on the failure of history to make a conscious impact on people; now they prefer loud music and youngsters who go around shooting at road signs. The parallel with *Last House on the Left* is striking. The film's mistake is to try to humanise Leatherface or, rather, the way it tries to do so. At one point in Texas, after dispatching a victim, Leatherface collapses into a chair and remains motionless, his head in his hands, inhibited and like a child awaiting punishment. He is much like Judd, the demented central character of *Death Trap*, who is happy when he can murder people without hindrance. When the young woman he has tied to a bed attracts the attention of another young woman by the noise she makes, Judd seizes up and is at a loss, perfectly represented by having him go and sit disconsolately in the corner, like Little Jack Horner. In *Texas 2* it is the sexual dimension of Leatherface's relation to the heroine Stretch which is problematic. By having him caress the inside of her thighs with his chainsaw, then prove unable to start it up, the film is suggesting we have an impotent adult, whereas Leatherface has not progressed beyond a pre-Oedipal attachment to the mother and is incapable of experiencing desire; like Norman Bates he has not had access to the circuit of desire via paternal law. This is recognised in the final shot where certain critics have interpreted Stretch waving a chainsaw over her head as a sign of her triumph. Nothing could be further from the truth; the fact that she behaves exactly like Leatherface, down to waggling her hips in an identical fashion, means that she has unconsciously identified with him to the point of now being psychotic herself.

Death Trap is not only neglected but misunderstood, due to the parallel it draws between Judd – who feeds to his crocodile any person who makes the mistake of stopping off at his hotel – and Leatherface. This is partially accurate but fails to come to terms with the representation of male sexuality in the film, a theme approached with care and subtlety by Hooper. The opening sequence in the brothel is remarkable and sets the tone – seedy, sordid, violent and uncompromising – for what follows. A young prostitute eyes her customer with suspicion and well she might: he is into brutal humiliation and, although Hooper only suggests it, rear penetration where the woman is on all fours. This 'animal' status is very much a sadistic male fantasy and one the film uses to denounce the treatment of women generally. When she refuses, the Madam fires her and offers the client 'two for the price of one'. It is as if she were the owner of a supermarket, with the 'girls' as consumer objects, to be consigned to the 'bargain basement' if they don't bring in the profits expected. When the prostitute stumbles on Judd's place, he recognises her and, going on the assumption that once a whore, always a whore, attacks her in exactly the same manner as the client, before taking a pitchfork to her, in a particularly nasty scene, then feeding her to the crocodile. Thus the female body as sexual object becomes an object for real consumption, with an implicit parallel being drawn between the behaviour of the client – who is not deranged – and Judd.

Masculine attitudes to women are at the centre of the film and this parallel is not the only one drawn. When a couple with a young daughter stop off at the hotel, Judd dispatches the husband and takes the wife prisoner, gagging her and tying her to a bed. Later Buck, the client from the brothel, becomes violent towards a customer in a bar after being humiliated by the Sheriff in front of his girlfriend: the male ego must be kept inflated under all circumstances. That Buck should take the young woman to Judd's for sex indicates just how alike the men are, despite their surface hostility to each other. The way Buck positions her body on the bed recalls the position of the imprisoned wife; for both him and Judd women are objects. In Judd's case this stems from a paranoid relation to women and sexuality, whereas the client is an 'average' male. The title *Death Trap* refers to the man-eating crocodile, but surely also to the destructive dimension of male desire when thwarted, such as when the woman refuses to play by the (masculine) rules. Significantly Judd says at one point: 'I knows the rules and I abides by them', a sort of mantra that fits in neatly with the Country and Western music he plays obsessively where masculinity is a fetish to be revered (and women, by implication, a threat to it). It is equally fitting that when Judd is eaten by the creature — the film shows that there is a need for poetic justice in such a bleak world! — all that remains of him is his wooden leg, an object now of as little value as the young prostitute.

iv) LARRY COHEN

I shall consider the *It's Alive* trilogy, *God Told Me To*, *Return to Salem's Lot* and *The Ambulance*. A combination of critical indifference and bad distribution has resulted in the unavailability of certain films, as is also the case with Hooper.

Conflicting views as interesting as they are productive surround discussions of *It's Alive*. Both Robin Wood and Tony Williams argue that the film is a radical critique of the patriarchal family (Wood 1986: 98–102; Williams 1997: 121–6), whereas Carol Clover argues it 'could hardly be more pro-life, pro-family'. (Clover 1992: 77) It is surely a political error to assume a film is 'pro-life' because it suggests abortion is not the solution, especially when the formula connotes far-right fundamentalists. At the same time the tendency in left-wing circles to represent the family as the seat of all that is negative in society comes perilously close to being as reactionary as the notion that the family is the seat of virtue. Keeping this in mind, what is *It's Alive* 'about'?

I suggest it has less to do with the family and monsters, real or ideological, than with the concept of society as a spectacle where we are invited to consume images as if these were more real than life itself, as if life were nothing but a series of images. I say this for two reasons. Firstly, the husband works in public relations and is forced to take a vacation after the controversy aroused by the birth of his 'killer baby' so as not to harm the firm's image. Significantly, a secretary looks at him as if he were a freak, an interesting example of how responsibility is shorn of its social, economic and historical roots (of which more presently). Secondly, towards the end of the film, Cohen insists on the inscription 'Stop Children' on a school bus. Clearly this is a warning to motorists, but in the context of the film it takes on another meaning where children are blamed for the problems created by society and their parents. Thus the verbal signifiers evoke a signified that is a reversal of the real responsibility of adults. It is the sort of unconscious message that people accept in order to be able to designate scapegoats; elsewhere Jews or blacks, here 'freaky' children.

Early in the film the wife says, 'we both want it. You won't feel trapped as you did last time'. This remark has rightly prompted Clover to call the family 'failed or unwelcoming', but to draw an odd conclusion, that 'a proper family would never have considered terminating a pregnancy'. (Clover 1992: 77) This surely misses the pressures brought to bear on couples to have children irrespective of their desires, as if being childless were a sign of sterility, not doing one's duty, and so on. That Cohen does not make explicit why the father felt 'trapped' must be taken as an attempt to draw attention to the unconscious forces at work to make people in general conform. *It's Alive* is a consistent attack on conformity on every level; it is 'pro-life' inasmuch as it refuses to see a 'freak' birth as a threat to humanity whose values in the film are shown to turn on power and money. Those who are anxious to eliminate the child fulfil exactly the same ideological function as the zombie hunters in *Night of the Living Dead*: to suppress an element whose presence is the return of the repressed of the real and dominant place accorded to profit in modern society.

Medical science and the pharmaceutical industry are represented as having a purely rational and calculating approach to the problem. The child is treated much as a product of labour that has gone wrong and therefore cannot be exploited commercially. If the doctor and the laboratory unite to destroy the 'creature', it is to erase all traces liable to explain what went wrong. As the husband and other fathers discuss pollution prior to the child's birth, Cohen is clearly both referring to the tragic cases of deformed babies in the late 60s due to criminal negligence on the part of certain companies and looking ahead to current concern over the environment. Then as now a single logic was at work: profit. The film pillories patriarchal capitalism and leaves us in no doubt as to who is responsible and who the victims are. 'It's not my child', says the father at one point, refusing to see it as his flesh and blood, as if to do so would contaminate him morally and turn him into a freak. The fact that he wants to be like everyone else is a telling comment by Cohen on the real social function of public relations; how people are led to relate in particular ways conducive to the reproduction of values such as ideological conformity and consumerism. 'Reproduction' must be controlled in every field in as far as babies are future consumers. That women are seen as simple producers of babies, whereas men have a more 'responsible' role is implicit in the medical expert's call to the husband to 'disassociate himself emotionally'. No attention is paid to the wife whose emotional 'investment' reaches the stage where she is heading for a breakdown.

How can we read the scene near the end where the husband, after a quarrel with his wife, says, 'I'm going to take my son upstairs'? Obviously he now accepts the child, but only within existing patriarchal parameters: the 'my' speaks volumes as connoting power structures and phallic rights depending on prolonging notions of people as goods and chattels for the correct economic functioning of society. Here it is not a question of *It's Alive* being 'pro-life' but of the father adopting that outlook where it is he who has a 'God-given' right to take decisions alone. In *It Lives Again* this repressive role is assumed by the authorities who track down mothers likely to give birth to such a child, in order to kill it. In this case they too are 'pro-life' in the current reactionary sense; a woman's right to dispose of her body is refused when 'not in the public interest', to quote a phrase used whenever civil rights and the right to information are curtailed in the interests of the survival of dominant economic and political forces. It is surely pertinent that the expert from *It's Alive* returns and is rearing two infants in the hope they will breed, thus reducing them to a variation of 'raw material' for profit, guinea-pigs in some obscene laboratory experiment. This return is that of the repressed; what capitalism hides from the public in order to naturalise and perpetuate its control over lives through 'expert knowledge' and the dissemination of images destined to make individuals conform to how they believe others see them.

The ability of capitalism to evolve and exploit today what it had no time for yesterday (and vice-versa) is patent in *Island of the Alive*, the least complex of the three. Abandoned on an uninhabited island – a sort of 'Jurassic Park' for freaks – the children have grown up and bred in a radioactive environment. They have now become valuable for political reasons. However, other capitalist forces are at work and send hunters to kill the children so that the drug responsible for their physical condition can be commercialised under another name. The contradictions inherent to a system based on the tensions between the ideology of the 'free individual' and real economic interests are clear, but the film has also abandoned much of what made *It's Alive* so dense and intense a movie.

Many of the qualities of the first film are to be found in *God Told Me To*. The Christ-figure in the film is an alien whose notion of what is good for humanity has a distinctly earthly ring: his disciples are chosen from among the denizens of Wall Street for whom fear is the key. Cohen has the brilliant idea of making the hero – the policeman who investigates the mass killings – the alien's brother, totally unaware of his heritage, but I wonder if the anti-Catholic aspect of the film does not tend to obfuscate the complex interaction of sex, society and gender in producing the potentially destructive presence of guilt. The scene where the hermaphrodite alien invites his brother to mate with her/him would have more impact if the cop were an atheist; hysteria would be seen as the inevitable outcome of a masculine position questioned by a feminine position within patriarchy. The religious trappings tend to get in the way (for an alternative analysis, see Williams 1997: 128–35).

The dominant place of religion in *God* clearly stems from Cohen being a Jew, an atheist and a radical and it turns up in another guise in his vampire movie *Return to Salem's Lot* where that politically incorrect director, the late Samuel Fuller, plays a character hunting down former Nazis. The film is politically subtle and plays intelligently with notions of history as a determining force and as an ideological weapon. The fact that the American flag is in sight as the townspeople vampirise someone driving through shows that Cohen has learned the lesson of the opening of *Night of the Living Dead*, although he is more explicit than Romero. However, one cannot but appreciate the way Cohen interrogates the past. Just as the Puritans left Europe to find a haven of tolerance in North America, then took to persecuting the Indians and inventing witchcraft as a means of social repression, so the vampires preferred to let the Puritans think they had perished at sea in order to hide, escape persecution and bide their time. The film even succeeds in articulating the political and economic dimensions of history. At the end of the film Fuller poses a most pertinent question for these history-denying postmodern times: 'In 500 years, who'll believe in Nazis?' And one vampire, who just happens to be the wife of the town's judge and patriarch, points out that 'vampire life and financial security go together'. Just think of the value of a piece of real-estate after 300 years! Vampires are the ultimate in capitalist exploitation (as Karl Marx realised without knowing it when he made the comparison between the two); the proletariat can toil for them and be bled dry by them and time is always on their side.

This deserves to be kept in mind when watching *The Ambulance*, which marks an interesting return, in a modern, realist setting, of the theme of the 'mad scientist'. However, the inherent conservatism of the 30s and the need to centre films on the experiments of a character represented as devoted but mad or as just plain insane have given way to an anonymous economic machine whose victims are treated in a way that bears a resemblance to the activities of Dr Moreau in *Island of Lost Souls*. As with the other directors discussed in this chapter, the megalomania of a crazed individual is now the calculating brutality of a private network of clinics bent on using diabetics in experiments whose aim is purely mercantile. If the film is unsettling, it is not because the rampant paranoia is the product of the feverish imagination of a young comic-book illustrator whose illusions of becoming famous turn into delusions of persecution. Quite the reverse: we have every right to be paranoid in a society whose correct economic functioning depends on citizens taking as normal everyday events the most dangerous attempts on their liberties. Nor must we forget that during the 50s Americans who were in no position to protect themselves became guinea-pigs in experiments destined to determine the results of radiation on human beings. Cohen's last excursion into horror to date is a welcome antidote to what I would call the 'Roswell syndrome': a combination of irresponsible anti-Government paranoia overdetermined by an equally paranoid belief in alien incursions into our lives.

v) JOE DANTE

Dante is a neglected director whose work shows a refreshingly new approach to horror and a genuine concern with many of the issues foregrounded in this chapter. His love for the popular culture of the 50s does not necessarily mean that he reduces it to a fetish, as *Matinee* shows. Thus the Cold-War paranoia of the Cuban missile crisis of 1962 is akin to the fear of alien attacks during the 50s. The character of producer/director Lawrence Woolsey is less a homage to the undeserving William Castle than an attempt to recreate 50s movies in a manner meaningful to audiences today. The comic dimension stems not from smug superiority but from a desire to criticise the rampant paranoia of the decade by inviting us to distance ourselves from the period without losing sight of the nature of the crises evoked. Such comedy also suggests an anti-militarist stance, explicit in the negative representation of certain toys (the 'Commando Elite') in *Small Soldiers*. Thus, in the film within the film — *'Mant!'* — in *Matinee*, the character played by Kevin McCarthy (the hero of *Invasion of the Body Snatchers*) is called Colonel Ankrum, a reference to actor Morris Ankrum, the officer in *Invaders from Mars* and *Earth versus the Flying Saucers*. The former is an intriguing representation of national paranoia filtered through a child's relationship to his parents, an important theme in Dante. *Piranha*, his first fictional film, is more openly political.

That the army and the war in Vietnam are pilloried in the film is perhaps less important (I shall return to it in the next section) than the way the complicity between army, government and free enterprise can result in loss of life in the cause of secrecy; in this case holiday-makers at a new resort being devoured by the piranhas that have escaped from an abandoned military site. Thus the unemployed hero used to work in a smelting plant which was closed down by the government and given to the army. Having served for top-secret activities, it was sold off to the resort. As he says, 'somebody's making money'. This theme of redundancy as a source of profit is given an added and highly political twist by the nature of the Army experiments: breeding piranhas to be introduced into the river system of North Vietnam to destroy it. The use of radiation in the breeding has produced a mutant both larger and even more vicious; the shots of characters being eaten alive are graphic. The scientist who has stayed to survey the plant tells the hero why he accepted such a monstrous assignment: 'a blank cheque, no scrounging for money, no academic politics; you don't know what that means to a scientist'. Such 'freedom' based on money provided by a government less mindful of human rights is another form of voluntary servitude where genuine responsibility is transformed ideologically into not having to account for one's actions. When the Nazis did it, it was a war crime.

Piranha is remarkable for the way it alternates, thanks to a dense and intelligent script by John Sayles, exposition, investigation, suspense and horror. There is not a moment's respite, yet the themes and the political comment never get lost along the way. The Colonel in charge of the secret site is now the literal 'silent partner' of the owner of the resort, since he covers up the danger to the resort with the help of an opportunistic female scientist. 'There'll be other wars', she says, the film anticipating the use of illegal weapons by the States in the Gulf War and NATO in Kosovo. Here, at least, the authorities do not evoke 'humanitarianism'; for the General it is 'necessary to destroy in order to save' and for the scientist 'some things are more important than a few lives'. The ending is bleak, with the suggestion that the piranhas will proliferate in the sea. The film does not so much exploit *Jaws* as rewrite it politically. *Piranha* also reinstates the mad scientist and is a remarkably alert example of 'eco horror', eschewing the temptation to reduce this theme to giant versions of everyday creatures. Like *Tremors* and *Arachnophobia*, it is effective, intelligent and frightening, although its humour is grim rather than tongue-in-cheek. The genuinely unpleasant *Squirm*, however, has no comic relief.

Discussions of *The Howling* have focused on the special effects, the highly atmospheric scenes in the werewolf colony run by psychiatrist George Waggner and the innumerable cinephilic private jokes: characters named after directors who have a werewolf in their filmography, cameos by Forrest Ackerman and Roger Corman (the man who is waiting to make a phone call, itself a reference to producer William Castle in an identical scene in *Rosemary's Baby*) and the ubiquitous Dick Miller as Walter Paisley, the name of the character he played in *Bucket of Blood*. I prefer to draw attention to the way the script (written by Sayles) pillories New Age ideologies and sects, especially in the light of the seemingly libertarian, but in fact repressive, function of the psychiatrist. His idea is to find a 'space' for werewolves to feel at home, but what he actually says and does needs to be deconstructed. Discussing Marsha, the film's nymphomaniac, he claims that her sexuality must be 'channelled' and that she has 'a long way to go'. What is this if not the repressive, normative superego imposing a certain vision of pleasure in keeping with his theories? Ultimately he is the stern father figure – having, appropriately, access to an opportunistic TV talk show to publicise his theories – striving to regiment sexuality in order to control people. When the werewolves revolt, they turn into a sort of primal horde refusing the castrating patriarch.

Both *Gremlins* and *Gremlins 2* attack aspects of Reaganian ideology. In the former, xenophobia takes the form of Dick Miller hating foreign cars and the bank manager telling the hero's father that 'the world's changing: you've got to be tough'. If the father is sympathetic, he submits unconsciously to the ideology of success by striving to invent a device likely to make him rich, whereas in the fight against the gremlins the wife, armed with traditional kitchen utensils, proves more effective. This is surely an instance where it would be obtuse to interpret the *use* of the family as a *defence* of family values, especially as the family's landlord is a woman interested only in money. This is taken up in *Gremlins 2* where the shop of the Chinaman who owns the mogwai becomes part of a real-estate project. A huge office-block stands on the site, a world unto itself, just as its owners are a law unto themselves. I see here, among other things, a reference to the 'Starliner Towers' in *Shivers* (see the chapter on Cronenberg). Interestingly, everything in the building is automated – a subtle comment on the wonders of technology making workers redundant – but things keep going wrong before the gremlins effect their own takeover. Doors failing to function suggest that the unconscious economic drive for order and control is doomed to failure, although it does have precise and negative effects, such as firing workers on the spot. Just as the gremlins in the first film can be seen as the return of the repressed of infantile drives refusing any constraint, so here we have the return of the repressed of proletarian labour. That the gremlins are dangerous can be seen as a negative appraisal of children and workers; it can also be construed as a sign that surplus repression can trigger off reactions that nobody can control and that this is where modern society is heading.

vi) REMAKES AND VARIANTS

The remake of *Night of the Living Dead* goes on the assumption that it is necessary to render explicit what Romero carefully implied. Thus the attack on Barbara is clearly sexual, which simply eliminates the important sub-text of family tensions and violence. The fact that Barbara herself becomes the central and most determined character is a sign of the influence of feminism (and, perhaps, radical film criticism) but needs to be tempered by the far more complex use made of Fran in *Dawn of the Dead*. More interesting and productive is *Return of the Living Dead*, which cleverly alternates monumentally sick humour and superbly creepy and atmospheric sequences in a cemetery. The film is less a spoof of *Night* than a successful working-through of a number of elements from the Romero film which it presents as a factual record: Romero was forced to hide the truth about the army which secretly put a number of zombies into storage. When a canister is accidentally broken, the gas which escapes with the zombie inside reanimates corpses in a morgue. Unfortunately, they have not seen *Night* and can only be destroyed by being burned. The ashes, however, are not scattered to the winds but, thanks to a downpour, sink into the adjacent cemetery and revive the corpses. They turn out to be able to talk, a new element that the film exploits for ghoulish humour but also to disturbing effect.

The living dead are true to their predecessors and attempt to break into the morgue. The besieged occupants pull one in and tie her down so as to find out what has happened. The film treats us to the top half of a woman's skeleton having a conversation with her captors. She explains that the appetite for living brains is due to the fact that only this can relieve 'the pain of being dead'. This unexpected revelation sets up a parallel between *Return* and the unsettling and underrated *Pet Sematary* which brings together repressive family values and anxiety over death. The heroine in that film refers to her dying sister as the family's 'dirty secret': everyone wanted her out of the way and the parents were absent when she finally died. The hero and heroine lose their child in an accident and the film turns on his refusal to accept this death and the pain involved in learning to come to terms with the inevitability of one's own demise. The 'pain of being dead' in *Return* takes on a genuinely disturbing significance when approached in these terms. That the sequence with the talking corpse is emotionally charged comes from this element: reason tells us that a corpse cannot feel pain. The explicitly political *Dead of Night* (aka *The Night Walk*) has a soldier killed in Vietnam brought back to life by his mother's wish. Now a vampiric zombie, he literally brings home to America what the White House did to Vietnam, until his mother, now deranged, drives him to the cemetery where, visibly disintegrating, he buries himself in the grave he has prepared.

For the directors under discussion here, army and politicians have not learned the lessons of Vietnam or of movies like *Dead of Night*. At the end of *Return* the army, on learning what has happened, simply destroys an entire neighbourhood of the town, relieved that only a few thousand died as a result. This callousness evokes the blanket bombing of Vietnam, a frequent theme of the period. The 'hit and run' sequences to destroy zombies in *Dawn* evoke the 'search and destroy' tactics of the American army in Vietnam, but it is *The Crazies* which goes furthest in this field. One of the characters was a Green Beret, a priest sets himself on fire, the troops that cordon off the contaminated town are called an 'army of invasion', and the reference to the need to explain things if one wants to avoid resistance evokes the notion of winning the 'hearts and minds' of the Vietnamese. In *The Crazies* the general attitude of the troops shows why America lost the war. The stupidity and cupidity of the Colonel in *Piranha* implies a similar criticism, as does the representation of the Bruce Dern character in *The 'Burbs*. That the hero of *House* should have lost a friend in Vietnam also unites the themes of retreating into one's private home to forget everyday politics and the paranoid notion of the American way of life coming under attack. Perhaps the most concise statement of this is in *The People Under the Stairs*, where the brother tours his house armed with a rifle and shoves the bayonet through the walls just in case someone is using the hidden passageway, itself a reference to the tunnels used by the Vietcong to move unseen and carry out their strikes. Another remarkable and underrated movie, *Dead and Buried*, stands this paranoia on its head by suggesting that zombies and the American way of life (or death) are the same thing.

Reference to Vietnam is not, however, the only way to introduce a political dimension, however implicit, into horror: *Children Shouldn't Play with Dead Things* does so via Charlie Manson. A theatre troupe spends the night on an island whose sole 'occupants' are buried in a cemetery. The owner and leader of the troupe dabbles in witchcraft and necromancy and has a marked taste for sick jokes and, more seriously, for necrophilia. Despite the fact that humour soon gives way to genuine horror − Clark, like O'Bannon, is deft at creating atmosphere by counting on the audience's fears of night, mist, graveyards and suggestive forward tracking shots − we should not lose sight of the parallel being created between Manson and the central character, Alan. The difference lies in the way they exert control over the communities they hold in thrall. Manson exploited psychic alienation and the mental state of his followers, Alan social alienation: do what I want or I shall put you out of a job and nobody else will agree to hire you. Alan's complete indifference towards the rights and dignity of the dead takes up the commodification of the individual under late capitalism, simple 'fodder' for the economic enrichment of the few. Various point-of-view shots in the film subtly suggest parallels between the living and the living dead, with one striking shot of the troupe trying to break into an abandoned house recalling shots from Romero's movies of the living dead acting in an identical fashion. This visual parallel indicates that anyone and anything can be transformed into a means for personal gain, of whatever nature.

The parallels within films made by the same director and between films made by a number of different directors merit attention. The self-conscious 'recycling' of aspects of *Night of the Living Dead* by *Return* — director O'Bannon also wrote *Dead and Buried*, whose director Gary Sherman made in Britain the admirable *Death Line* (Humphries 1974) where zombie cannibals are represented as victims of class exploitation — is both the sign of common political and artistic sensibilities and a metaphor for the central theme of the period: cannibalism as the logical extension of a consumer society where commodification extends to every aspect of everyday life. This is perfectly captured by the slogan of the central character in *Motel Hell*, a film which brings together aspects of *Psycho*, *Deranged*, *The Texas Chainsaw Massacre* and *Mother's Day* in a suitably black fashion: 'it takes all kinds of critters to make Farmer Vincent's fritters'. Passers-by are kidnapped, their vocal chords cut, and are then planted in his garden with their heads covered as if they were tender plants and fed with ecologically produced food until they are 'ripe' to be removed and transformed into hamburgers. The outrageous tongue-in-cheek approach, which makes certain sequences all the more disturbing, should not deflect attention from the film's deadly seriousness. Vincent lives with his sister — see *The People Under the Stairs* — in a climate of decided incestuousness: a painting of them represents an apparently married couple. Their TV is permanently tuned to an evangelist programme, a prescient example of the role far-right fundamentalists were to play in politics. That Vincent believes in treating all God's creatures in the same way highlights the close link between this particular brand of Protestantism and capitalist ideology. Humans are raised like animals or vegetables, thus mirroring the way the average working person is exploited as a body destined to produce goods for the profit of the few and the feeding of the many. Like *Texas* and *Dawn*, *Motel Hell* (a lesser film, nonetheless) takes to its logical conclusion the concept of the unrestrained drives underpinning capitalism and how they are passed off as God's work. 'The fact that you're here with us proves it was pre-ordained' can be applied to watching TV or being turned into a vegetable prior to becoming fare for a fast-food joint. As with *Psycho*, *Texas* and *Dawn*, the film illustrates the intimate link between economic drives and the death drive. The implicit incest theme in turn suggests a form of libidinal 'recycling' where no evolution is possible but where the system reproduces itself in a vicious circle of production, profit and death from which any notion of meaningful sexuality and human relations has been banished. Indeed, the human subject as the origin of society is elided in favour of money.

The radicalism of so much horror throughout the 70s can hardly come as a surprise; the political climate militated in favour of dystopic visions of society. Considerably more surprising is the continuation of this trend into the early 90s, in the light of a conservative backlash represented in aspects of the 'slasher' movie from the end of the 70s. I have chosen to concentrate on progressive films made by progressive directors from *Night of the Living Dead* to *The People Under the Stairs* because they place us in a position which obliges us to think differently if we are to try to make sense of what is being portrayed. These films are genuine attempts by intelligent people to communicate their views to as wide an audience as possible and it is something that we shall find only sporadically in the films discussed in the following chapter.

7

SLASHERS, SERIAL KILLERS AND
THE 'FINAL GIRL'

—⊶◦⊷—

'A true classic: never goes out of style'. With these words the serial killer whose spirit is imprisoned in the doll in *Bride of Chucky* kills a policeman by stabbing him repeatedly, thus rendering a homage to *Psycho*, 'slasher' films and that most trusty of weapons, the butcher's knife (*The Toolbox Murders* goes out of its way to be different: the killer carries a toolbox around with him and dips into its contents to perpetrate his assorted murders). The notoriety of certain films – stemming from their high body count and the amount of gore – should not lead us to forget that the central characteristic of the 'slasher' film is the act of stalking victims (Dika 1990); and that death by strangulation can also take place (one such murder occurs in *Halloween*). Rather than see the remark from *Chucky* as mere cynical exploitation, I prefer to highlight the dimension of repetition, very much present since *Halloween* and *Friday the 13th* and not simply in the seemingly endless number of sequels made to cash in on the unexpected success of the originals. At the risk of transforming repetition into *déjà vu*, I shall open with a discussion of these two films.

i) *HALLOWEEN* AND *FRIDAY THE 13TH*:
SETTING THE SCENE

Despite the attention paid to the opening of Carpenter's film, where an invisible killer butchers an adolescent girl, I feel that something is missing from the commentaries. Why the killing? What is the function of the ending of the film where Michael keeps coming back from the dead?

William Paul has put his finger on the inconsistencies of certain critical exegeses by drawing attention to the vexed question of sexual motivation when the murderer is a boy of six: 'Reading sexual desire into this without accounting for the age of the child seems to me only slightly less perverse than the sequence itself'. (Paul 1994: 485) Quite. If we go on the assumption that the film is a reactionary denunciation of promiscuous teenagers, then we talk ourselves into a corner: little Michael can have no idea of what his sister and her boyfriend are about to do upstairs. And if we propose the equation 'a child watching = the primal scene', then we are drawing a conclusion that fails to recognise as much as it acknowledges. I shall not deny that *Halloween* suggests that virginal girls are socially superior to sexually experienced ones – although I would argue that it is progressive (and politically incorrect) to suggest that a girl of eighteen might wish to give priority to her studies over sex – and that the film elides any social dimension of psychosis. Nor shall I marginalise the important and intimately linked themes of the gaze, the primal scene and sexual aggression. We need to go further if we are to understand this film.

To evoke sexuality, desire and the primal scene when discussing a child of six means that we take literally the notion of repression and the unconscious: Michael has no idea of *why* he kills his sister. For a start, Michael is not present in the bedroom: he goes up to kill her only after the boyfriend has left. And if they have indeed had sex, as the shots of the boy putting on his shirt and the girl, dressed only in her panties and combing her hair happily, surely connote strongly, then it was a rapid affair: the opening sequence lasts four minutes, which reduces the sex act to a few seconds if we take the time of the story for real screen time. If, however, we view the sequence as *subjective*, then other factors are at stake. Unconsciously Michael is killing, not his sister, but his mother for choosing someone else. Surely it is of the greatest importance that Michael should put on a mask, hardly a way of hiding his identity; his sister must recognise him. The mask then symbolises Michael's refusal to be looked at, to become the object of the other's look, to recognise the other as having the same rights and desires as himself. Michael has not passed beyond the mirror stage and cannot let anyone into his world as this would be to destroy himself as narcissistic centre of the world and his relation with his mother as the sole relationship that matters. We need to go beyond a structural reading of Michael's psychosis to a social one.

Paul has insisted on the loneliness of suburban life and the fact that Michael feels abandoned. (Paul 1994: 322–3) That Michael should be wandering about outside is odd, but not if we note that his sister has forgotten about him for other matters. A sense of social alienation is thus overdetermined by psychic alienation: the sister-as-mother abandoning the son in favour of another. Hence the fundamental role of the point-of-view shots; by placing us where Michael is, *Halloween* forces us to recognise what it is like to be alone on the streets, a tactic reversed later when the heroine desperately seeks shelter as Michael stalks her. Here, the film misrecognises its own textual strategy and turns Michael into an individual case rather than a social phenomenon. It is surely significant that there is a sudden change in point of view during the murder of the sister; we are in the place of the killer and see through the mask. Then the look moves to the right and we see an arm wielding a knife. Suddenly, if only for a moment, we are watching the murder and not participating in it. What is happening here? Both the opening and the closing shots of the film are taken from across the street; we see the house, firstly from the standpoint of Michael (later revealed to be aged six), then of Michael, as an adult, breathing heavily, apparently still alive at the end. Much has been written of the dubious ethics of having spectators identify with the killer after forcing us to identify with the victim, a case of having one's cake and eating it, creating an imaginary position within a real social system. It is in this context that the theme of repetition proves helpful.

In the final confrontation Michael is stabbed in the neck with a knitting needle, his eye is gouged out with a coat-hanger, he is stabbed in the stomach and shot several times. On each occasion he falls to the ground and lies, always in the same position, as if dead. Then he rises and seeks to kill again, except for the last time when he disappears. *Halloween* apparently moves into the realm of the supernatural, but another interpretation is possible. Michael is the exteriorisation of our fear of loneliness and being attacked and of our need, determined by social and psychic alienation, to experience fear through fiction the better to exorcise it in reality. These repeated acts of being killed and returning are a metaphor for spectatorial desire, the desire to be frightened in the knowledge that such things cannot happen in real life, precisely because it is real life that produces the anxiety of loneliness and abandonment inherent in a society that talks of the family but cares about it only when it can be used as a weapon every bit as murderous as Michael's knife. The ideology of social upward mobility symbolised by chic suburbs is one based on the elimination of one's rivals, where 'keeping up with the Joneses' means digging their graves. Unfortunately, this progressive economic insight has been repressed in favour of the purely mercantile one of cashing in on success via the sequel-as-repetition. For Freud, the repetition of an act is the carrying out in another form of a desire that has been repressed: we are condemned to repeat what we fail to understand. Social alienation has reached such a point that audiences rush back to see more killings, oblivious to the fact that they are encouraging the destruction of precisely those values – collective commitment as an antidote to loneliness and fragmentation – to which they unconsciously aspire.

The role of the gaze in *Halloween* demands a closer look: the ambiguity mentioned above is at work elsewhere. At one point a girl (soon to be a victim) spills food on her dress, removes her clothes and dons a nightdress. As she undresses, the camera is placed outside the window looking in and we see her in her panties, from behind, looking for a change of clothes. We are not alone: to the right of the screen is Michael,

Figure 9   Watching Michael watching a future victim. *Halloween*. Copyright © 1978 Falcon Films/Compass International – Debra Hill.

also watching her. We/the camera are just behind him. Shortly after, the girl is on the phone and the camera places us in the room with her. Suddenly, Michael appears outside the French window (left ajar, of course) and looks in. Two aspects of the shot are to be noted. Firstly, Michael is looking at the girl: we are therefore watching Michael watching her, as in the previous shot. Secondly, Michael's gaze encompasses us the spectators. If this heralds Michael as a danger to everyone, the fact we are again in a privileged position connotes something else. We realise the girl will soon fall victim to Michael, which enables us to deny the voyeuristic status conferred on us by the earlier shot: hence the change in point of view. Thus the spectators can both enjoy the earlier sight of the girl undressing and later feel safe from any danger insofar as we can identify with her, while knowing we are safe. Thus the object of scopophilia becomes the victim and is punished in our place. Spying on girls undressing is fine, provided the looker is not a psychotic. Both the spectator and Michael 'possess' the girl's body by their looks, but the spectator's is repressed in favour of the killer's, thus enabling us to have our cake and eat it, safely distanced from the action and its potentially disturbing implications.

Halloween is given serious critical treatment, partly because its reflexive nature — the function of the look — lends itself perfectly to an articulation of theory and close analysis, but also because of its status as the first slasher. *Friday the 13th* is considered to lack the intellectual dimension of the earlier film, which is inaccurate. It is just as impressive in the way it implicates the viewer, drawing us from the opening into a world of nightmare from which we shall emerge only at the expense of repressing certain elements the film itself is anxious to leave in the dark. Certainly the use of night creates the sort of anxiety intimately connected with the representation of the primal scene, overdetermined by the unsettling fact that audiences have difficulty in finding their bearings, thus rendering them even more fragile, like the characters. The fact of placing us in the position of the killer overcomes this by conferring on spectators an imaginary power and control (Dika 1990: 68) which obviously serves to exteriorise anxiety and to make the other pay for it: a classic tactic whose sadistic component is patent. On occasion, however, the system breaks down.

By placing the viewer alternately in the position of the stalker and that of the victim, the slasher movie accomplishes several things: it bestows upon us that imaginary power of a sadistic nature I have just mentioned; it encourages us to empathise with the victim and it enables us, by eliminating the killer, to 'work through' this contradictory position in such a way as to repress the unpleasant implications of being a killer, while at the same time not having to accept our position as a victim. In other words, the textual position masks a social position where people are more likely to be victims of the other's economic aggressivity than wielders of absolute power (or knives). It is here that *Friday the 13th* fails to play the game. At one point a girl at the camp goes to the toilet after having sex. The camera tracks in slowly towards her from our point of view, as if someone is/we are approaching her. She looks up, not into the camera but off-screen left in the direction of a sound. This is repeated in an almost identical fashion shortly after where another girl goes to the toilet: the character does not look into the camera and there is no shot-reverse shot indicating some menacing figure about to stab her. Thus the film places the spectator in a position of potential aggressor, only to reveal that the danger lies off-screen. By so doing it suggests that the danger exists for us too – the off-screen being the favourite place for lurking monsters – and that our supposedly homogeneous subject position is in fact a split one, a split which corresponds to our split position as spectators outside the text and as spectators inscribed within the text by various modes of identification.

As this tactic is not used systematically, it would be endowed with coherence only if the film insisted on a crucial element all too easily forgotten in the suspense of the showdown between the heroine and the killer, the mother of Jason who drowned at the camp years before. The fact that Jason perished because those in charge of the camp failed to honour their social responsibilities and that his mother worked as cook for the camp's owners introduces class explicitly. That middle-class audiences can scream 'Kill her!', calling on the heroine to dispatch the mother (Dika 1990: 66), thus taking up Jason's call to his mother to kill the heroine – the deranged mother imagines herself as avenging her dead son and hears his voice – is a revealing and terrifying instance of people collaborating in their own alienation and misrecognising the fact that they could just as easily be victims. The film's sliding into the supernatural – Jason still haunts the camp – is surely the return of the repressed of class antagonism; those the very traces of whose labour is elided come back, like the zombies who kill Murder Legendre at the end of *White Zombie* and those in Romero's trilogy, to exact their revenge.

ii) RECURRING THEMES, RECURRING STRUCTURES

What lessons can we draw from the above? Caution should be exercised before attributing to *Halloween* and *Friday the 13th* the 'paternity' of the slasher movie: criticism loves nothing more than an origin, an unconscious manifestation of the both repressive and reassuring – hence conservative – function of the father-figure under patriarchy. Before moving on to consider other films, it is already possible to take up the implications of the concept of origin. What renders the most accomplished slashers so frightening is not the nature of the murders but the fact of not knowing who is committing them nor where – or how – he or she will strike next. *Friday the 13th* is even more unsettling than *Halloween*: at least we see Michael whose identity, despite his mask, is known to us. However, even he has the disconcerting habit of appearing out of nowhere. This is to be distinguished from the matter of shock tactics as a narrative device, to which I will return below. The spectators are particularly implicated in the atmosphere of fear engendered when they are ignorant both of the identity of the killer (Mrs Voorhees puts in a very late appearance and is not immediately identified as the killer) and of where he or she is. Here the slasher film also plays, more or less skilfully, with elements other than the off-screen, such as doors opening by themselves and sounds, both floorboards, windows and doors that creak and, especially, sounds that cannot be identified or located and which create less fear than anxiety. One film which exploits this to great effect is *When a Stranger Calls*, where the sound in question is none other than the human voice. (Zizek 1991: 127–8) The repeated phone calls where the babysitter is asked 'have you checked the children?' leads both her and the police she ends up calling to barricade the house and try to track where the calls are coming from. When they do find out, it is too late: the killer has been using another line from within the house and has already murdered the children in their beds. This radical undermining of the codes of the genre and what we expect upsets the spectators' subjective relationship to the film. The notion of danger coming from anywhere is to be taken literally and is far more unnerving when it is located within the supposedly reassuring home.

In order to make more explicit what can be at stake in such situations of uncertainty, I shall use the example of *Blue Velvet*. I am thinking of the sequence near the beginning of the film where the hero meets up one evening with his fiancée and they walk along a dark street. Jeffrey has just been interrogated over the ear he has found, which perforce creates for the spectator a climate of anxiety: is the couple in danger? Lynch carefully insists on the banality of the situation and on the romance surrounding the two characters so that we can feel at ease, a state of mind to adopt with circumspection in a Lynch movie. Suddenly, and for no apparent reason, Lynch places the camera on the other side of the street, whereas until now it has been on the pavement just in front of the couple. This change of position corresponds precisely to the subjective point-of-view shots we are accustomed to in slashers, with some unknown and therefore deadly presence peering from behind a tree across the road at his future victim. The reference to *Halloween* is clear and prepares us psychologically for unexpected and unpleasant events, without any knowledge of what they might be or when they might happen. The shot communicates to us the presence of something beyond our control, just as flushing the toilet in Dorothy Vallens' flat will unwittingly precipitate Jeffrey into a subjective position, literally and psychically, that he is totally unprepared for.

If we return now to our two 'founding' texts, we must recognise that at least two films pre-date these two classics: *Black Christmas* and *Massacre at Central High*. The former opens with a shot of a large, gloomy house (more in keeping with classic horror settings, although *Hell Night* is also situated in such a dwelling). The camera places the spectators outside, then in the place of a man breathing heavily, an element taken up in the very last shot of *Halloween*. *Black Christmas* differs from later slashers by not having adolescents and young adults as sole victims. Not so *Massacre at Central High*, even if its interest lies in the way the elements have been taken over and transformed by later films. Almost the entire film takes place within the confines of a posh California school where a group of well-heeled bullies rules over the other youngsters, imposing a fascistic sense of order that, significantly, is adhered to by the victims out of cowardice and to which they subscribe wholeheartedly once the hero has eliminated the bullies, responsible for crippling him to punish his refusal to conform. Although the film foregrounds class – the bullies torment a boy from a poor background, then destroy his car without which he cannot get around – it is more interested in the social and psychological conditions that encourage victims to collaborate in their own humiliation and deprivation of rights. The graphic nature of certain killings and the theme of cold-blooded revenge return in later films, but in *Central High* we are constantly obliged to sympathise with the killer, the only person in the film ready to defend his right to be different.

Central High is thus rather an entry into the progressive cycle of Hollywood movies of the 60s and 70s, but its themes, characters and settings push it in the direction of the slasher movie. A revealing aspect of the film, indeed, is the cover of the videotape, which figures a maniac wielding an axe, an image totally absent from the film, but one that exploits dishonestly what we have come to define as the 'slasher movie'. A late addition to the genre that resembles *Central High* more closely than is apparent is *Dead Man's Curve*, with its clever use of actor Matthew Lillard (one of the killers of *Scream*) and its insistence on the sorts of pressures which result when youngsters can get into a prestigious university only if they are awarded a scholarship, thus highlighting the theme of success: one person's upward mobility is brought about at the expense (of the lives) of his or her rivals.

As we shall see now, class is a theme of some importance in the slasher.

iii) CLASS

Despite appearances, *Halloween* has something to teach us here. The total lack of compassion on the part of Dr Loomis for Michael suggests a heartless person devoid of any notion of suffering and upbringing. That the film shows him to be right must not prevent us from insisting on an element skated over: in a Hollywood movie the refusal to evoke class is a 'structuring absence' and a minor detail can be the displaced manifestation of repression. If this is the case, the rejection by Loomis of any consideration other than Michael as the embodiment of evil would be the indication that *Halloween* is representing on the mode of denial a 'foreign body' considered to be alien to mainstream Hollywood. Elsewhere, however, class does not disappear so easily as Michael at the end of *Halloween*.

My Bloody Valentine is interesting in the way it takes up elements and transforms them into their opposites in the name of the concerns of the slasher movie. The film is set in a mining community where five miners were buried alive for six weeks as a result of an explosion. Just as Jason drowned because of a lack of supervision by those in charge of the camp, so blame for the accident can be laid at the door of two supervisors who left the mine without checking the level of gas. One miner survived by resorting to cannibalism, spent a year in an asylum and now returns to kill the supervisors. Can it be a simple coincidence that a character who has been safely 'put away' – or removed from society so that people should forget who was really responsible – returns to the scene of the crime in so many films? *Halloween* asks us to believe that Michael returns to his home town to take up the killing where he left off at the age of six, which is ample justification for considering the film as reactionary. In *My Bloody Valentine* the real crime is effaced in favour of an act – cannibalism – so monstrous that its very evocation inspires disgust. However, at one point the film unwittingly represents the real social relations resulting from capitalism by having clothes and miners' suits dropping from the ceiling as if they had a life of their own. This neatly sums up commodity fetishism where those whose labour produce goods and hence wealth are absent, whereas the products of their labour become self-sufficient. This theme had already been treated in *Death Line*, but at a time – 1972, the same year as *Last House on the Left* – when it was still acceptable to present class and economics explicitly.

Driller Killer opens with a headline: 'State Abandons Mentally Ill to City Streets'. Since the painter hero has a nightmare where he is attacked by a man with a drill, we are entitled to ask who is mentally ill and what mental illness is. The nightmare may constructively be interpreted as a return of the guilt of the primal scene, with the murderous wielder of the drill standing in for the father punishing the child for its desire. This, however, is not represented in individual terms but is linked to the notion of urban paranoia. Winos and tramps are the driller killer's victims. This is both a projection of castration anxiety brought on by the nightmare as punishment for a forbidden desire for the mother and a realisation of society's unconscious desire: the elimination of 'undesirables'. The painter's psychic alienation therefore takes on a precise social hue. He becomes society's agent to eliminate those elements who are a constant reminder of society's failure to integrate: exclusion and elimination are the outcome of generalised alienation. That one shot should show him holding his drill as if it were a six-gun expresses neatly the theme of 'regeneration through violence'.

This is arguably also the theme of *I Spit on Your Grave*, the controversy surrounding which has masked its place within the genre. (Clover: 114–24, 160–5) The problem with the film lies in its implicit condemnation of rural life as opposed to town life, the former the home of white trash, mental defectives and mindless superstitions (this is the real theme of *Pumpkinhead*). Once we approach the town/country opposition, not as one with fixed, inherent values but as an imaginary opposition determined by social and economic criteria, *I Spit on Your Grave* moves beyond the 'rape revenge' sub-genre. We learn early in the film that two of the future rapists are so bored they have seen a movie twice. This is surely a classic example of ideological misrecognition: the men are incapable of any analysis of their real social situation and can thus use boredom as an excuse. The situation also subtly hints at an attitude towards women determined by images and fiction, themselves inscribed into social discourses concerning the places occupied by men and women. It is hardly surprising, then, that one of the rapists should accuse the victim of being at the origin of the act: 'you coax a man into doing it'. This is classic stuff, but insufficient for grasping what the film shows us. The pump attendant who is the first to be attracted to the heroine – carefully presented in a non-seductive way – says he hates people who don't work. I would argue that this is the truth speaking unconsciously in an inverted form: his buddies are unemployed. What he hates and fears is not them but what he might become. He transforms this social anxiety into resentment at the expense of the woman, symbol of city life and therefore wealth (and as her high heels show at the beginning, she is both literally and metaphorically 'well heeled'). The man is so completely subjugated by patriarchy – the ideology of success on the one hand, the inferiority and immorality of women on the other – that he cannot see the future victim in terms other than as an object to be passed from one hand to another, goods existing only to be exchanged for money or sexual pleasure. The woman's victory after eliminating the men in particularly horrible ways is a devastatingly ironic instance of the survival of the economic fittest: masculine initiative and knowhow are in a woman's capable (and deadly) hands. She is perhaps the ultimate in 'Final Girls', and it is this concept and its numerous ramifications that shall concern us next.

iv) THE 'FINAL GIRL'

This, one of the central notions in contemporary theoretical approaches to the modern horror film, we owe to Carol Clover. (Clover 1992: 21–64) She writes:

> The image of the distressed female most likely to linger in memory is the image of the one who did not die: the survivor, or 'Final Girl'. She is the one who encounters the mutilated bodies of her friends and perceives the full extent of the preceding horror and of her own peril; who is chased, cornered, wounded; whom we see scream, stagger, fall, rise, and scream again. She is abject terror personified ... She alone looks death in the face, but she alone also finds the strength either to stay the killer long enough to be rescued (ending A) or to kill him herself (ending B). But in either case, from 1974 on, the survivor figure has been female. (35)

It is worth noting in passing that in writing 'scream, stagger, fall, rise, and scream again', Clover insists on the importance of repetition we discussed above when considering *Halloween*. Fear *of* the slasher and fear *for* the heroine are intimately linked in a desire to experience fear and overcome it. Between Sally in *The Texas Chainsaw Massacre* (1974) and Stretch in *The Texas Chainsaw Massacre 2* (1986) we have Laurie (*Halloween*), Alice (*Friday the 13th*), Marti (*Hell Night*), Valerie (*Slumber Party Massacre*) and Nancy (*Nightmare on Elm Street*). An early version of the 'Final Girl' can be traced back as far as *The Sadist* (1963). A girl is the only survivor of the killer and, after a prolonged chase, escapes when he falls down a disused mineshaft. She fits in to Clover's 'ending A'. Rather than repeat all that has been written on the topic, I wish to address certain issues raised in different films.

The matter of gender is paramount inasmuch as we have not a hero, but a heroine battling against overwhelming odds and saving, if not her chums, at least herself and dispatching the monstrous killer into the bargain. One reason for her victory, it is argued, is that she is not promiscuous. This factor suggests that virtue is preferable to vice, but perhaps we can recast this in terms of subjectivity and not binary oppo-sitions; Laurie and Marti define themselves socially in relation to their friends of both sexes, whereas the 'promiscuous' girl gives rull rein to narcissism and therefore to selfish individualism. The 'Final Girl', in other words, is more altruistic and socially responsible. The association in film after film of promiscuity with sudden death does not mean we have to follow suit; other unconscious factors are at work. Take *Hell Night* whose heroine is virtuous, unlike most of the other characters. She is also an excellent mechanic, a typically masculine trait. One girl is not only randy but wanders around in sexy underwear. She is clearly earmarked for butchery and, sure enough, we have a point-of-view shot of the murderer approaching the bed where she is lying. However, we can reject this simplistic representation and interpret the shot as a masculine fantasy of rape, where the victim is represented as willing in order to hide the true nature of masculine aggressive tendencies. The male interprets 'provocative' attire as an invitation, which ignores how women are encouraged daily by advertising to be 'beautiful', 'desirable' and so on, discourses determined mostly by men and certainly by capitalist patriarchy. Both men and women submit unconsciously to the ideology of the Other and act accordingly. Woe betide any woman who fails to conform! This is Laurie's case; she has short hair and wears severe long socks. In certain contexts that would be enough to connote her as lesbian.

Fear, as we have seen, is the key theme of the slasher film. If such films teach audiences to want to be afraid in order to overcome this fear and then come back for more (films), then the films become ways of acting out fears that refuse to go away but are not recognised as such. In other words, being afraid while watching a slasher film is socially and psychi-cally determined and means something else. It is possible to interpret what is at stake thanks to Clover's claim that adolescent boys identify with the 'Final Girl' because she is behaving in a masculine way (I am simplifying considerably here). This, however, must be approached with caution in order to be aware of the social and ideological contradictions resulting in any form of identification, particularly when a person of one sex identifies with a person of the other sex. I would suggest that adolescent boys getting a kick out of identifying with adolescent girls indicates an unconscious and properly Utopian refusal to submit to the socially and culturally determined stereotyping of active, decision-taking males and passive, submissive females. It indicates a desire for a shared experience over narcissistic self-assertion. At the same time it also suggests that the heroine is 'really' the hero, while at the same time remaining feminine. Is not this what happens at the end of *Alien*? Is Ripley rendered positive as a woman because we are shown that traditionally masculine qualities — force, courage, intelligence, resourcefulness — can be a woman's qualities too? Or is the film suggesting insidiously that, as these are indeed 'traditional' masculine qualities, Ripley is rather a hero than a heroine? This ambiguity, of course, can come into existence only as a result of redrawing gender lines in a potentially subversive way, so the film ends on a more conservative note. Is not the shot of a nearly naked Ripley another way of saying men have nothing to fear as Ripley *is* only a woman, after all?

Hysteria is a key notion here. By that I mean male hysteria, where the man asks himself if he is a man or a woman because of certain values he embraces and because he rejects phallocentric notions of virility and prefers values socially coded as 'feminine'. This is what is at stake in the sort of identification with the 'Final Girl' that Clover foregrounds. It can help explain reactions in cinemas where youths egg on the killer: unconsciously identifying with the victims (metaphors for social and class victims such as themselves), they are in fact both recognising the feminine within them and rejecting it stridently (= hysterically). Let us return to the ending of *Friday the 13th* in this context. If Alice is the 'Final Girl', so in a distorted way is Mrs Voorhees; her initiative and activity have enabled her to avenge her son and, in so doing, she becomes masculine and therefore doubly guilty socially and ideologically. That Alice should decapitate her can be seen as the castration of the castrating woman and a return to socially normal gender roles. Mrs Voorhees is punished consciously for being a killer and unconsciously for being masculine. And Alice, having functioned in an assertive, masculine way, can return to her 'real' function as a young woman worthy of assuming her 'proper' social role.

I have insisted above on the function of subjective, point-of-view shots and the way the spectator's gaze coincides, thanks to the camera, with that of killer or victim. Clover writes of the 'Final Girl' that 'her triumph *depends* on her assumption of the gaze' and that this phallicises her symbolically. (Clover 1992: 60–1) This encapsulates nicely what I have elaborated in the previous paragraph and I want to consider two films which call into question the masculine-based order of the gaze: *Slumber*

Party Massacre and *Eyes of a Stranger*. That they do so in radically different ways may be due to the fact that the former was written and directed by two women, although that (as I argue later) does not necessarily make for a progressive film inviting the audience to deconstruct those binary oppositions that condition our way of representing men and women and interpreting their social functions. The interaction of class, gender and ideology is one that must be taken seriously, given the unconscious subject positions imposed socially on all of us.

At one point in *Slumber Party Massacre* the three teenage heroines (alone in the home of one of them) undress and get changed into typically 'sexy' clothes: a dress with a slit up the thigh, a low-cut nightie. There is no reason for this on the level of the story but every reason on the level of the narrative and point of view: two boys are looking in the window and goggling at the sight. Only we know they are there, so the girls are not dressing up for an audience of boys. We have here the convergence of a private and a collective fantasy; each girl dresses according to how she wishes to appear in society; and they do so collectively as this feminine identification with what boys are expected to want from girls is socially and unconsciously determined. Taken as such, it would be at best ambiguous, encouraging audiences to indulge in negative views of the behaviour of teenage girls. However, this would be to neglect an earlier scene, one of the most remarkable in modern horror and one that involves the same two boys.

The scene involves the first victim of the killer who, armed with a power drill, will invade the house at the end and attempt – unsuccessfully – to kill the heroines. The two boys are present in the scene, in the act of ogling the buttocks of a girl standing on a ladder. One of them makes a remark to the effect that girls 'love it', a reference to girls wanting to be ogled and seduced. He then puts this common male fantasy into practice and is unceremoniously rejected. The boys walk off and the girl is at once snatched up by the killer (who is hiding in a van) and butchered, with a shot-reverse-shot showing us the killing and, from within the van, the boys disappearing into the distance. The killer is thus acting out the desire of the boys, with the point-of-view shots placing the audience both inside the van and outside watching the helpless victim die. Here, then, we are both killer and victim and spectators at the horrible death of a girl whose fate becomes the extreme version of the sexual fantasy of young males. In this context it is revelatory that the killer, prior to attacking a female victim, says 'You know you want it', taking up what the boy said in the sequence in question and making explicit to the spectators the implications for women when masculine drives are uncontrolled. Interestingly, at the end of the film, the boys offer to go and get help but are manifestly terrified. They make the offer because it is what is expected socially of them, but it is the three girls who join forces and kill the killer. Their courage is based on the need to defend themselves because there is nobody to turn to. It is not determined by social codes that, in other circumstances, transform chivalry into a desire for domination.

A similar scene of undressing occurs in *Slumber Party Massacre 2* but is more ambiguous, functioning rather as pure spectacle for the film's audience due to the lack of any element corresponding to the killing in the van in the earlier film. The film does imply, however, a criticism of parents' attitudes, in that they are either absent or over-possessive. Thus the killer, a rock singer who wields a guitar with a power drill at the end and who kills off couples as soon as they have sex, can be interpreted as the obscene father figure (of whom more later), bent on murder and mayhem for his own pleasure. He represents pure drive, allowing no social constraint to stand in his way, thus symbolising both parental laxism — enjoy yourselves, kids! (I refer readers back to my comments on the father's complacency towards his daughter in *Last House on the Left*) — and parental severity based on a social superego that imposes certain codes of behaviour on youngsters and takes no account of their desires. In this case the spectacle of the girls dancing, drinking and stripping becomes an unconscious rejection of the lack of concerned parental guidance.

This, I would suggest, is the main theme of *Eyes of a Stranger*. The main characters are the killer and a young woman who looks after her younger sister, blind as a result of being kidnapped and raped years before. The film raises the question of responsibility and centres it on women forced to defend themselves. The fact that the younger sister regains her sight as a result of her struggle against the killer during her sister's absence crystallises the problem mentioned above: laxism or over-protectiveness, with both being harmful. The film criticises social structures, the family, and the law, but it is the attitude of the elder sister which turns the film into an attack on the way women are determined by factors beyond their control. It was when the elder girl, not yet adult, had been left in charge of her sister that the latter was raped. She had left her alone and ever since has blamed herself for what happened. She is, in fact, blaming herself for not having fulfilled a role as substitute mother, where she has been unconsciously determined from childhood for the maternal function and nothing else. Her guilt stems from not having been a 'proper mother' and the fact that she leaves her sister alone again, thus exposing her to the killer, indicates a desire to relinquish a social function that has become purely repressive, one that keeps the blind sister in a state of dependence of the kind that the girls in *Slumber Party Massacre II* are rejecting, without fully realising it, when they throw off social and family restraints along with their clothes. This desire, however, can only be positive when it flows from an adult attitude based on responsibility to oneself and others.

At one point in *Eyes of a Stranger* the elder sister is watching a horror movie on TV when she is attacked, but it is only her boyfriend playing a prank. Earlier he had frightened a waitress by wearing a mask and the entire film turns on the male need to frighten women the better to dominate them. This aspect contrasts sharply with particularly tiresome elements of many slashers where hands suddenly come into the frame and grab a character by the shoulder, only for it to be revealed that the hand belongs to a friend and not some killer. *Halloween: Twenty Years After* is depressingly dependent on such dishonest tactics. This drive to scare audiences with cheap thrills finds another form in the annoying tendency of characters in slashers to wander off alone down long, dark corridors, although everyone knows a killer is loose. I suggest we see such devices as a form of drive, a wish to obtain satisfaction without the obstacle of social restraint, an irresponsible and infantile form of behaviour on the part of the films' makers that finds its antidote in films such as *Slumber Party Massacre* and *Eyes of a Stranger*. The question of a film-maker's responsibility brings us to *Dressed to Kill*.

v) THE CASE OF *DRESSED TO KILL*

The controversy surrounding this intelligent but somewhat ambiguous movie turns on the opening sequence in the shower and the subsequent murder of the character represented there, played by Angie Dickinson. I propose to ask certain questions without which we are likely to fall into a number of traps, while recognising that much of what we are shown

cannot but create a certain complicity with these traps. The ending of
the shower sequence, where Dickinson is seized and raped, indicates that
a fantasy is being represented, but whose, hers or ours? Let us go back
to the beginning and to the slow tracking shot towards the open door of
the bathroom, which continues until we enter and see a female figure
soaping herself in the shower. A man on the left is shaving. We must be
aware simultaneously of the question of spectatorial voyeurism being
set in place here and the possibility that she is fantasising about being
attacked by a man. This in turn raises the question of why, to which I
shall return presently. It is striking that the object of her gaze cannot be
determined: is she looking at the camera, thus encouraging the male
spectator to fantasise about himself as lover, or at the man shaving
whom we learn is her husband? A shot-reverse-shot from within the
shower indicates clearly that she is indeed looking at him, but that in no
way removes the split nature of the object of her gaze. There is no law
that forces a director to respect the Hollywood code of point-of-view
shots, especially if the aim of the sequence lies elsewhere, which it does.

The word 'shower' immediately evokes *Psycho*, but the decidedly
romantic music indicates a sort of anti-*Psycho*, whereas the way De Palma
films the murder of Dickinson in the lift is an exact copy of the murder of
Marion Crane and the fleeing of her killer after. This music returns at the
museum where she encounters the man she later accompanies to his flat.
This would seem to indicate that her fantasy is one of being seduced by
another man and this interpretation is justified, based as it is on the way
the sequences in question are shot. But it leaves aside too many elements
to be convincing. One explicit element of the shower sequence is that
the woman is deriving pleasure by caressing her breasts and sex. This
is crucial: for a woman to obtain satisfaction in the absence of a man is
difficult for many men to accept. However, a man is present, although he
is not making love to her. Thus another set of questions must be asked: is
her fantasy of rape what she craves or is it her way of representing the
brutality of her husband during the sex act? It is clear from the following
scene, where she and her husband are making love, that she is not
satisfied but only simulating, and that he is oblivious to this: he pats her,
complacently rather than affectionately, on the cheek. I would therefore
offer a further interpretation to those implicit in the questions just asked
about the rape in the shower and would argue that the woman is
punishing herself because she unconsciously accepts the ideology that a

woman's pleasure cannot exist without a male and that the brutal assault on her is both an indication of her husband's egoism in bed and her own masochistic position, one imposed by a patriarchal society.

We return here to what we have already seen: women are encouraged to have a certain image of themselves and their relation to sex is determined elsewhere and unconsciously assumed by them. This is precisely what is at stake in the museum; her clear desire to be seduced by the man must be seen in the context of what has already transpired and suggests, on the one hand, her sexual frustration and on the other, the fact that a woman who seeks solace outside marriage is no better than a whore who deserves whatever fate befalls her. Is it not patent that, by making the Nancy Allen character a call-girl, De Palma is denouncing this ideology of which women are the victims? I suggest we take literally the word 'image'. As she moves through the rooms of the museum, clearly distraught at losing contact with this man who attracts her, the Dickinson character is framed on two occasions in front of a picture of a naked woman who manifestly takes up the shots in the shower. Since her movements are accompanied by systematic tracks forward, De Palma is calling our attention to the shower sequence and the element of fantasy. This is surely evidence that the film is portraying Dickinson not as a 'loose woman' but as a woman who is a victim of her frustrations and the sense of guilt visited on her by a hypocritical society. She is literally assimilated — and has literally assimilated herself — to a picture, an image of women which corresponds, precisely, to a male fantasy: turning them into objects and then fetishising them through art so as to be able to use the latter as a justification for voyeurism. In which case, are we not justified in claiming that the murder of Dickinson, by a man who cannot stand the feminine aspects of his being and who is therefore as much a hysteric as a psychotic, deserves rather to be interpreted as the elimination of one of society's victims by another? The adulterous woman and the transvestite are examples of the other and their punishment ineluctable. Caine butchering Dickinson is not simply a matter of the insane male slasher punishing a woman for reminding him of something he cannot accept but is also a man punishing a woman for something society cannot tolerate.

Moreover, the transvestite psychiatrist is both a reference to *Psycho* (Norman's cross-dressing) and an ironic comment on the blindness of the psychiatrist in Hitchcock's film faced with aspects of Norman's case

Figure 10   A stalker plying his trade. *Don't Answer the Phone*. Copyright © 1980
Scorpio Productions/Crown International – Michael D. Castle, Robert Hammer.

which he cannot contemplate. He is also, perhaps, one in a long list of
characters represented in films that foreground the morbid influence a
mother or father can have on a male character, to the point of transforming him into a killer. The list would include *When a Stranger Calls*,
The Toolbox Murders, *Maniac*, *The Boogey Man*, *Don't Answer the Phone*
and *Alone in the Dark*.

vi) 'FATHER KNOWS BEST': THE FUNCTION OF FREDDY KRUEGER

In his superb book *Nightmare on Main Street*, Mark Edmundson writes:
'Walk down into the basement of Nancy's house and you find Freddy's
boiler room. Walk a flight down from the first floor at school and you're
there, too'. (Edmundson 1997: 55) This deceptively simple summary of
the omnipresence of Freddy goes to the heart of the matter by
suggesting, on the one hand, that he represents the dark side of both
characters and society and on the other hand that Freddy is a sort of

double, capable of materialising anywhere and in any form, realising the worst nightmares of all and sundry, nightmares that, as I shall try to show, are desires that dare not speak their name. I wish to elaborate on the notion of Freddy as double, particularly as the double of the parents of the adolescents inhabiting Elm Street and of the values they take for granted. I shall appeal to a psychoanalytical framework to do so, going on the assumption made explicit in the introduction that the unconscious is always both social and historical.

It is commonplace in writing about slashers to assume that the films are punishing promiscuous teenagers for giving free rein to their sexuality. We have already seen how problematic this approach is, however true it can be shown to be on particular occasions. The problem with it lies in the unquestioned belief that cause and effect in real life are linked in identical fashion in movies. The dangers inherent in this approach can be seen in *Nightmare on Elm Street* in the sequence where Tina — the girl attacked by Freddy in the film's prologue — has sex with her boyfriend in her mother's house. She is immediately butchered by Freddy. Once we grant Freddy a particular status, such killings take on a different hue, although punishment is very much the order of the day. It is surely worth noting that the young couple literally take the place of Tina's mother and her lover: they occupy their bed and behave as if they were adults. By assuming this social function, they are not transgressing the adult rule that youngsters should not have sex, but are taking upon themselves the function they are destined to fulfil later in life, when they will be expected to be married and have children. They are therefore being punished for preempting the adults' social and phallic rights, for exercising a certain liberty that adults consider theirs to grant or withhold. By killing Tina, Freddy is issuing a warning to adolescents which is social rather than simply sexual in nature. Youngsters are to behave as their parents expect.

This, however, is only part of the story and highlights Freddy's function as a purely repressive father-figure, the stern, puritanical, social superego. Clearly that hardly corresponds to how he is represented. Slavoj Zizek has described Freddy as 'the obscene and revengeful Father-of-Enjoyment' (Zizek 1991: 23), demanding obedience from everyone, using people's bodies at will and denying everyone the right to sexuality which is his prerogative. When Freddy says 'Come to Freddy', he is obviously saying 'Come to Daddy', but not just any Daddy; Freddy is pure drive, the drive for absolute and complete satisfaction of any and every whim imaginable. What he wants he gets, and he gets it by any means at his disposal. Freddy is the epitome of the American way of life: success is yours if you want it badly enough. Nor should we forget that Craven conceived Freddy as the 'bad father'.

This is why bisexuality functions so prominently in certain films of the series, as we shall see. Freddy does not submit to the law, which prohibits incest, for the simple reason that he takes himself for the law: 'This is God!' he exclaims in the film's prologue, showing his phallic fingers to Tina. Freddy is the father the girls desired in the pre-Oedipal stage. He now returns to satisfy this desire because it suits him to dispose of women as he sees fit: to rape them, then cut them up. Freddy is America's fictional Jack the Ripper – he punishes and enjoys it because he knows that society unconsciously desires such punishment for its black sheep – but just how fictional he really is must wait until later. I have mentioned incest and suggest we see Nancy's relation to Freddy as profoundly incestuous, although we must place this in a social context. Nancy's parents are separated and she lives with her mother. At one point she takes a bath and is attacked by Freddy in one of the most blatantly sexual episodes of the series: Freddy's fingers swim through the water like the shark in *Jaws*. Far more revealing than this, however, is the fact that she locks the door. This is doubtless important for the story – Nancy must fight off Freddy alone – but it is a crudely cognitivist approach that I reject. Nancy locks the door both because she desires to be alone with Freddy and because she wishes to have a private life of her own. Towards the end of the film, when fleeing from Freddy, she suddenly gets bogged down on the stairs and cannot advance. Freud saw such cases of immobility in dreams, accompanied by pronounced anxiety, as a manifestation of intellectual paralysis due to the subject being faced with contradictory and incompatible desires. Nancy flees from Freddy *because* there is something about him she desires, that part representing her own father. Her hysterical screams when Freddy attacks and clearly rapes her mother are triggered off precisely because she understands the nature of her own desire for Freddy as father.

In mentioning Nancy's need for a private world, I was also referring back to my remarks concerning adolescent desires not to submit to parental law. Nancy locks the bathroom door to keep her mother out of her life, creating a situation where she is not constantly forced to tell her everything, as a young child is expected to do. It is precisely for this reason that Tina is killed off and the scene in the cemetery where Nancy is with both her parents gives us a clue as to what is happening. When she describes Freddy, her parents look anxiously at one another: they know but the children do not. In other words, the parents are keeping the children in the dark, withholding from them the very information that could help them, not to fight Freddy, but to understand what sort of society they are living in. Let us not forget at this point that Freddy too was a victim, pursued and burned to death by outraged parents because a loophole in the law has allowed a child molester to go free. He is also a victim because of his class origins, a fact that the film disavows precisely in the way it insists upon it. Can we not see in the continued commercial success of the series, with Freddy becoming a hero for the very adolescents he pursues, slices and dices, the manifestation of a rebellion on the part of the young that the neoliberal ideology of 'anything goes' (Freddy's credo) has taken over for its own political and economic ends? Before answering that question, some remarks should be made about other films in the series.

The gay sub-text of *NES 2: Freddy's Revenge* has been analysed carefully (Benshoff 1997: 246–9), so I want to insist on the notion of Freddy as 'obscene father'. When the hero Jesse — note the nicely bisexual name — dreams he goes to a gay bar and meets his football coach, he is expressing at once a recognition of his homosexual tendencies and his fear of being thought of as gay. The killing of the coach by Freddy can hence be seen as a punishment, not for the man's gayness, but because he is encroaching on Freddy's territory: Freddy, like the pre-Oedipal child, is indifferent to the sex of the person he desires (to kill), although the films hardly present things this way. All he wants is to go beyond the pleasure principle into forbidden territory, a very human striving and one without which the human race would become extinct. Socially, however, that would upset the patriarchal, capitalist apple-cart, so audiences are encouraged to work out through fiction what is denied them in real life. This helps explain the scene in *NES 3: Dream Warriors* where Freddy assumes the form of a sexy nurse to seduce and murder Joey: he encourages the boy to express his sexuality, then punishes him hideously for doing so. There is more to the sequence than that, however, as we have already seen the nurse/Freddy in the company of a male nurse who takes sexual advantage of a woman hospitalised for drug abuse. The word 'abuse' is hardly coincidental; one form of abuse favours another. Is there any difference between Freddy practising child abuse and someone abusing their authority to obtain illicit sexual pleasure? This renders explicit the social criticism underpinning the series.

Wes Craven's New Nightmare is remarkable for the way it represents the repression inherent to our societies, where 'repression' condenses the sexual and the social, indeed shows us how it is impossible to separate the two (which Freud spent decades explaining). Just as Nancy's parents kept the truth from her and exposed her to something far worse, so Nancy, now a mother, has retained the sense of guilt transmitted to her by her parents and transmits it to her son Dylan. At one and the same time she communicates unconsciously to him her fear of sleeping, thus traumatising the child, and transfers onto him her incestuous attachment to her father. Dylan, as object of his mother's desire, feels guilty at rejecting his father who now returns, of course, in the form of the vengeful Freddy, ever ready to punish sadistically that which society has produced but which it cannot face up to and must repress. The sort of guilt represented in the series is of the kind that someone has to pay for but which nobody can recognise.

I asked earlier just how fictional Freddy is and we can find the answer in the way merchandising has exploited the character. Ian Conrich has written of 'the successful release of Freddy from the fictional world of the film into a consumer society reality'. (Conrich 2000: 224) Referring to the fabrication of certain objects such as dolls and cut-outs made to resemble Freddy, he continues: 'The object is here allowed to finally triumph over the subject, with the subject desiring either to resemble Freddy, or to acquire products that recreate parts of Freddy's identity'. (230) We find here a condensation of what has been written about the character of Freddy and of remarks made in other contexts. Freddy as double is transformed into objects that in turn transform filmgoers into Freddy clones. They become the doubles of a double and lose all sense of social identity, crucial under capitalism for alienating consumers while encouraging them to adopt a purely imaginary position in society which eliminates political awareness, the whole point of the postmodern concept 'game'. And Freddy loves games, as a detailed analysis of *NES 6: Freddy's Dead* has shown. (Sconce 1993: 111–14) Ultimately, then, Freddy is on the side of the law, but it is that of drives and *jouissance* and not of social responsibility.

vii) PSYCHOTICS IN OUR MIDST

Although our main concern in this section is with serial killers, we shall see that other psychotics, who cannot be defined as serial killers, have features in common that need to be elucidated. It is not a matter of moving outside the gore and butchery of the slasher: films such as *Henry: Portrait of a Serial Killer* and *Seven* contain scenes more harrowing than anything in a slasher. Rather it is a question of interrogating the representation of psychotics who could be our neighbours, who seem to function normally within society yet whose presence and grisly activities introduce doubts as to society's functioning, doubts that can be resolved in a conservative fashion by ridding society of the pathological foreign body, or left intact in a way that questions the foundations of society itself. Certain issues involved can be grasped through *Bad Influence*, *The Hand that Rocks the Cradle* and *The Boys Next Door*.

The smooth-talking and seductive psychopath who represents the exteriorisation of the hero's unconscious desire in *Bad Influence* is meant to suggest that all is not well in the world of the yuppie, but if he is simply not unsettling enough, it is due not to incompetence on the part of the actor and the director but to the film's unconscious ideological conservatism. Ultimately we are told that it is best to marry a bland young woman whose father is very rich, avoid sex with temptresses of foreign origin and, especially, never have group sex, as the psychotic does. The 'bad influence' is a purely individual matter and disappears with the killer's death. If *The Hand that Rocks the Cradle* is every bit as conservative, it unwittingly introduces elements that its reductive discourse cannot contain. The psychotic portrayed in the film gets taken on by a family to look after their baby and, more generally, their home; she lives in. It is soon apparent that her purpose is to destroy the couple and take the husband for herself. Why? In answering this question the film shows a total lack of compassion determined by social blindness. The wife was a victim of her husband's philandering; he took advantage of his position as a gynaecologist to make advances to his patients. As a result of complaints from several women, including the wife, he commits suicide. The news is broken, most brutally, to his wife, provoking a miscarriage. She then loses her home and all her possessions when her husband's victims receive damages. That something should snap in a woman who, through no fault of her own, loses husband, child and home in one go, seems to escape the film's makers who have no time for old-fashioned notions of sympathy and understanding. Moreover, that the film was written by a woman shows that women can be just as adamant in their defence of the most reactionary and repressive aspects of capitalist patriarchy as men. It is not the sex of a film's makers that matters but their awareness of class, politics and economics.

Such awareness is apparent in *The Boys Next Door*, directed by a woman and written by two men. Both Bo and Roy are warped by resentment caused by the fact they have only work in a factory to look forward to and by the social and academic success of their high-school companions who reject them because of their anti-social behaviour. The film's strength and intelligence lie in its refusal of the slightest complacency towards the two boys and in its foregrounding of the havoc wrought by the work ethic in a system that ruthlessly marginalises whole sections of society in the name of freedom and success. Roy's father has totally submitted to his own alienation, spending his evenings drinking himself into a stupor in front of the TV. The boys show their contempt at one point for an elderly woman forced to live in the streets, betraying the same ideology as white racists who, condemned to social and intellectual mediocrity, need to find scapegoats in blacks to feel worthwhile. For Roy, notions such as restraint and discipline rhyme with their own failure, so he reacts by giving free rein to his drives: self-expression takes the form of wanting to rape any girl in sight and to shit in the middle of the street. This is a narcissistic regression to the oral and pre-Oedipal stage so devastatingly represented by Leatherface. It also shows that Roy is the reverse of the paternal coin: one submits to order, the other to drives. Both serve the interests of patriarchy and capitalism. We are dealing here with a topic central to a number of key serial killer movies and it is revealing of the insight displayed by *The Boys Next Door* – a disturbing movie that few people remember – that it should quote the statements of a real-life serial killer: 'if I had a rifle now, I could make you do just about what I wanted; all my life that is what people have been doing to me'. We shall try to unravel the implications of this remark.

A useful starting-point is the early serial-killer movie *Badlands* which will provide us with a theoretical framework. The central characters also go on a killing spree in search of something that forever escapes them and which the boy cannot put into words. I propose to cast this in terms of Lacan's theory of the object *a*, eternally lost because inexistent, the maternal phallus that would provide the character with that imaginary plenitude without which he cannot exist and to achieve which he kills incessantly. We can see *Badlands* as the neo-horror rendering of the eternal pursuit by Wile E. Coyote of the Road Runner, that ultimate example of the object *a*. (Donald 1989: 145) In *Natural Born Killers* Micky is the effect of a grimmer image, that of the headless corpse from a horror movie that surges from his unconscious and shows him to be subjected to the death drive. The reference to the maternal phallus evokes the notion of a return to an ideal state of early fusion with the mother, a state that is reminiscent of total stasis and non-evolution, of death itself. This fusion includes the notion of incorporation by the other, which is exteriorised in serial killers in the form of an extreme aggression that cannot but lead to the extermination of the other, in a context of social and psychic alienation. (Humphries, 2002) It is reveal-ing that the killer of *Freeway* justifies his murderous attacks by accusing the adolescent girl whom he intends to make his next victim of being the aggressor. That she gets the better of him shows that the 'Final Girl' need not be boyish and sexually inexperienced; here she is neither.

The serial killer is an effect both of the mirror-stage and of the ideol-ogy of social and economic success. The other is thus a constant threat to be eliminated, hence the need to kill repeatedly and the function of cannibalism, the ultimate form of incorporation. For capitalism each indi-vidual is free to strive to succeed, which can only mean the elimination of social and economic rivals. Push this 'logic' to its literal and unconscious conclusion and you have the serial killer. The problem, of course, is that a killing solves nothing and the killer must begin the whole infernal process over again, a sort of recycling of leftovers. This gives to the notion of repetition its real and horrifying significance, one which we can apply to Leatherface, Michael Myers and the central characters of *The Hitcher* and *Henry: Portrait of a Serial Killer*. It also lends a special, literal meaning to the expression 'the death drive' in films where a literal car drive results in the killer confronting the real meaning of his search: his own destruc-tion as the only possible outcome. The ending of *Seven* is exemplary here, where the killer forces his mirror image Brad Pitt to shoot him.

The Hitcher creates a fascinating link with slasher movies by having the eponymous central character shot or run down by the boy, only to keep on rising again, as if from the dead. What is he if not the everyday equivalent of Michael Myers? The logic of repetition and the logic of the death drive are indissociably linked; the purpose of endless series of movies built round a given character thus finds a meaning both psychic and economic. Films such as *Henry*, *The Hitcher* and *Freeway* are a welcome antidote to the politically correct *Silence of the Lambs* which invites audience complicity with the very figure the film designates as dangerous. Perhaps it would be more accurate to say that, by having a sexually deviant killer offset by the elegant and eloquent Hannibal Lecter, the film encourages the worst sort of prejudice. The ending of the disreputable *Hannibal* suggests yet another series in the making, with the aestheticisation of violence and horror justifying economic opportunism and vice versa.

To conclude this chapter, I wish to comment on an aspect of contemporary horror that is as revealing as it is interesting: the use of sequences that seem to be part of reality, then turn out to be nightmares. Clearly this is systematic in the *Nightmare on Elm Street* series, but I want first to return to the ending of *Carrie* commented on in Chapter 5. Referring to its effect on audiences, William Paul writes: 'It was as if the movie continued to have some hold on us (much as Sue's mom held onto Sue), exerting a *control* that reached us even in the *cold reality* of the illuminated auditorium'. (Paul 1994: 409) I have stressed 'control' and 'cold reality' as these are the concepts I shall develop briefly here.

The scene: a diner called 'Mom's', with Donald Pleasence as a cleaver-wielding religious maniac. At one point Martin Landau is hanging upside down and Pleasence brings the cleaver down on his crotch. Landau wakes up screaming. It was 'only' a nightmare. Later in the film a woman evokes her fear of the dark as a child: 'there was something that I couldn't see, that wanted to get me – in the closet, outside the window – the worst thing of all was the thing under the bed'. What is this 'memory' if not that of the guilt of the primal scene, with the child imagining retribution from its parents in the form of some nameless horror, nameless precisely because it represents the impossible desire of incest? This brings us back to the notion of the 'Obscene Father' symbolised by Freddy Krueger, except that the nightmare in *Alone in the Dark* stages an encounter with both parents: note the name of the diner. Near the beginning of *Nightmare on Elm Street* Craven's camera tracks slowly to the right, moving from a shot of Nancy's mother waving outside the house, across the lawn to a shot of the little girls skipping. This last image is the film's signifier of fantasy, but here the unbroken track suggests an equation between the everyday and fantasy that demands our attention. Rather than suggesting that there is no difference and leaving it at that in a typically postmodern gesture, the film insists on the simple and neglected fact that fantasy is firmly anchored in reality: the woman's comments on her fear of the dark in *Alone in the Dark* and Paul's incisive comment on *Carrie* are perfect instances of this. What I want to stress is that the content of the fantasy stems directly from parental repression of infantile desire and, hence, sexuality, with its concomitant social implications: maintaining children in a state of ignorance beyond that of childhood and adolescence in the name of the status quo. What Paul and other critics insist on as a 'failure of closure' in certain films, represented by the sudden revelation that what we have been watching is a nightmare, can be productive if it leads audiences to reflect on their relation to the text and to the text's representation of sexual and social repression. We shall see these notions returning in varied and unexpected ways in the films of David Cronenberg.

8

DAVID CRONENBERG AND SPECIAL EFFECTS

~~⌒⌒~~

In the space of twelve years Cronenberg made seven horror films: *Shivers*, *Rabid*, *The Brood*, *Scanners*, *Videodrome*, *Dead Zone* and *The Fly*. If he can lay claim to being the most influential director of contemporary horror and, with Jacques Tourneur, the most important director in the history of the genre, then he is also the one who, since *Shivers*, has aroused the most extreme passions, controversy and hysteria. And, just in case we thought things had calmed down after the triumph of *Dead Ringers*, along came *Crash* like some implacable return of the repressed to show us we were wrong. Since much has been written about the director and the various subjects of controversy and general interest concerned, I do not propose to return to them systematically, although my remarks on *Shivers* and *Crash* will inevitably mention what seems to me to be at stake in all the fuss. Nor do I wish simply to sum up the themes we can pinpoint in Cronenberg's films. I wish to engage with both the violent rejection of his work and the tendency to depoliticise it through appeals to aesthetics and metaphysics. In this way I hope to suggest we can interpret the films coherently from the standpoint of 'the political unconscious' and defend the use of special effects as inherent to that concern and not just as so many images to be consumed like the fodder in the self-service restaurant of the opening sequence of *Scanners*.

I shall begin by quoting what is probably the most thought-provoking study of the director, that of Steven Shaviro, despite his silly and counter-productive injunction to 'avoid Freud' (Shaviro 1993: 67):

> Cronenberg's films display the body in its crude, primordial materiality. They thereby deny the postmodern myth of textual or

signifying autonomy . . . The machine . . . in *The Fly* is typical in this regard. Its ostensible purpose is teleportation: the quintessential postmodern fantasy of instantaneous transmission, of getting from one point to another without having to endure the inconveniences of bodily movement and the passage of time. (128)

What interests me here is less the juxtaposition of the body and technology than the critique of postmodernism. Rather than define the term as an abstract, theoretical concept, I shall refer to a certain number of shots repeated in a variety of forms in different films in an attempt to set the scene for an analysis of the ideological and political significance of bodies and technologies in Cronenberg.

It needs to be stated at this juncture that only certain films suggest a causal link between experiments with technology and the mutation of the body: *Rabid, Videodrome, The Fly, Dead Ringers, eXistenZ*. Other films tend to eschew such an explicit link by concentrating on the liberation of mental and psychic forces in ways that transform bodies: the appearance of the parasite in *Shivers*, Nola Carveth's 'family' in *The Brood*, the effects of telepathy – exploding heads and mind control – in *Scanners*. This distinction between two apparently different strands in Cronenberg's approach to horror (physical and psychic) is just that: only apparent. There is at work a 'deep structure', essentially unconscious, which shows that the films can be read as a political analysis of the exercise of power and control, where social, cultural, technological and economic aspects of everyday life are bound together in a particular way. I shall sum my argument up in the following terms. The body is transformed by the above aspects into an object over which the subject has no control. As such it functions as a metaphor for the worker or small businessman, scientist or intellectual, the fruits of whose labour are stolen from him as he assists helplessly, as if an outsider, while simultaneously misrecognising his real subject status.

At one point in *Scanners* we see, from a helicopter, the headquarters of the multinational ConSec. It is represented as what I propose to call a 'high-rise, high-tech' building, an example of modern architecture set in almost bucolic surroundings, with lawns and trees. As such it refers back to the 'Starliner' Tower in *Shivers*, not only visually but also thematically, a symbol of wealth cut off from the outside world. A similar visual effect is produced by the plastic-surgery clinic seen near the beginning of *Rabid*.

To these motifs should be added the mall in *Rabid*, the mall with the self-service restaurant in *Scanners*, the dingy, derelict and generally rundown buildings where Dr Ruth brings together the scanners and where Seth Brundle carries out his experiments in *The Fly*. Finally, we have the systematic juxtaposition in *Videodrome* of luxury, modern skyscrapers and just such rundown buildings of two or three storeys. I shall argue that this is neither a coincidence nor a desire to represent faithfully modern Toronto — to do so would be to abandon any attempt to understand how films function in favour of some pre-given 'nature' or 'reality' — but a clue to the very special way bodies and technologies are linked dialectically in Cronenberg. The fact that architecture is represented as 'ideology at work' is a clear anti-postmodern aspect of his films. As *Shivers* affords the most systematic representation of many points at issue, I shall start there.

i) *SHIVERS* AND ITS IMPLICATIONS

The film opens with a four-minute sequence presented as an advertisement for life in the new, luxury 'Starliner Tower' residence. Among the remarks made to seduce potential buyers are the following:

'Day-to-day living becomes a luxury cruise'.
'The noise and traffic of the city may as well be a million miles away'.
'Explore our island paradise: it belongs to you and your fellow passengers alone'.
'Cruise without ever leaving the great ship "Starliner": it's all here'.

Let us now take the following remark by Fredric Jameson, in the context of his analysis of the luxury, high-rise hotel The Westin Bonaventure situated in downtown Los Angeles:

... the Bonaventure aspires to being a total space, a complete world, a kind of miniature city; to this new total space, meanwhile, corresponds a new collective practice, a new mode in which individuals move and congregate, something like the practive of a new and historically original kind of hypercrowd. (Jameson 1991: 40)

My contention is that the residence in *Shivers* functions ideologically like the real-life hotel: as a place where all one's immediate needs and desires seem to be satisfied — it has a laundry, supermarket, medical centre, swimming pool, and so on — to the extent that not only does one not have to leave it but one can even forget the outside world exists. Thus the parasites both represent the satisfaction of certain needs and suggest that a self-contained world is destructive of any genuine, intersubjective human contact. They are thus far from being the simple exteriorisation of unbridled lust and selfish, destructive drives.

It is here, then, that I part company with those who interpret the parasites as a form of liberation of sexual needs denied expression by an over-repressive society and those who interpret *Shivers* as a denunciation by Cronenberg of sexuality in general and female sexuality and the body

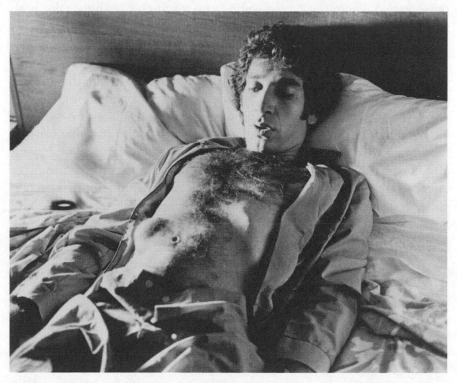

Figure 11 Parasites coming from within. *Shivers.* Copyright © 1974 Cinepix/ DAL — Reitman Productions/Canadian Film Development Co. — Ivan Reitman, André Link, John Dunning.

in particular. The former approach, to sum it up crudely, constitutes the 'anything goes' syndrome; the latter totally fails to take into account the contradictory and conflicting nature of desire, as an unconscious phenomenon become manifest in diverse fashions. In an attempt to mark out the theoretical territory and to facilitate the discussion of the different films, I shall bring together a psychoanalytical and ideological reading by referring again to the mirror stage discussed in the context of the vampire in Chapter 1. The subject becomes aware simultaneously of his or her body as an entity giving meaning and cohesion to previously inarticulate motions and of his or her dependence on the (m)other. This other can then be viewed alternately by the subject as a person one needs in order to function meaningfully in society and as an obstacle to be removed in order to comfort the narcissistic notion of the subject as an individual, independent self. This, in turn, can be seen in terms of self-preservation where the subject enters into a form of deadly rivalry with the other whose elimination becomes necessary in order to assure survival and success. If we interpret this in economic and political terms, we have the definition of capitalism: get rid of economic rivals, if necessary by war, in order to ensure one's own triumph. I shall argue that, in one form or another, it is this negative, destructive and narcissistic basis of consumer capitalism that is being represented in multifarious ways in Cronenberg's films. The inherently contradictory nature of capitalism and the similar effects it produces on subjects can be grasped only by paying attention to the constant co-presence within characters and scenes of unconscious conflicts whereby the subject at once submits to a certain social logic and resists it. The Utopian nature of this resistance will hopefully enable us to obtain some notion of what Cronenberg's cinema is 'about'.

I shall offer myself the luxury of being provocative by claiming that it is only along these lines that one can give meaning to the films in question. The undecidability of where reality ends and hallucinations begin in *Videodrome* must not be seen as some simple representation of the ambiguity of the image nor as some profound attempt to denounce manipulation (though both are the case). Rather we are dealing with the unconscious manifestation of a subject-position split between a desire to grasp reality in economic terms as the first step towards a genuine collectivity and a wish to protect itself socially and psychically by transforming these images into something ideologically seductive that fetishises the individual as (narcissistic) centre of the world. The reader will appreciate that this would entail detailed analyses of each film, which is far beyond the scope of this chapter. I can only attempt here to draw attention to factors indicating an insistent Utopian strain in Cronenberg, by which I mean a striving within the films against the alienation of the subject under capitalism and towards some form of genuine subjectivity. We shall see that this Utopia can be nostalgic, a reactionary longing for some pristine freedom from control that never really existed, but also progressive, an alternative to surplus repression, to the transformation of the subject into a simple consumer; indeed, into a commodity for the other's pleasure and (ab)use.

By 'progessive' I do not mean 'positive', not the first epithet I would have recourse to in an attempt to summarise Cronenberg's cinema. One example will have to suffice. The heroine in *Rabid* is the victim of

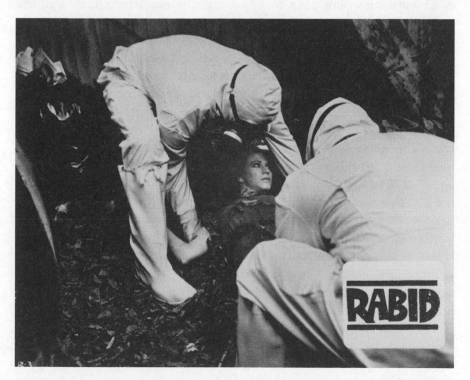

Figure 12   A victim of mad science on the rubbish dump. *Rabid.* Copyright © 1976 Cinepix/CinemaEntertainment/Dilbar Syndicate/Canadian Film Development Co. – John Dunning.

experiments carried out by a man far more interested in his masculine status than anything else and we should surely pay heed when a nurse – a woman – points out to him the dangers involved. If Rose becomes a literal consumer, then at the end of the film she is transformed into literal rubbish by being thrown into the garbage truck, not so much an object of consumption as one of the latter's leftovers. That this ending which represents so starkly the fate of woman in an arrogant man's world should recall so vividly the ending of *Night of the Living Dead* – where the hero/victim is black – is enough to give food for thought and make us at least hesitate before trying to pigeonhole the director as reactionary, obsessed, sick and so on. There is no hope here, but nor is there any facile pessimism, rather an unblinking attempt to analyse the social forces leading to the tragedy.

This is perhaps the moment to return to *Shivers*, the most controversial of Cronenberg's films prior to *Crash*, and the one which, thanks to the extremity of its vision, best enables us to map out 'the political unconscious'. To do so, I shall quote again Jameson's comments on the hotel. Referring to the elevators which move up and down, transporting residents and visitors from reception desk to revolving penthouse bar and without which no visit can be made, he describes them as 'the allegorical signifier of that older promenade we are no longer allowed to conduct on our own'. (Jameson 1991: 42) I suggest we approach in these terms the scene where the two elderly ladies, armed with an umbrella, take their constitutional around the lawns surrounding the Tower, their age at once setting them apart from most of the residents and insisting on the fact that this self-contained 'world' cannot answer all our needs and desires. Thus there are moments when we experience the wish to keep in touch with reality and nature, even if only in the form of carefully tended lawns, which conjure up that conservative past of the individual house with private garden but also symbolise the way such nostalgia has already been foreseen and taken in hand by advertising and housing projects. In which case the 'older promenade' comes over as the signifier of the bourgeois notion of individual freedom taken literally by those who reject the spurious 'collectivity' of the Tower but who are not consciously able to analyse the negative effects it has on them, except in some meaningless (yet necessary) escape to 'Nature'.

It is then surely significant that it is on the umbrella carried by these elderly ladies that Nicholas vomits the parasite. For these creatures should not be seen as symbols of something else — a penis, a turd, or both — but rather as the textual manifestation of the ideological contradictions striving for expression and mastery within the logic determined by 'late capitalism' and the Utopian resistance to it. Surely the parasites represent *drives*, where the subject's libido seeks the immediate satisfaction of its aims, without constraints of any kind. As such, their sexual nature is clear but not in the classic terms employed. Drives belong to the pre-Oedipal stage of the subject's development where, amongst other factors, it seeks to fuse with the parent that is the object of its affection at the expense of the other parent. This is one definition of *jouissance*. The characteristic of the drive is that it is unstoppable. One of the most arresting aspects of *Shivers* is the way contaminated residents hurl themselves gleefully upon non-contaminated residents in an attempt to possess them, to take them over, to transform them into images of their contaminated selves. The self asserts its identity at the expense of the right of the other to maintain his or hers, which we can, once again, see in terms of economic rivalry. I refer readers back to my comments on Leatherface and *The Texas Chainsaw Massacre*.

It is precisely here, however, that we must pause and ask ourselves questions about the circumstances of the parasites' progress. The advertisement for the Tower seeks to seduce by offering everything that one can desire, but this mentality is already ideological: it goes on the assumption that desire is based on plenitude and harmony, whereas it is constituted in and by a lack and cannot exist otherwise. If desire were satisfied once and for all, the subject would simply cease to exist; it would have literally nothing left to desire. In other words, desire sets its face firmly against drives and it is drives, not desire, that the advertisement adresses. For the aim is both to satisfy in advance anything the future resident needs, which comes down to blocking off desire completely and to fetishise the individual as someone unique and dependent on no other person, which comes down to unconsciously eliminating the other. The future resident is therefore at one and the same time rendered infantile by an enterprise that unconsciously sets itself up as a mother substitute and castrated symbolically insofar as he or she cannot express any desire that has not been foreseen by the promoters. The residents are doomed therefore to function under the control of the strictest repression where absolutely no freedom of thought or choice is possible. As Jameson points out,

> ... market as a concept rarely has anything to do with choice or
> freedom, since those are all determined for us in advance, whether
> we are talking about new model cars, toys, or television programs;
> we select among those, no doubt, but we can scarcely be said to
> have a say in actually choosing any of them. (Jameson 1991: 266)

The film therefore gives a new twist to Marcuse's notion of 'surplus
repression' where capitalist logic goes beyond the constraints needed to
allow a certain social cohesion: if sexual drives could be expressed freely,
society would collapse into anarchy, violence and (self-)destruction. Seen
in these terms, the parasites do take on a liberating force, a form of
rebellion against a version of order, regimentation, control and constraint
whose sole purpose is to impose commodities on people in order to create
surplus value for the capitalist and surplus repression for the rest of us.

The film's ambiguity is perfectly summed up in the final sequence
where the sole survivor of the contamination is finally taken over in the
swimming pool, prior to the great exodus from the Tower to spread
the parasite abroad. Here we have simultaneously a new collectivity
which refuses the fragmentation of society into discrete units symbolised by flats within isolated towers and the triumph of drives whose
satisfaction heralds the end of desire in favour of a sexual – read:
economic – free-for-all where one self's drive is another's destruction.
Like the promenade discussed above, there is at work a nostalgic return
to the past that recalls Marcuse: 'The memory of gratification is at the
origin of all thinking, and the impulse to recapture past gratification is
the hidden driving power behind the process of thought'. (Marcuse
1955: 42) As with *Psycho* we are dealing with a literal death-drive, 'an
unconscious flight from pain and want. It is an expression of the eternal
struggle against suffering and repression'. (Marcuse 1955: 41) Cut off
from a conscious grasp of the past and history, this drive can only turn
into a vast collective suicide; there can be no rules or constraints enabling
the temporary non-satisfaction of a drive as a gesture to the existence and
rights of the other. The 'collective' nature of the residence under the
control of the parasites is a sort of parody of 'group therapy' where each
person is forced to talk/act in the name of 'self-expression', the manifestation of a ferocious superego imposing freedom. Thus the parasitic
Nicholas rapes his wife: 'You're my wife; make love to me'. Such a

collectivity is therefore purely imaginary and has nothing political about it. It represents perfectly the random difference and political indifference of postmodernism.

ii) THE WORLD OF DAVID CRONENBERG

We can perhaps best sum up the ending of *Shivers* by defining it as the unconscious representation of the unsolvable contradiction between the subject's desire for genuine contact and the self's narcissistic striving to transform such contact into the annihilation of the other as rival. We shall have the occasion to return in some detail to the theme of contact, both literal and figurative, but must resume here our opening gambit concerning the buildings on show. The first shot we have of the clinic in *Rabid* is of an ultra-modern block whose windows, which cover most of its surface, repel any attempt to see in and only reflect the trees standing outside. Thus the building reflects Jameson's remark about the glass structure of the Bonaventure, creating a boundary between inside and outside, whose reality from the point of view of literal vision blocks off all human contact. This artificial creation of boundaries is, however, an integral part of the fragmentation of society, of the Taylorisation of labour where each worker executes one job without having any overall notion of the purpose of what he or she produces. Significantly, and despite his having some control over his professional activities, the plastic surgeon tends to separate experiments from results, as if he has no responsibility for the latter, a manifestation of his alienated status as a paid worker. Not for nothing is reference made to 'a pack of hungry investors' in a context where the surgeon has stated: 'I don't want to become the Colonel Sanders of plastic surgery'. This fascinating link between aesthetics and commodities – or aesthetics as commodity – is pursued in different ways by the film. As we have already seen when discussing cannibalism in horror, the notion of consumption within capitalism is to be taken literally. Here Rose, the film's heroine/victim, is transformed into a vampire, feeding off new victims, just as the plastic surgeon fed off her in the name of progress and science. This is further elaborated in the mall sequence where Rose is approached as sexual object by a young man, a form of seduction mirroring the capacity of capitalism to transform any person or object, even a concept like 'sexuality', into a commodity. That Rose should vampirise a man in a porn cinema is a neat reversal of the dominant situation, but also shows that subjects function within a vicious circle: consume or be consumed.

The mall sequence in *Rabid* contains a scene where an overzealous policeman opens fire and kills innocent bystanders: excessive order – surplus repression – thus leads to a breakdown of order. It also looks ahead to the remarkable opening of *Scanners* with its garish and inhuman self-service restaurant, itself embedded in a mall. What is ironic here is the dehumanising aspect of the surroundings where two bourgeois ladies look with disgust upon the derelict hero, without recognising that their tendency to transform him into something subhuman, barely more than an object, is the result of just that transformation of human relations into commodities which is responsible for the mall in the first place. My use of the word 'derelict' is not innocent: according to its grammatical function, the word designates both a tramp and the rundown, abandoned aspect of a building. This juxtaposition within language itself of the human and the non-human is exploited by Cronenberg in several films in the shape of the buildings where Dr Ruth brings scanners together to hide them from ConSec, where Seth Brundle has installed his laboratory in *The Fly* and where Max Renn has his office in *Videodrome*. Here, too, O'Blivion's daughter refers to those who turn to the 'Cathode Ray Mission' for succour as 'derelicts', thus showing that charity exists as an ideology masking the objective nature of the economic status quo. The activities of the various characters are not treated identically: Brundle is not a pornographer like Renn. Something else is therefore happening and I would suggest we have the co-presence – very marked in *Videodrome*, where Cronenberg, via camera movements unnecessary for the simple story-line, insists on the contiguity of luxury skyscrapers and dingy old dwellings – of the old and the new, the lingering on of one economic system, now deemed part of pre-history and doomed to destruction by a new system. Renn the old-fashioned individual capitalist versus the tentacular all-embracing capitalism represented by Convex, 'an articulated nightmare vision of how we as individuals feel within the new multinational world system'. (Jameson 1992: 26) Similarly, Ruth is hired by ConSec to inquire into scanners and also carries out experiments in secret in a derelict building symbolising both his mistaken belief that his two activities are completely separate from each other and a nostalgic

Utopian longing for a time when alienation and repression of an explicitly political kind were not the only order of the day. Yet Ruth and Darryl Revok have the same purpose: power. The former is exalted, the latter totalitarian, but very much his father's son. Brundle, like Renn, represents individual initiative (a thing of the past) and considers himself independent because he is left alone by the firm that subsidises him, failing to understand that his desire to remain cut off from the outside and the very nature of his experiments – which eliminate time and space – are the effects of that very economic cause of which he is an unconscious effect.

Ultimately Cronenberg's mad scientists – and his cinema, more than any other, is the continuation of this key theme of the 30s – turn inexorably into adjuncts of the machines, instruments and methods of which they consider themselves to be the origin. This notion finds its supreme expression in the Mantle twins in *Dead Ringers*, notably in Beverly's insane recourse to what he calls 'radical technology', or the invention of monstrous instruments destined to find out why certain female bodies are 'abnormal', why they do not fit in with what the science/ideology of gynaecology defines as female. In his encroaching psychosis, Beverly transforms reality into what he thinks it should be, a pathology due certainly to the insufficient resolving of the Oedipal complex and of the narcissistic dimension of the mirror stage resulting in a crisis of identity, but also to alienation of an economic kind where success and wealth mean transforming the other into a body to be exploited. Thus the crisis of identity which has been repressed since early childhood returns and turns against the twins who thus suffer exactly that commodification they have long visited on women.

Just as the Mantles want to control women via instruments, the ultimate boundary separating them, so the plastic surgeon in *Rabid* uses the discourse of beauty to turn women into what they think they should look like, according to the masculine discourse on female beauty. The pseudo-therapy of Dr Raglan in *The Brood* obliges patients to express their emotions, a form of subtle control where you convince people they are expressing themselves freely, whereas they are submitting to a particularly extreme form of social repression. It is therefore fitting he should be killed by 'the brood', symbols of his exploitation of Nola Carveth's body, who turn on him like so many 'revolting bodies', the products of the labour of her body exacting revenge for the mercantile exploitation Raglan has carried out in the name of science. In *Scanners* political and economic power in the future will be wielded thanks to medicine, yet unborn children will be raised to obey 'evil' scanner Darryl Revok in a new fascist state, minds and bodies permanently alienated. Perhaps the most striking image of this in all Cronenberg is the scene in *Videodrome* where Convex places the 'hallucination helmet' on Renn's head, transforming him into an uncanny lookalike of the fly in the 1958 film: a human body with a non-human head. Except here it is an inorganic head, thus neatly condensing Renn's anxiety to turn clients into profit-making machines and his own subsequent exploitation. And in *The Fly* Brundle is not only turned into an insect but one that also fuses with his pod; he is literally objectified. Earlier he has claimed that every person wants to be 'turned into something else'. Not 'someone else', so his remark is an unconscious condensation of people conceived as com-modities and of that Utopian desire for change that cannot articulate itself politically but which, thanks to language, is materialised imposing on the subject a meaning he cannot grasp but which determines his being.

This is the appropriate point to return to the theme of contact via a fascinating and unnoticed ambiguity in *Dead Ringers*. It is assumed that Claire Niveau asks Beverly to tie her up for sex out of masochism. I would agree that a woman who accepts to be tied up thus has clear masochistic leanings, but we should remember how Nicky Brand in *Videodrome* unconsciously submits to the image men impose on women. There is nothing in the dialogue of *Dead Ringers* to indicate that she makes such a request. In which case we are justified in arguing that Beverly makes the proposition and that Claire consents. The difference, from the standpoint of our analyses here, is crucial: it suggests that the need to control the female body is paramount at all times, and not only during professional examinations and surgery. If she accepts, this is due to an unconscious submission to the male discourse determining a woman's 'place' within the sex act. In other words we must take seriously the twins' discussion on sex when children, professing a liking for the idea that sex is possible without contact. The alienation of the twins, both psychic (their identity problem) and social (the fetishisation of instru-ments as signifiers of success and money), has reached the stage where they can contemplate the female body as a pleasurable extension of surgical tubes and clamps, while at the same time convincing themselves Claire cannot have an orgasm otherwise. Certainly the film tends to encourage this interpretation, which only means that Cronenberg is unconsciously submitting to commodification through his representation of female sexuality.

What is remarkable about Cronenberg's cinema is its welcomingly unsentimental and non-idealistic representation of contact, which is always mediated by the Other. By that I mean that Cronenberg rejects any mystical notion of communion as something existing between two single individuals. Think of the function of the telephone in *Shivers*. We take this invention of technology for granted, fetishising it as an object functioning miraculously without the intervention of past labour and knowledge. And yet this banal instrument is the only means of contact with the exterior world once the residents start taking one another over, the exterior world which becomes as distant as a planet, as if the Tower were indeed cruising in space where, as the poster for *Alien* reminds us, 'nobody hears you scream'. Thus the phone becomes what it always was: a potential means for genuine intersubjectivity and human contact, a function repressed in a supposedly self-contained world where people identify with the signifiers of luxury and consumption and become mere effects of them. The current proliferation of mobile phones needs to be considered in this light.

The Lacanian concept of the big Other is represented in *Scanners* by the voices that Cameron Vale cannot keep out and which Darryl Revok attempts to expel by boring a hole in the middle of his forehead. We are dealing therefore with the positive and negative functions of these voices. Revok is paranoid, the voices functioning to remind him of his dependence on others (the Other as language itself), a dependence he rejects. This is the meaning of Ruth's remark that he was self-destructive when young: now he is destructive. For Lacan, the most extreme manifestation of narcissism is suicide: the subject reacts with such violence against the other of the mirror stage – the other that takes the form of his own image – that he must destroy him. In so doing, he is destroying himself. Revok has projected this extreme form of identification onto the outside world and is thus ready to annihilate anyone who does not submit to his narcissistic image of himself. This is a fascist attitude to which we shall return later when discussing *Dead Zone* and *Videodrome*. It is also one with precise economic ramifications, as can be construed from the fact that, even when hiding in a quiet suburb, Cameron and Kim are not safe from Revok. *Scanners* suggests that no area of human endeavour (including the unconscious) remains outside the control of global capitalism.

It is precisely in such a context that we can see how futile and misguided are the accusations of being reductive often aimed at psycho-analysis: without the concept of the unconscious we deprive ourselves of the possibility of understanding how people can be manipulated against their will, made to submit to strategies of control that work against their social and economic interest. In *Dead Zone* we have a virtual textbook representation of the way the ego identifies with the powerful leader. Gerg Stillson cunningly expresses a general dissatisfaction with politics and politicians, having understood that what people want to hear is a discourse demanding honesty and integrity. He then represents himself as its emblem. Each supporter of Stillson thus identifies unconsciously with the desire of each other supporter to find a sort of 'Saviour' and projects that desire onto the outside world, where the signifier 'Stillson' becomes invested with the necessary meaning and mission. There is, then, a form of contact at work in *Dead Zone*, but it is one that, in the name of the collectivity, poses an even greater threat to it than the selfishness and cynicism of existing politicians. The brilliance of the film is to propose the most banal form of contact possible, so banal that one hardly even thinks of it: it is precisely at the moment when he grasps a person's hand that Johnny is able to read the future. This literal contact thus becomes the central manifestation in Cronenberg of the Utopian thrust, of a collective, unconscious desire for a return to human values unmediated by that ultimate fetish money and the repression it entails. The boundaries indispensable for maintaining social and psychic frag-mentation – and therefore a repressive social order – suddenly collapse.

It is this, rather than the humanist denunciation of Nazism, that high-lights the links between capitalism and fascism in *Dead Zone*. We have seen it in *Scanners*, but in so extreme a form – Revok – that its true sig-nificance is easy to miss. *Videodrome*, however, is more explicit, whatever criticisms we can make of the film's ultimate refusal to distinguish reality and hallucination. At one point Renn is interviewed, most discreetly, on a TV panel show about his activities as a producer of video porn. He insists on the economic aspect, stressing that his is a 'small' business: 'In order to survive, we have to give people what they can't get elsewhere'. Shaviro has given a perfect description of Renn: 'sleazy, competitive, aggressive, and tough in a self-congratulatory way'. (Shaviro 1993: 144) There is a clear parallel between the hard-core porn peddled by Renn and the hard-core violence peddled by 'Videodrome': a naked woman being flogged by a masked man in a small room devoid of decor. In other words: no production values in order to make a profit and 'give people what they can't get elsewhere'. Another parallel can be drawn: the actors and actresses do it because they have no real choice. Or, rather, the 'choice' is between that and unemployment, or worse. The role of the woman and the man is to bring *jouissance* to the viewer who thus identifies with the sadistic big Other. Economic and political forces overdetermine one another, encouraging viewers to assist passively in their own exploitation via the intermediary of a surrogate scapegoat. For to identify with such sadism is unconsciously to be an accomplice in (one's own) exploitation. In *Videodrome* it is not Convex, but Harlan – the stooge planted on Renn – who defends the fascist line about North America going soft while the rest of the world gets tough. Convex will transmit 'Videodrome' so that viewers will identify with the sadism of the strong and want to see the weak suffer. Hardly surprising, then, that the programme should be said to be broadcast from Malaysia, a Third World country destined under global capitalism to suffer so that workers in the developed world can think themselves strong, while in fact these latter workers will also suffer in the long run. This becomes patent when we learn the programme is being broadcast from Pittsburg (incidentally, the home of Romero's zombies). Hardly surprising either that Convex should control Spectacular Optical which makes missiles for NATO and spectacles for the Third World. *Videodrome* – made in 1982 – is extra-ordinarily prescient: what was Kosovo, if not NATO versus the Third World, where, in the name of humanitarianism, thousands were bombed out of existence?

The whole question of looking is addressed unequivocally in *The Fly* and *Crash* in the most disturbing ways. The credit sequence of the former presents the spectator – for it is our view that is primarily concerned – with hazy images that seem to represent larvae or bees busy in their hive. When the image comes into focus, we realise that what we have been looking at – without 'seeing' it – is a convention with people milling about. Cronenberg cuts to Seth Brundle, insisting apparently on his eyes, but in reality on his look: he is looking off-screen and addressing someone who is revealed by the next shot to be Veronica, the journalist who will become pregnant by him. If I draw attention to the look, it is because it tends to be neglected in favour of Jeff Goldblum's striking and prominent eyes, but we should not allow ourselves to misinterpret the clue. Several strands of this remarkable film are tied together here. Firstly, there is the notion of a humanity that is already dehumanised. Later we understand this is also Brundle's case; he hates vehicles but is a slave to the ideology of technology as change and therefore progress (a common but imaginary 'cause/effect' syndrome). This leads him to fail to recognise, like his computer (on which he counts as a fetish), that flesh, be it that of a baboon, is not an object devoid of 'poetry'. It is this that makes a subject more than just a body, but Cronenberg seems to glide over the question; Brundle reprogrammes his computer to take the difference into account, but we do not learn how he did so.

Secondly, the look is the locus of desire itself: we see what we desire, not necessarily what is actually there. Hence the role played by the look of Brundle-as-Fly in the last scene. For it is precisely not his eyes that Cronenberg shows us here, any more than it was in the film's opening shot, but his look. Now completely transformed, Brundle is nevertheless capable of symbolic thought by pointing the rifle against his fly's head. He remains, until the bitter end, a subject, with human thoughts and feelings. What makes the ending so completely overwhelming, the most horrific of any film, is that the most radical boundary of all, that between a human and an insect, is in place yet does not function. It is a subject, not a body, who suffers.

Crash is a film of extremes, whether it be staging the fatal accidents of famous personalities, filming the corpses of victims of car accidents, or desiring to be involved in an accident in order to experience *jouissance*. The links between looking, filming, sexual ecstasy and the most literal representation of the death drive yet put on film were obviously too much for many critics, for whom *Crash* functioned as the return of the repressed reminiscent of the *Peeping Tom* scandal, but what needs to be stressed in the context of this chapter is the way the Ballard character relates to women. Just as Vaughan humanises cars and dehumanises corpses via his camera, so Ballard (significantly, a director of advertisements) poses his look on the particular form of the Rosanna Arquette character, complete with limbs encased in metal prostheses. When he makes love to her — in a car, of course — what fascinates him is not the woman, not even as a vehicle (pun intended) for his sexual pleasure, but her body as an object, an extension of the metal fixtures. For Ballard, the modern world is one of steel; planes and cars are far more human for him than any person. That this modern world turns on (instruments of) death is a further example of that physical and psychic mutilation with which *Dead Ringers* ends and which sums up perfectly the way Cronenberg's cinema represents the dehumanisation of desire by drives.

The aesthetic, ethical, economic and political aspects of this cinema are brought together in the use of special effects.

iii) WHAT PRICE SPECIAL EFFECTS?

I would argue as follows concerning Cronenberg's cinema. Inasmuch as it turns on the interaction and interdependence of the body and technology where both human and economic relations are inextricably tied up with the representations and functions of these twin themes, his cinema is a rare example of special effects being an integral part of the vision proposed, rather than some optional or optical extra. I have no intention here of making a list of 'good' special effects as opposed to 'bad' special effects, although it is necessary to give examples of radically different — indeed, opposing — uses of this particular brand of technology. One readily comes to mind: Romero's trilogy of zombie movies. Here one cannot distinguish between the make-up and the meaning and function of the zombies within the films. Their lobotomised behaviour as perfect capitalist consumers is represented by their automatic gait, their unseeing eyes and, especially, that compulsion to repeat that which, containing as it does no variant whatsoever, is the textual manifestation of the pleasure principle, that 'death drive' I have referred to above when discussing *Shivers*. I am not trying to make Cronenberg an objective ally of Romero on the Left. Romero's attacks on capitalism and consumerism are perfectly conscious, whatever unconscious meaning we can attribute to various details and their implications. Cronenberg is, rather, a humanist of a sceptical and arguably conservative hue who denounces extremism but seems unaware of the profoundly subversive thrust of his own movies.

How different this is from those special effects which are simply grafted onto the storyline as objects of fascination to be consumed passively in a state of rapt wonder and amazement. The fact that movie buffs, journalists and film theorists alike wax ecstatic over intergalactic warfare, aliens bringing sweetness and light to an eager humanity and dinosaurs gobbling people up must not lead us to assume we are under some obligation to consider such effects as aesthetically successful because they look so 'real', so 'natural', so 'pleasing' to so many spectators. This discourse has been with us for some time, ever since it has been considered 'modern' to scorn the special effects of *King Kong* as old-fashioned, for the simple reason that they can be *seen* to be effects. The current praise for and interest in the virtual image and its like is the purest case of fetishism and alienation we have encountered to date in film criticism. The traces of labour have been effaced so as to leave a smooth surface from which all has been removed except the ability to repress all knowledge of time in favour of a self-contained space (like the 'Starliner' Tower) functioning in a temporal void. Anxiety over humanity's future (increasingly problematic) is transformed into a fascination not unlike that of the spectators watching 'Videodrome'. Special effects are the cinema's equivalent of the ideology of 'the end of history'.

It is for this reason that *eXistenZ* is such a letdown in the context of the films discussed here. Ultimately it partakes of just that discourse I have mentioned, where the spectator is left with the feeling that, if we cannot tell the difference between game and reality, then it does not really matter as reality has been turned into a game anyway. If we displace the centre somewhat, however, we find a more interesting state of affairs: the game functions as a sort of drug and its addicts become literal computers. The words and gestures of the players are determined by this technological 'hook-up'. The player is asked to let himself go, in other words to submit to those very same destructive drives represented in *Shivers.* We are back in the field of pre-Oedipal narcissism: if anyone tries to prevent you from obtaining satisfaction, eliminate them. This is what keeps capitalism and surplus repression going. People get rid of their stress and aggressiveness on a purely imaginary mode and genuine change is blocked.

Ultimately, however, *eXistenZ* is simply ambiguous. What are we to make of the hero's refusal to be 'penetrated' by a bioport? A fear of feminisation due to a concept of virility verging on hysteria? Or a refusal to abandon himself, not to pleasure, but to *jouissance* as a negation of intersubjectivity and genuine human contact? The film's overall thrust is one of pessimistic stoicism concerning reality, virtual or otherwise. As such it partakes of that ideology of postmodernism which creeps into *Videodrome* too. It is therefore with *Videodrome* that I wish to conclude, to show that we must not see Cronenberg simply as a sexual reactionary or a special effects wizard.

Firstly, I want to draw attention to the concept of 'hysteria' as it can be construed textually and constructed theoretically. The male hysteric — Renn in the film — asks himself the question: 'am I a man or a woman?' By doing so he gives voice unconsciously to the socially determined fear of being gay, which produces symptoms within the hysteric, incribed onto his body as so many signifiers of psychic conflict (like the warts that appear on the body of the wretched patient tormented by Raglan in the opening sequence of *The Brood*, on the grounds that he may not be sufficiently masculine). *Videodrome* represents this by what is certainly one of the most extraordinary examples of special effects in all of Cronenberg's films: what critics rightly call 'the vaginal slit' that appears in Renn's midriff and into which tapes are aggressively thrust. What I find so exemplary about this scene is the way it draws together all the themes and concerns we have discussed so far. Tapes pulsate as they take on a life of their own, whereas the human body is transformed into an object. This co-presence within Renn's body of the male and the female, the very notion of being 'penetrated', translates magnificently the way people are commodified under capitalism, as well as their 'visceral' reaction; an attempt to reassert themselves via aggressiveness towards the other. Hence Renn's anxiety over Nicky Brand's masochism: burning herself with cigarettes. As a pornographer fascinated by 'Videodrome', he unconsciously recognises in Nicky a trend present in every human being, a trend which can turn into its opposite (the sadism we have already discussed) or which can transform the psyche of the person who identifies with it. Renn is afraid of resembling Nicky to the point of 'becoming' a woman, which is precisely what happens to him in relation to Convex. In more general terms, the male strives desperately to show how masculine he is by transforming the female into a passive object to be penetrated. Is it necessary to insist here on how hysterical the Mantle twins are?

I do not believe there can be any question of wide-eyed fascination and passive consumption of the images of special effects in Cronenberg, however blasé we have become. Thus I want to conclude on a final political twist provided by *Videodrome* in the form of a pun. Convex talks of making 'missiles for NATO and spectacles for the Third World'. Clearly he means 'eye glasses', but 'spectacles' can also be interpreted as 'shows put on for the gaze of spectators': after all, Convex's multinational is called 'Spectacular Optical' and he even puts on a show for clients. Thus, images in general and special effects in particular are 'spectacles' conceived to deceive and put to sleep those whom multinationals wish to exploit to the hilt, such as the spectators who find in such sinister spectacles as 'Videodrome' the imaginary individual solution to the real contradictions of existence.

CONCLUSION:
WHERE DO WE GO FROM HERE?

—∽◦∽—

The state of things is not conducive to optimism, let alone enthusiasm: with the exception of Shayamalan, no major talent has emerged in the last decade and the occasional important film (of which more later) seems to be an isolated phenomenon leading nowhere. I do not feel it is being nostalgic to deplore the failure of the careers of Romero and Hooper whose early movies changed the face of horror and did lead somewhere. That the latest Hooper films have gone straight to video is doubtless a sign of the times and hardly an encouraging one for film-makers and spectators. Cohen seems to have been reduced to silence as far as horror goes and it is legitimate to express anxiety over the career of Dante, given the relative failure of *Small Soldiers*. That Dante has been true to his vision over a period of twenty years and has managed to negotiate box-office flops is hopefully an indication of things to come. Which leaves us with the case of Craven.

Wes Craven's New Nightmare showed two things: that Freddy Krueger was a most complex character; and that Craven was able both to respect that fact and turn in an intelligent and thoughtful farewell to his 'bad father'. Such is not the case with the *Scream* trilogy. The problem lies in the fact that *Scream* itself was already highly derivative, whereas the ramifications of the character of Freddy have been shown to be considerable (I am not thinking of the commercial exploitation of him). Thus the outstanding moments in *Scream* are the brilliantly orchestrated opening, a veritable condensation of everything 'slashers' have shown us, and the sequence where we watch the youngsters watching *Halloween* on television, with the killer in the background watching them. However, far less is made of the 'spectacular' nature of this than in *Halloween*, although the revelation that there are two killers should not have come as a surprise: the filming of the comings and goings of the killer(s) in the opening and elsewhere showed that Craven was asking us to keep our eyes open. That, however, is not sufficient to launch a series. *Scream 2* is opportunistic, while *Scream 3* totally fails to make anything of its 'reflexive' nature, unlike such earlier films as *Targets* and even *Fade to Black*. Ultimately, self-parodic elements fail out of a lack of conviction, whereas *Scary Movie 2* has more in common with 'bad taste' movies like *Big Daddy* and *There's Something about Mary* than with the horror genre. From that standpoint, the ultimate 'horror' movie is *Very Bad Things.*

Another recent tendency, and one that it is too early to judge, is the decision to undertake systematic remakes of horror classics. Thus Dark Castle Productions have started to remake William Castle movies. The first of these, *House on Haunted Hill*, is deft, sophisticated and scary, which is far more than can be said of the original. The second in the series is *13 Ghosts*. Kismet Classics will film no fewer than ten films by the late Mario Bava, of which I expect nothing, given the quality of the originals. Moreover, Bava's stylistic intentiveness and his ability to create a thoroughly morbid atmosphere is unlikely to be well served by contemporary Hollywood. We should not forget that his *Blood and Black Lace* (1964) is the forerunner of 'slasher' and 'stalker' films, but who in Hollywood is capable of equalling that early achievement? Certainly not Carpenter. Those who were ready to give Australian import Jamie Blanks the benefit of the doubt after the dismal *Urban Legend* will not repeat their mistake after the incompetent and opportunistic *Valentine*. Similarly, *I Know What You Did Last Summer*, the abysmal quality of which can be blamed on crass direction and a mindless script, shows that Williamson's script for *Scream* said everything he had to say and that both he and Craven believed in the project.

That inanities like *Frequency* and *Final Destination* can be made is hardly likely to foster hope for the future of horror and fantasy in Hollywood. The former might have been worthwhile if the story had turned out to be wishful-thinking, a fantasy on the part of the father along the lines of *The Sixth Sense*. What we have instead is a deplorable piece of neo-liberal ideology where the past is rewritten to fetishise the private at the expense of history and the collective, the latter being reduced to a baseball match. *Final Destination* is a piece of obscurantist nonsense whose only 'idea' is that death is an agency that has a 'plan' for each of us. The film's makers should have taken a look at the brilliant *Fearless* (Peter Weir, 1993), a sober, intelligent and genuinely disturbing look at the effect on someone of suddenly being faced with possible death and what it does to him. Ultimately, *Frequency* and *Final Destination* complement one another: the former is an attempt to change the past to correspond to desire, the latter to deny death by foretelling the future. Both represent a refusal to think in the present.

However, all this pales into relative insignificance compared with that outrage *Shadow of a Vampire*, the most objectionable horror film to be inflicted on us in recent years. Once again, we are dealing with a film that has one 'idea' and a totally crazy one: that Max Shreck, who played the vampire in Murnau's *Nosferatu* (1922), really was a vampire. So we are treated to Willem Dafoe, shuffling around snuffling like a werewolf with a head cold, prior to the 'revelation' of yet another crazy notion concerning the effects of drugs on Murnau himself. That the director was a drug addict is totally irrelevant. What the film shows us is Murnau himself ending up believing in the vampiric status of Shreck and sinking gradually into psychosis as he films the actor disappearing, like the Count at the end of *Nosferatu*. One wonders how the psychotic Murnau recovered to direct one of the most widely admired films in the history of the cinema, *Sunrise*. The whole enterprise is one of boundless stupidity and pretentiousness and will hopefully disappear, like Nosferatu, in a puff of smoke.

If we turn now, thankfully, to those movies worthy of extended interest, we can note the persistence of themes foregrounded in the previous chapters: *The Sixth Sense*, *Sleepy Hollow* and *What Lies Beneath* all turn on parent-child relations, particularly the question of the father. The frightening aspects of the Shayamalan film concern precisely this: the boy's hallucination of a female presence suggests a guilt complex over his close relationship to his mother, her conflictual relationship with her husband and the child's place in this emotional struggle. Just as the mother in the hallucination displays her slashed wrists, so the boy's body bears similar traces. This is arguably the condensation of guilt through identification and of one residue of the mirror stage where the child remains obstinately attached to the mother. In retrospect, what is perhaps the most remarkable aspect of *The Sixth Sense* is the fact that, in a climate inauspicious for experimentation (especially for a first film), Shayamalan could conceive and carry through the daring idea of planting clues about the ending – Bruce Willis having lunch with his wife who takes no notice of him for the simple reason that he's dead – without alienating audiences who flocked in droves to see this disturbing and demanding movie.

Sleepy Hollow interrogates the notions of the 'bad father' and the symbolic debt. The hero's nightmare involves a cruel father and a victimised mother, suggesting an incestuous relationship between mother and child underscored by the idyllic dream prior to the nightmare. It is hardly coincidental that Burton should film the headless horseman and the father in the nightmare in identical fashion; shot from behind so that his head is invisible, the father is another implacable, indestructible force. This is precisely where the dimension of the symbolic debt comes in. The horseman is the 'bad' father returning to claim such a debt: the family was robbed of its rightful heritage by powerful landowners. The heroine remarks to the detective hero at one point that everyone in the village is linked by blood or marriage, so guilt is part and parcel of a heritage handed down from generation to generation. Everyone hides the fact in order to preserve the patriarchal status quo. However, the wife of the current leading landowner oversteps the mark by wanting the heritage for herself. By killing her hermit sister to this effect, she violates patriarchal law; her position is an unacceptably masculine one of decision and action. That the horseman carries her off as a substitute for the heroine is surely a displacement; she is really being punished for refusing to submit to the social and cultural dimension of the symbolic debt. *Sleepy Hollow* is a film on patriarchal capitalism in the making: the hero restores the law by marrying the heroine and looking after the son of the man killed by the headless horseman.

What Lies Beneath concerns both family relations and the notion of death. Thus the mother finds her life reduced to mindless banalities once her daughter leaves home: she is deprived of the only reason for her social function as mother. If the scenes where she sees 'herself' in the bath water are so frightening, it is because they show her as a woman old enough to be, precisely, her own mother (and the bathroom scenes recall *The Shining*). The shots thus condense the encroaching meaningless of her existence and the fact of dying; her daugher gone, this is all she has to look forward to. The film thus remarkably represents another aspect of the mirror stage: by overcoming our narcissistic attachment to the mother and realising the Oedipus complex, we unconsciously recognise our own mortality. It is not pleasant to have it reactivated in such a fashion. We should not allow ourselves to be side-tracked by the supernatural element of the film: the mother is convinced the vision is the ghost of the girl who has disappeared and visits her mother in turn. That she could interpret an old face for such a young one is surely indicative of a generation problem prompted by the fate of women under patriarchy and the fear of mortality. Significantly, her husband allowed himself to be seduced by the girl because he too is afraid of getting old. Similarly, the woman neighbour who suffers from hysteria is already overwhelmed by precisely the life of suffocation and death that now awaits the heroine. Each woman in the film sees herself in another woman, with no possibility of escape. The final shot of the mother laying flowers on the grave of the girl who disappeared (the fact that the husband, responsible for her death in an accident, sees her body as a rotting corpse perfectly conveys his neurotic fear of death) is a fitting summary of the themes of this unusually bleak movie.

Unbreakable is perhaps even more impressive than *The Sixth Sense* and concerns death and its impact in ways as sophisticated as *Fearless*. The exceptional status of both the Samuel L. Jackson and Bruce Willis characters – what does it mean to have a body that can break like glass? how does it feel to be the sole survivor of a train crash? – leads the former to see the latter as an ideal mirror image. This is a notion perfectly illustrated by the use of the camera in the sequence where Jackson is born: our attention is drawn to the characters via shots in a mirror. Shayamalan resorts to this in a different manner during the train journey where Willis talks to a young woman. Never are we shown them together: instead the director moves the camera so as to frame one or the other. Why? Because this way of shooting underlines for the spectator, through uncanny repetition, how the character can come to believe there is something special about him (he is unique, alone), whereas it could just as easily have been the woman who survived. It is precisely this unconscious desire to be different that attracts Jackson to Willis: he can live out through him on an unconscious imaginary mode the lives of the superhuman heroes he has identified with in comic books. Hence his aggressive reaction to a customer in his shop who wants to buy an original drawing for his son. Jackson unconsciously recognises the truth of his own unhealthy fascination since childhood and rejects it by throwing the man out. The 'supernatural' element of *Unbreakable* can thus be taken symbolically by spectators as representing their own need for immortality.

I have come across only one film that takes up that radical, critical strain I have analysed in previous chapters: *Terror Tract*. In its three episodes, which move from the frightening to the satirical, the film openly attacks life in suburbia and, crucially, its economic dimension via the representation of the pressures on real-estate agents to 'perform' according to instructions. The film thus functions as a totally negative version of *Poltergeist* and the ending, showing neighbours shooting or running each other down, gives the impression of entering territory where *The 'Burbs* feared to tread. A close analysis of the 'Bobo' section, where a little girl adopts a monkey she finds in the garden, with devastating and tragic results, will enable us to judge the pertinence of the film.

The father's excessive attachment to his daughter, who unconsciously submits to his every whim, functions until they clash over the monkey. The father is right to insist on the reality principle: the monkey belongs to someone and she can keep it until it is claimed. We are dealing with a child who has reached an age where she can and will express her own desires, here symbolised by the animal. It becomes the manifestation of the girl's subjectivity, desperately seeking expression faced with a father who desires in her place (the child is in a state of mental anorexia where the adult blocks off desire to the point where death/suicide can ensue), while claiming it is in her best interest. Thus, after the monkey has caused havoc and come close to killing him and the father is in a position to kill it, his daughter shoots him. This is the only way she can preserve the subjectivity of her identity through desire. By killing the animal, the father would have forced the girl to regress to the pre-Oedipal stage she has overcome. Now, as a result of her father's death at her hands, she retreats into a catatonic state to escape the Real of desire, that of her father's incestuous attachment passed off as 'devotion'. Interestingly, *Terror Tract* manages also to represent modern paranoia via the 'siege' mentality of the father: the security of the house must be maintained at all costs. Hence he too has unconsciously recognised in the monkey his daughter's desire for emancipation. By trying to keep the animal out, he is in reality showing his determination to keep his daughter in and to control her movements, desires and so on. Significantly, he possesses a sophisticated rifle and condenses in his attitudes the characters we have seen in films as different and separate in time as *Night of the Living Dead* and *The People Under the Stairs*, *The Stepfather* and *Parents*.

Unfortunately, even several swallows do not make a summer: the addition of the truly intriguing *Blair Witch Project* (how to create a growing sense of horror without showing anything) to those films analysed above does not change the basic situation. Only with Shayamalan can it be said that something exciting has arrived in Hollywood, but it is a sign of the times that the political thrust of the 70s and, to a lesser extent, of the 80s is missing. It is patent that we shall see no more films of the calibre of *The Texas Chainsaw Massacre*, which represents for the present writer everything that a horror movie can and should be. I shall therefore conclude by repeating my question: where do we go from here?

FILMOGRAPHY

❧

2000 Maniacs	Herschel Gordon Lewis	1965
The Addiction	Abel Ferrara	1994
Alice, Sweet Alice (aka Communion)	Albert Sole	1977
Alien	Ridley Scott	1979
Aliens	James Cameron	1986
The Alligator People	Roy Del Ruth	1959
Alone in the Dark	Jack Sholder	1982
The Ambulance	Larry Cohen	1990
American Psycho	Mary Hanson	2000
The Amityville Horror	Stuart Rosenberg	1979
An American Werewolf in London	John Landis	1981
April Fool's Day	Fred Walton	1986
Arachnophobia	Frank Marshall	1990
Attack of the 50-Foot Woman	Nathan Hertz	1958
Attack of the Crab Monsters	Roger Corman	1957
Attack of the Giant Leeches	Bernard Kowalski	1959
Audrey Rose	Robert Wise	1977
Bad Influence	Curtis Hanson	1990
Basic Instinct	Paul Verhoeven	1991
The Basket Case	Frank Henenlotter	1981
The Bat Whispers	Roland West	1930
The Beast with Five Fingers	Robert Florey	1945
The Beast Within	Philippe Mora	1982
Bedlam	Mark Robson	1946

Before I Hang	Nick Grinde	1940
The Black Cat	Edgar G. Ulmer	1934
Black Christmas	Bob Clark	1974
Black Friday	Arthur Lubin	1940
The Black Room	Roy William Neill	1935
The Blair Witch Project	Daniel Myrick, Eduardo Sanchez	1999
The Blob	Irwin S. Yeaworth	1958
Blood Feast	Herschel Gordon Lewis	1963
Blue Velvet	David Lynch	1986
The Body Snatcher	Robert Wise	1945
Body Snatchers	Abel Ferrara	1993
The Boogey Man	Ulli Lommel	1980
The Boys Next Door	Penelope Spheeris	1984
Brain Damage	Frank Henenlotter	1986
The Brain Eaters	Bruno VeSota	1958
The Brain from Planet Arous	Nathan Hertz	1957
The Brain That Wouldn't Die	Joseph Green	1960
Bram Stoker's Dracula	Francis Ford Coppola	1992
Bride of Chucky	Ronny Yu	2000
Bride of Frankenstein	James Whale	1935
Bride of the Monster	Ed Wood	1955
The Brood	David Cronenberg	1979
A Bucket of Blood	Roger Corman	1959
Buffy the Vampire Slayer	Kate Rubel Kazui	1992
The 'Burbs	Joe Dante	1989
Candyman	Bernard Rose	1992
Carnival of Souls	Herk Harvey	1962
Carrie	Brian De Palma	1976
Cat People	Jacques Tourneur	1942
Children Shouldn't Play with Dead Things	Bob Clark	1972
Chopper Chicks in Zombietown	Dan Haskins	1989
Christine	John Carpenter	1983
Copycat	Jon Amiel	1995
Count Yorga, Vampire	Bob Kelljan	1970
The Craft	Andrew Fleming	1996

Crash	David Cronenberg	1996
The Crazies	George A. Romero	1972
Creature from the Black Lagoon	Jack Arnold	1954
Creepshow	George A. Romero	1982
The Crime of Dr Crespi	John H. Auer	1935
Cujo	Lewis Teague	1983
Curse of the Cat People	Robert Wise	1944
Damien: The Omen 2	Don Taylor	1978
The Dark Backward	Adam Rifkin	1991
Dark Eyes of London	Walter Summers	1939
The Dark Half	George A. Romero	1992
Daughter of Horror (aka Dementia)	Bruno VeSota	1953
Dawn of the Dead	George A. Romero	1978
Day of the Dead	George A. Romero	1985
The Day the Earth Stood Still	Robert Wise	1951
Day the World Ended	Roger Corman	1956
Dead and Buried	Gary Sherman	1981
The Dead Can't Lie	Lloyd Fonvielle	1988
Dead Man's Curve	Dan Rosen	1998
Dead of Night (aka The Night Walk)	Bob Clark	1973
Dead Ringers	David Cronenberg	1988
Dead Zone	David Cronenberg	1983
Death Becomes Her	Robert Zemeckis	1992
Death Line	Gary Sherman	1972
Death Takes a Holiday	Mitchell Leisen	1934
Death Trap	Tobe Hooper	1976
Demon Seed	Donald Cammell	1977
Deranged	Alan Ormsby	1974
The Devil Bat	Jean Yarbrough	1940
The Devil Commands	Edward Dmytryk	1941
The Devil Doll	Tod Browning	1936
Dolls	Stuart Gordon	1986
Don't Answer the Phone	Robert Hammer	1980
Doppelganger	Avi Nesher	1992
Dr Cyclops	Ernest B. Schoedsack	1939
Dr Jekyll and Mr Hyde	Rouben Mamoulian	1931
Dr Jekyll and Mr Hyde	Victor Fleming	1941

Dr X	Michael Curtiz	1932
Dracula	Tod Browning	1931
Dracula	Dan Curtis	1973
Dracula	John Badham	1979
Dracula's Daughter	Lambert Hillyer	1936
Dressed to Kill	Brian De Palma	1980
Driller Killer	Abel Ferrara	1979
Eraserhead	David Lynch	1976
The Evil Dead	Sam Raimi	1982
eXistenZ	David Cronenberg	1999
The Exorcist	William Friedkin	1973
Eyes of a Stranger	Ken Wiederhorn	1981
The Eyes of Laura Mars	Irvin Kershner	1978
The Face Behind the Mask	Robert Florey	1941
Fade to Black	Vernon Zimmerman	1980
Fatal Attraction	Adrian Lyne	1987
The Fearless Vampire Killers (aka *Dance of The Vampires*)	Roman Polanski	1967
Fear No Evil	Frank LaLoggia	1981
Final Destination	James Wong	2000
Firestarter	Mark Lester	1984
Flesh-Eating Mothers	James Aviles Martin	1992
The Fly	Kurt Neumann	1958
The Fly	David Cronenberg	1986
The Fog	John Carpenter	1979
Frankenhooker	Frank Henenlotter	1990
Frankenstein	James Whale	1931
Frankenstein Meets the Wolfman	Roy William Neill	1942
Frankenstein Unbound	Roger Corman	1990
Freaks	Tod Browning	1932
Freddy's Dead: The Final Nightmare	Rachel Talalay	1991
Freeway	Matthew Bright	1996
Freeway Maniac	Paul Winters	1994
Frequency	Gregory Hoblit	2000
Friday the 13th	Sean Cunningham	1980
Fright Night	Tom Holland	1989

From Beyond	Stuart Gordon	1986
From Dusk to Dawn	Robert Rodriguez	1995
The Funhouse	Tobe Hooper	1981
The Fury	Brian De Palma	1978
Games	Curtis Harrington	1967
The Ghost Ship	Mark Robson	1943
Ghostbusters	Ivan Reitman	1985
Ghosts of Mars	John Carpenter	2001
The Ghoul	T. Hayes Hunter	1933
The Gift	Sam Raimi	2000
God Told Me To	Larry Cohen	1975
Graveyard Shift	Gerard Ciccoritti	1986
Gremlins	Joe Dante	1984
Gremlins 2	Joe Dante	1990
Halloween	John Carpenter	1978
Halloween 3: Season of the Witch	Tommy Lee Wallace	1983
Halloween: Twenty Years on	Steve Miner	1998
The Hand that Rocks the Cradle	Curtis Hanson	1992
Hannibal	Ridley Scott	2001
The Haunted Palace	Roger Corman	1963
The Haunting	Robert Wise	1963
Hell Night	Tom de Simone	1981
Henry: Portrait of a Serial Killer	John McNaughton	1986
The Heretic	John Boorman	1977
The Hidden	Jack Sholder	1987
The Hills Have Eyes	Wes Craven	1977
The Hitcher	Robert Harmon	1986
Homicidal	William Castle	1961
House	Steve Miner	1986
House 3	James Isaac	1989
House of Dracula	Earl C. Kenton	1945
House of Frankenstein	Earl C. Kenton	1944
House of Usher	Roger Corman	1960
House on Haunted Hill	William Castle	1958
House on Haunted Hill	William Malone	1999
How to Make a Monster	Herbert Strock	1958

The Howling	Joe Dante	1980
The Hunger	Tony Scott	1984
Hush, Hush, Sweet Charlotte	Robert Aldrich	1964
I Bury the Living	Albert Band	1957
I Know What You Did Last Summer	Jim Gillespie	1997
I Married a Monster from Outer Space	Gene Fowler, Jr.	1958
I Saw What You Did	William Castle	1965
I Spit on Your Grave	Meyer Lanski	1978
I Walked with a Zombie	Jacques Tourneur	1943
I Was a Teenage Frankenstein	Herbert Strock	1957
I Was a Teenage Werewolf	Gene Fowler, Jr.	1957
Idle Hands	Rodney Flender	1999
In the Mouth of Madness	John Carpenter	1992
Invaders from Mars	William Cameron Menzies	1953
Invasion of the Body Snatchers	Don Siegel	1955
Invasion of the Body Snatchers	Philip Kaufman	1978
The Invisible Man	James Whale	1933
The Invisible Ray	Lambert Hillyer	1936
Island of Lost Souls	Erle C. Kenton	1932
Island of the Alive	Larry Cohen	1986
Isle of the Dead	Mark Robson	1945
It Came from Outer Space	Jack Arnold	1953
It Conquered the World	Roger Corman	1956
It Lives Again	Larry Cohen	1978
It's Alive	Larry Cohen	1973
The Keep	Michael Mann	1984
King Kong	Ernest B. Schoedsack	1933
The Lady in White	Frank LaLoggia	1988
Lake Placid	Steve Miner	1999
Last House on the Left	Wes Craven	1972
The Leopard Man	Jacques Tourneur	1943
Letters from a Killer	David Carson	1998
The Little Shop of Horrors	Roger Corman	1960

The Lost Boys	Joel Schumacher	1987
Lost Highway	David Lynch	1996
The Mad Genius	Michael Curtiz	1931
Mad Love	Karl Freund	1935
Man Made Monster	George Waggner	1941
The Man Who Changed His Mind	Robert Stevenson	1936
The Man with the X-Ray Eyes	Roger Corman	1963
Manhunter	Michael Mann	1986
Maniac	Dwight Esper	1934
Maniac	William Lustig	1980
Maniac Cop	William Lustig	1988
Maniac Cop 2	William Lustig	1991
Mark of the Vampire	Tod Browning	1935
Martin	George A. Romero	1976
The Mask of Fu Manchu	Charles Brabin	1932
Masque of the Red Death	Roger Corman	1964
Massacre at Central High	Renee Daalder	1976
Matinee	Joe Dante	1993
Misery	Rob Reiner	1992
Monkey Shines	George A. Romero	1988
The Monolith Monsters	John Sherwood	1957
The Monster and the Girl	Stuart Heisler	1940
Monster on the Campus	Jack Arnold	1958
The Monster Squad	Fred Dekker	1987
The Monster Walks	Frank Strayer	1932
The Most Dangerous Game	Ernest B. Schoedsack, Irving Pichel	1932
Motel Hell	Kevin Connor	1980
Mother's Day	Charles Kaufmann	1980
Mr Sardonicus	William Castle	1961
Ms. 45	Abel Ferrara	1981
The Mummy	Karl Freund	1932
The Mummy's Hand	Christy Cabanne	1940
Murders in the Rue Morgue	Robert Florey	1931
Murders in the Zoo	Edward Sutherland	1933
My Bloody Valentine	George Mihalka	1986
Mystery of the Wax Museum	Michael Curtiz	1933

Natural Born Killers	Oliver Stone	1994
Near Dark	Kathryn Bigelow	1987
Night Must Fall	Richard Thorpe	1937
Night of the Living Dead	George A. Romero	1968
Night of the Living Dead	Tom Savini	1990
Night Tide	Curtis Harrington	1961
Nightmare on Elm Street	Wes Craven	1984
NES 2: Freddy's Revenge	Jack Sholder	1985
NES 3: Dream Warriors	Chuck Russell	1987
NES 4: The Dream Master	Renny Harlin	1988
NES 5: The Dream Child	Stephen Hopkins	1989
Not of this Earth	Roger Corman	1957
The Old Dark House	James Whale	1932
The Omen	Richard Donner	1976
Parents	Bob Balaban	1989
Peeping Tom	Michael Powell	1960
The People under the Stairs	Wes Craven	1991
Pet Sematary	Mary Louise Lambert	1989
Phantom of the Paradise	Brian De Palma	1974
Phantoms	Joe Chappell	1998
Piranha	Joe Dante	1978
The Pit and the Pendulum	Roger Corman	1961
Poltergeist	Tobe Hooper	1982
Poltergeist 2	Brian Gibson	1986
Poltergeist 3	Gary Sherman	1988
The Premature Burial	Roger Corman	1962
Prince of Darkness	John Carpenter	1987
Prison	Renny Harlan	1989
Prom Night	Paul Lynch	1980
Psycho	Alfred Hitchcock	1960
Psycho 2	Richard Franklin	1983
Psycho 3	Anthony Perkins	1986
Pumpkinhead	Stan Winston	1986
Q – the Winged Serpent	Larry Cohen	1982

Rabid	David Cronenberg	1976
Race with the Devil	Jack Starrett	1975
The Rage: Carrie 2	Katt Shea	1999
Raising Cain	Brian De Palma	1992
The Rapture	Michael Tolkin	1991
The Raven	Louis Friedlander	1935
The Raven	Roger Corman	1963
Reanimator	Stuart Gordon	1985
The Return of Count Yorga	Bob Kelljan	1971
The Return of Dr X	Vincent Sherman	1939
Return of the Fly	Edward Bernds	1959
Return of the Living Dead	Dan O'Bannon	1985
Return to Salem's Lot	Larry Cohen	1987
The Rocky Horror Picture Show	Jim Sharman	1975
Rosemary's Baby	Roman Polanski	1968
The Sadist	Arch Hall	1963
Scanners	David Cronenberg	1980
Scary Movie 2	Keenan Ivory Wayans	2001
Scream	Wes Craven	1996
Scream 2	Wes Craven	1997
Scream 3	Wes Craven	2000
The Screaming Skull	Alex Nicol	1958
Serial Mom	John Waters	1994
The Serpent and the Rainbow	Wes Craven	1987
Seven	David Fincher	1995
The Seventh Victim	Mark Robson	1943
Shadow of the Vampire	Edward Merhige	2000
She Demons	Richard Cunha	1957
The Shining	Stanley Kubrick	1980
Shivers	David Cronenberg	1975
The Silence of the Lambs	Jonathan Demme	1991
Sisters	Brian De Palma	1973
The Sixth Sense	M. Night Shayamalan	1999
Sleepy Hollow	Tim Burton	1999
Slumber Party Massacre	Amy Jones	1981
Slumber Party Massacre 2	Deborah Brock	1987
Small Soldiers	Joe Dante	1998

Society	Brian Yuzna	1989
Son of Dracula	Robert Siodmak	1943
Son of Frankenstein	Rowland V. Lee	1939
Son of Kong	Ernest B. Schoedsack	1933
Squirm	Jeff Liebermann	1976
The Stepfather	Joseph Ruben	1987
Straitjacket	William Castle	1964
Supernatural	Victor Halperin	1933
Svengali	Archie Mayo	1931
Tales from the Dark Side	John Harrison	1991
Tales of Terror	Roger Corman	1962
Targets	Peter Bogdanovich	1967
Teenage Caveman	Roger Corman	1958
The Terror	Roger Corman	1963
Terror Tract	Lance Dreesen, Clint Hutchison	2000
TerrorVision	Ted Nicolaou	1986
The Texas Chainsaw Massacre	Tobe Hooper	1974
The Texas Chainsaw Massacre 2	Tobe Hooper	1986
The Texas Chainsaw Massacre: The New Generation	Kim Henkel	1996
Them!	Gordon Douglas	1954
They Live	John Carpenter	1988
The Thing	Christian Nyby	1951
The Thing	John Carpenter	1981
Tightrope	Richard Tuggle	1984
The Tingler	William Castle	1959
The Tomb of Ligeia	Roger Corman	1964
The Toolbox Murders	Dennis Donnelly	1978
Tower of London	Rowland V. Lee	1939
Tremors	Ron Underwood	1989
Two Evil Eyes	Dario Argento, George A. Romero	1990
Unbreakable	M. Night Shayamalan	2000
The Undead	Roger Corman	1957

The Undying Monster	John Brahm	1942
Urban Legend	Jamie Blanks	1999
Valentine	Jamie Blanks	2001
Vamp	Richard Wenk	1986
The Vampire Bat	Frank Strayer	1933
Vampires	John Carpenter	1995
Vampire's Kiss	Robert Bierman	1989
Videodrome	David Cronenberg	1982
The Walking Dead	Michael Curtiz	1936
The Wasp Woman	Roger Corman	1959
Werewolf of London	Stuart Walker	1935
Wes Craven's New Nightmare	Wes Craven	1995
What Lies Beneath	Robert Zemeckis	2000
Whatever Happened to Baby Jane?	Robert Aldrich	1962
What's the Matter with Helen?	Curtis Harrington	1971
When a Stranger Calls	Fred Walton	1979
White Zombie	Victor Halperin	1932
The Wolf Man	George Waggner	1941
Wolfen	Michael Wadleigh	1980

BIBLIOGRAPHY

Adorno, Theodor (1974), *Minima Moralia*, London: Verso.

Baldick, Chris (1987), *In Frankenstein's Shadow. Myth, Monstrosity, and Nineteenth-Century Writing*, Oxford: Clarendon Press.

Benshoff, Harry M. (1997), *Monsters in the Closet. Homosexuality and the Horror Film*, Manchester: Manchester University Press.

Berenstein, Rhona J. (1996), *Attack of the Leading Ladies. Gender, Sexuality, and Spectatorship in Classic Horror*, New York: Columbia University Press.

Bernard, Kenneth (1976), '*King Kong*: a Meditation', in Ronald Gottesman and Harry Geduld (eds), *The Girl in the Hairy Paw*, New York: Avon, pp. 122–30.

Biskind, Peter (1983), *Seeing is Believing, or: How Hollywood Taught us to Stop Worrying and Love the Fifties*, New York: Pantheon Books, pp. 102–59.

Brottman, Mikita (1998), *Meat is Murder! An Illustrated Guide to Cannibal Culture*, London: Creation Books International.

Carroll, Noel (1990), *The Philosophy of Horror*, London: Routledge.

Clover, Carol J. (1992), *Men, Women and Chainsaws. Gender in the Modern Horror Film*, London: BFI Publishing.

Conrich, Ian (2000), 'Seducing the Subject: Freddy Krueger', in Alain Silver and James Ursini (eds), *Horror Film Reader*, pp. 223–35.

Copjec, Joan (1994), 'Vampires, Breast-Feeding, and Anxiety', in Copjec, *Read My Desire. Lacan against the Historicists*, Cambridge, Massachusetts: The MIT Press, pp. 117–39.

Craft, Christopher (1997), ' "Kiss me with those red lips": Gender and Inversion in Bram Stoker's *Dracula*', in Nina Auerbach and David J. Skal (eds), *Dracula*, New York: Norton Critical Edition, pp. 444–59.

Crane, Jonathan Lake (1994), *Terror and Everyday Life. Singular Moments in the History of the Horror Film*, London: Sage Publications.

Creed, Barbara (1993), *The Monstrous-Feminine. Film, Feminism, Psychoanalysis*, London: Routledge.

Dadoun, Roger (1989), 'Fetishism in the Horror Film', in James Donald (ed.), *Fantasy in the Cinema*, pp. 39–61.

Dika, Vera (1990), *Games of Terror. Halloween, Friday the 13th, and the Films of the Stalker Cycle*, London and Toronto: Associated University Presses.

Donald, James (ed.) (1989), *Fantasy and the Cinema*, London: BFI.

Dyson, Jeremy (1997), *Bright Darkness. The Lost Art of the Supernatural Horror Film*, London: Cassell.

Edmundson, Mark (1997), *Nightmare on Main Street. Angels, Sadomasochism and the Culture of Gothic*, Cambridge, Massachusetts: Harvard University Press.

Elsaesser, Thomas (1989), 'Social mobility and the fantastic: German silent cinema', in James Donald (ed.), *Fantasy and the Cinema*, pp. 23–38.

Freeland, Cynthia A. (2000), *The Naked and the Undead. Evil and the Appeal of Horror*, Boulder, Colorado: The Westview Press.

Freud, Sigmund, *The Standard Edition of the Complete Psychological Works*, London: Hogarth Press, 24 volumes:

SE 17, 'The Uncanny', pp. 217–52.

SE 18, 'Beyond the Pleasure Principle', pp. 7–64.

SE 20, 'Inhibitions, Symptoms, Anxiety', pp. 87–172.

SE 21, 'Fetishism', pp. 152–7.

Grant, Barry Keith (ed.) (1984), *Planks of Reason. Essays on the Horror Film*, Metuchen, New Jersey: Scarecrow Press.

Grant, Barry Keith (ed.) (1996), *The Dread of Difference. Gender and the Horror Film*, Austin: University of Texas Press.

Grant, Barry Keith (1999), 'American Psycho/sis. The Pure Products of America Go Crazy', in Christopher Sharrett (ed.), *Mythologies of Violence in Postmodern Media*, Detroit: Wayne State University Press, pp. 65–83.

Grant, Michael (ed.) (2000), *The Modern Fantastic. The Films of David Cronenberg*, London: Flicks Books.

Halberstam, Judith (1995), *Skin Shows. Gothic Horror and the Technology of Monsters*, Durham: Duke University Press.

Hardy, Phil (ed.) (1996), *The Aurum Encyclopedia of Horror*, London: Aurum Press.

Hawkins, Jane (2000), *Cutting Edge. Art-Horror and the Horrific Avant-Garde*, Minneapolis: University of Minnesota Press.

Hogan, David J. (1986), *Dark Romance. Sexuality in the Horror Film*, Jefferson, North Carolina: McFarland.

Humphries, Reynold (1974), 'Death Line (aka Raw Meat)', *Cinefantastique*, 3: 2, 28.

Humphries, Reynold (2000), 'The Semiotics of Horror: the case of *Dracula's Daughter*', *Interdisciplinary Journal for Germanic Linguistics and Semiotic Analysis*, 5: 2, 273–89.

Humphries, Reynold (2002), 'On the Road Again. Rehearsing the Death Drive in Modern Realist Horror Cinema', *PostScript*, 21: 3, Summer.

Jameson, Fredric (1991), *Postmodernism, or the Cultural Logic of Late Capitalism*, London: Verso.

Jameson, Fredric (1992), *The Geopolitical Aesthetic. Cinema and Space in the World System*, London: BFI.

Jancovich, Mark (1996), *Rational Fears. American Horror in the 1950s*, Manchester: Manchester University Press.

Kellner, Douglas (1996), 'Poltergeists, Gender and Class in the Age of Reagan and Bush', in David E. James and Rick Berg (eds), *The Hidden Foundation*, Minneapolis: University of Minnesota Press, pp. 217–39.

Krzywinska, Tanya (2000), *A Skin For Dancing In. Possession, Witchcraft and Voodoo in Film*, London: Flicks Books.

Lowry, Edward and deCordova, Richard (1984), 'Enunciation and the Production of Horror in *White Zombie'*, in Barry Keith Grant (ed.), *Planks of Reason*, pp. 346–89.

Marcuse, Herbert (1955), *Eros and Civilization*, London: Sphere Books.

Mulvey, Laura (2000), 'Death Drives: Hitchcock's *Psycho'*, *Film Studies*, 2: Spring, 5–14.

Newitz, Annalee (1999), 'Serial Killers, True Crime and Economic Performance', in Christopher Sharrett (ed.), *Mythologies of Violence in Postmodern Media*, Detroit: Wayne State University Press, pp. 65–83.

Newman, Kim (ed.) (1996), *The BFI Companion to Horror*, London: Cassell.

Paul, William (1994), *Laughing Screaming. Modern Hollywood Horror and Comedy*, New York: Columbia University Press.

Petley, Julian (1999), 'The Monstrous Child', in Michele Aaron (ed.), *The Body's Perilous Pleasures*, Edinburgh: Edinburgh University Press, pp. 87–107.

Pinedo, Isabel Christina (1997), *Recreational Terror. Women and the Pleasures of Horror Film Viewing*, New York: SUNY.

Prawer, S. S. (1980), *Caligari's Children. The Film as Tale of Terror*, New York: Da Capo Press.

Punter, David (1996), *The Literature of Terror*. Volume 2: *The Modern Gothic*, London and New York: Longman.

Rasmussen, Randy Loren (1998), *Children of the Night. The Six Archetypal Characters of Classic Horror Film*, Jefferson, North Carolina: McFarland.

Rhodes, Gary D. (2001), White Zombie. *Anatomy of a Horror Film*, Jefferson, North Carolina: McFarland.

Rodley, Chris (ed.) (1992), *Cronenberg on Cronenberg*, London: Faber and Faber.

Russell, David J. (1998), 'Monster Roundup: Reintegrating the Horror Genre', in Nick Browne (ed.), *Refiguring American Film Genres. Theory and History*, Berkeley and Los Angeles: University of California Press, pp. 223–54.

Schneider, Steven (2000), 'Monsters as (Uncanny) Metaphors: Freud, Lakoff, and the Representation of Monstrosity in Cinematic Horror', in Alain Silver and James Ursini (eds), *Horror Film Reader*, pp. 167–91.

Schneider, Steven (2002), *An Auteur on Elm Street: the Cinema of Wes Craven*, London: Wallflower Press/New York: Columbia University Press.

Sconce, Jeffrey (1993), 'Spectacles of Death. Identification, Reflexivity and Contemporary Horror', in Jim Collins, Hilary Radner, Ava Preacher Collins (eds), *Film Theory Goes to the Movies*, London: Routledge, pp. 103–19.

Senn, Bryan (1996), *Golden Horrors. An Illustrated Critical Filmography, 1931–1939*, Jefferson, North Carolina: McFarland.

Shaviro, Steven (1993), 'Contagious Allegories: George Romero' and 'Bodies of Fear: David Cronenberg', in Shaviro, *The Cinematic Body*, Minneapolis: University of Minnesota Press, pp. 83–104; pp. 127–55.

Silver, Alain and Ursini, James (1993), *The Vampire Film*, New York: Limelight Editions.

Silver, Alain and Ursini, James (eds) (2000), *Horror Film Reader*, New York: Limelight Editions.

Simpson, Philip L. (1999), 'The Politics of Apocalypse in the Cinema of Serial Murder', in Christopher Sharrett (ed.), *Mythologies of Violence in Postmodern Media*, Detroit: Wayne State University Press, pp. 65–83.

Simpson, Philip L. (2000), *Psycho Paths. Tracking the Serial Killer through Contemporary American Film and Literature*, Carbondale: Southern Illinois Press.

Skal, David J. (1993), *The Monster Show: a Cultural History of Horror*, London: Plexus.

Skal, David J. (1998), *Screams of Reason: Mad Science and Modern Culture*, New York: Norton.

Svehla, Gary J. and Susan (eds) (1995), *Bela Lugosi*, Baltimore: Midnight Marquee Press.

Svehla, Gary J. and Susan (eds) (1996), *Boris Karloff*, Baltimore: Midnight Marquee Press.

Tudor, Andrew (1989), *Monsters and Mad Scientists. A Cultural History of the Horror Movie*, Oxford: Basil Blackwell.

Twitchell, James (1985), *Dreadful Pleasures. An Anatomy of Modern Horror*, Oxford: Oxford University Press.

Vale, V. and Juno, Andrea (eds) (1986), *Incredibly Strange Films*, San Francisco: Re/Search Publications.

Waller, Gregory A. (1987), *American Horrors. Essays on the Modern American Horror Film*, Urbana and Chicago: University of Illinois Press.

Weaver, Tom (1993), *Poverty Row Horrors. Monogram, PRC and Republic Horror Films of the Forties*, Jefferson, North Carolina: McFarland.

Wells, Paul (2000), *The Horror Genre. From Beelzebub to Blair Witch*, London: Wallflower Press.

Williams, Linda (1996), 'When the Woman Looks', in Barry Keith Grant (ed.), *The Dread of Difference*, pp. 15–34.

Williams, Linda Ruth (1999), 'The Inside-out of Masculinity: David Cronenberg's Visceral Pleasures', in Michele Aaron (ed.), *The Body's Perilous Pleasures*, Edinburgh: Edinburgh University Press, pp. 30–48.

Williams, Tony (1996), *Hearths of Darkness. The Family in the American Horror Film*, London: Associated University Presses.

Williams, Tony (1997), *Larry Cohen: the Radical Allegories of an Independent Filmmaker*, Jefferson, North Carolina: McFarland.

Wood, Robin (1976), 'The Shadow Worlds of Jacques Tourneur', in Robin Wood, *Personal Views*, London: Gordon Fraser, pp. 209–23.

Wood, Robin (1986), *Hollywood from Vietnam to Reagan*, New York: Columbia University Press, pp. 70–201.

Worth, D. Earl (1995), *Sleaze Creatures. An Illustrated Guide to Obscure Hollywood Horror Movies, 1956–1959*, Key West, Florida: Fantasma Books.

Zizek, Slavoj (1991), *Looking Awry. An Approach to Jacques Lacan through Popular Culture*, Cambridge: Massachusetts: The MIT Press.

INDEX